Contributions to Finance and Accounting

The book series 'Contributions to Finance and Accounting' features the latest research from research areas like financial management, investment, capital markets, financial institutions, FinTech and financial innovation, accounting methods and standards, reporting, and corporate governance, among others. Books published in this series are primarily monographs and edited volumes that present new research results, both theoretical and empirical, on a clearly defined topic. All books are published in print and digital formats and disseminated globally. This book series is indexed in Scopus.

Ruihui Xu · Dawei Zhao

Digital Transformation of Private Equity in China

Springer

Ruihui Xu
Research Institute
People's Bank of China
Beijing, China

Dawei Zhao
Research Institute
People's Bank of China
Beijing, China

ISSN 2730-6038 ISSN 2730-6046 (electronic)
Contributions to Finance and Accounting
ISBN 978-981-99-8481-7 ISBN 978-981-99-8482-4 (eBook)
https://doi.org/10.1007/978-981-99-8482-4

This Springer imprint is published by the registered company Springer Nature Singapore Pte Ltd.
The registered company address is: 152 Beach Road, #21-01/04 Gateway East, Singapore 189721, Singapore

Preface

In the recent 30 years, China's private equity industry has made significant progress and attained remarkable achievements, especially with the advancement of China's capital market reform. It has been playing an essential role in promoting the development of a multi-level capital market, serving the real economy, and enriching the public investment channels. Meanwhile, China's regulatory framework also secures its healthy and orderly development. The framework consists of three parts: supervision by central government regulatory departments, prudential supervision, and risk resolution by local government financial authorities over certain types of financial intermediaries in its jurisdiction, and self-regulation by industry associations.

Private equity investment, an essential part of a multi-level capital market, is a necessity for enhancing financial support for the real economy and China's economic development. Building a high-quality and dynamic private equity market is conducive to continuously stimulating technological innovation and improving corporate governance. On the one hand, the integration between technology and the financial industry has been deepening, and technology has become an essential means to enhance financial service quality and efficiency. In this regard, answers to the following questions will be critical concerns of the industry at present and in the future: how to introduce digital technologies into the private equity industry's business innovation and operation management process? How can digital technology be used to promote the comprehensive digital transformation of the private equity industry?

On the other hand, digital technologies (represented by the Internet, big data, artificial intelligence, and blockchain) have injected new impetus for the development of the private equity industry but also brought unknown risks and posed new challenges to the regulation of the private equity industry. However, it is still unclear how to utilize digital technology to improve the regulatory means and tools of the private equity industry. How to use digital technology to prevent the risk of the private equity industry? The answers to the questions have theoretical significance and practical value for healthy development and supervision of the private equity industry in China.

Digital Transformation of Private Equity in China systematically studies and discusses the current situation and development trend of technology application in the private equity industry. First, it summarizes the current development status of the private equity industry and outlooks the industry's future development trend. Second, it studies the application of digital technologies in critical areas such as regulation, compliance, and anti-money laundering in the private equity industry. Third, it discusses how digital technologies such as big data, artificial intelligence, and blockchain will change the private equity industry and thus promote its digital transformation and development. Fourth, it systematically reviews the digital technology application in the private equity industry in the United States, the United Kingdom, Japan, Singapore, and other countries and summarizes the experiences that have significance for China.

Digital Transformation of Private Equity in China provides an overview of the private equity industry and a study of digital technology applications such as the Internet, big data, artificial intelligence, and blockchain but also analyze practical cases of technology applications. Therefore, this book has a broad audience, especially scholars and practitioners. It is a valuable reference for researchers in related fields, and it can also provide some insights into technology applications for practitioners in the private equity industry.

The authors of *Digital Transformation of Private Equity in China* are front-line researchers specializing in fintech research and application. We hope the book will stimulate more research and applications of digital technology in the private equity industry, contribute to the digital transformation of the private equity industry, and further support the development of the real economy and a multi-level capital market.

Beijing, China

Ruihui Xu
Dawei Zhao

Contents

1 Private Equity in the Age of Fintech 1
1.1 Current Development of the PE Industry 1
1.1.1 Definition and Characteristics of PE 1
1.1.2 PE in China 2
1.2 Issues to Be Concerned About High-Quality Development of the PE Market 5
1.2.1 Clarify the Positioning of the PE Industry Development 5
1.2.2 Perform Efficient Risk Management in PE 5
1.2.3 Strengthen the Post-Investment Management 6
1.2.4 Improve the Exit Mechanism of PE 6
1.3 The Combination of Fintech and the PE Industry 7
1.3.1 Key Features of Fintech 7
1.3.2 Advantages of Fintech Applications in the PE Industry 8
1.3.3 Cases of Fintech Application in the PE Industry 9
1.3.4 Issues of Digital Technology Application in the PE Industry 11
References 12

2 Technology Innovation and Private Equity 15
2.1 Development and Dilemma of PE Investment in a New Stage 15
2.1.1 PE Market Snowballs and Shows a Positive Trend 16
2.1.2 Dilemma of China's PE Industry 17
2.1.3 Technology Innovation Boosts the Development of the PE Industry 18
2.2 Big Data and PE 20
2.2.1 Big Data Technology, Industry, and PE Mutually Benefit Each Other 20
2.2.2 Big Data Technology Promotes the Development of the PE Industry 21

2.3 Mobile Internet Activates PE Business 22
2.4 AI Assists in Efficient Decision-Making 23
2.5 Blockchain Increases Business Trust 25
References 27

3 Private Equity Investment in Fintech 29
3.1 The Importance of PE Investment in Fintech 29
3.1.1 PE Investment Model in Fintech 29
3.1.2 PE Promotes Technology Innovation 31
3.2 Overview of PE Investment in Fintech 32
3.2.1 Global Fintech and PE 32
3.2.2 PE Investments in the Fintech Subcategories and Different Regions 34
3.3 Fintech Investments Through Special Purpose Acquisition Companies 37
3.3.1 The Concept of SPAC and Listing Rules 38
3.3.2 Overview of Fintech Investments Through SPAC 41
3.4 Cases of PE Investment in Fintech 41
3.4.1 Foreign Cases 41
3.4.2 China Cases 45
References 49

4 Technology Applications in Private Equity Regulation 51
4.1 Regulatory Framework of China's PE Industry 52
4.1.1 China Securities Regulatory Commission: Industry Supervision 53
4.1.2 The Asset Management Association of China: Industry Self-Regulation 54
4.1.3 Local Financial Bureaus: Current Supervision Status and Future Trend 54
4.2 Risk Issues in the Development of China's PE Industry 55
4.2.1 Some Institutions Do not Standardize the Review of Qualified Investors 56
4.2.2 Some Reported Fundraising Method Does not Match the Actual 56
4.2.3 Some Institutions Use Investor Funds Illegally 57
4.2.4 Some Institutions Have Inadequate Information Disclosure 57
4.2.5 Some Institutions Promise to Guarantee the Principal and Return to Investors in a Disguised Way 58
4.2.6 Some Information is not Updated or not Timely Updated 58
4.3 Policy Suggestions for Establishing a Digital Regulatory System in the PE Industry 59
4.3.1 The Main Tasks 59

4.3.2 The Principles and Objectives 60
4.3.3 A General Framework of a Digital PE Investment Regulatory System 62
4.3.4 Additional Suggestions for Building a Digital PE Investment Regulatory System 62
References 66

5 Technology Applications in Private Equity Compliance Management 67
5.1 The Origins of Technology Application in PE Compliance Management 68
5.1.1 Service Transformation During the Expansion of the PE Industry 68
5.1.2 Compliance Operations Become a Pain Point, and the Cost of PE Investment Further Increases 69
5.1.3 With Technology Empowerment, Compliance Technology Provides Solutions 72
5.2 Development of Compliance Technology 73
5.2.1 The Foundation of Compliance Technology Has Been Continuously Consolidated 73
5.2.2 The Importance of Compliance Technology Application is Highlighted 74
5.2.3 Compliance Technology Has Rich Application Scenarios 75
5.3 PE Investment Compliance System 75
5.3.1 Key Compliance Issues of Fund Managers 78
5.3.2 Key Compliance Issues of Fund Products 78
5.4 The Practice of Technology Application in PE Compliance Management 79
5.4.1 An Investment Management System Provides A Comprehensive Solution for Compliance Operations 79
5.4.2 Electronic Contracts Normalize Contract Signing 81
5.4.3 Electronic Database Serves Suitability Management 81
5.4.4 Intelligent Matching for Compliance Fundraising 84
5.5 Issues of Compliance Technology Application and Policy Suggestions 85
5.5.1 Major Issues 85
5.5.2 Policy Recommendations 86
References 87

6 Technology Applications in Private Equity Anti-Money Laundering 89
6.1 The Connotation of Money Laundering 89

6.2 Current Anti-Money Laundering Regulations in the PE Industry ... 90
6.2.1 Money Laundering Characteristics of International PE Funds ... 90
6.2.2 Current Situation and Problems of Anti-Money Laundering Regulation of PE Funds in China ... 92
6.3 Application of Technology in AML in the PE Industry ... 96
6.3.1 The Positive Effect of Technology on AML ... 97
6.3.2 Challenges of AML with Fintech ... 99
6.3.3 Application of Digital Technology in AML in PE Investment ... 100
References ... 103

7 Status and Development Trend of Big Data Technology Application in the Private Equity Industry ... 105
7.1 The Development and Status of Big Data Technology ... 105
7.1.1 Key Features of Big Data ... 106
7.1.2 Classification of Big Data ... 108
7.1.3 The Main Applications of Big Data Technology in Business ... 112
7.2 Application of Big Data Technology in the PE Industry ... 113
7.2.1 Application of Big Data Technology in the Project Searching and Screening Stages ... 113
7.2.2 Application of Big Data Technology in Project Evaluation ... 115
7.2.3 Application of Big Data Technology in Post-Investment Management ... 115
7.2.4 Key Elements of Big Data Technology Applied to PE Investment ... 116
7.3 Trends of Big Data Technology in the PE Industry ... 117
7.3.1 Importance of Big Data Will Gradually Exceed Personal Social Networks ... 117
7.3.2 Teams of Data Scientists Will Become an Integral Part of Changing the Governance Structure of PE Companies ... 118
References ... 118

8 Status and Development Trend of Artificial Intelligence Application in the Private Equity Industry ... 121
8.1 The Development of AI Technology ... 121
8.2 Policy Environment of AI and PE Industry ... 124
8.3 The Current Market Situation of the PE Industry ... 126
8.3.1 The Demand for Equity Assets Has Surged ... 126
8.3.2 The Pain Points of the Traditional PE Industry ... 127
8.4 Application Scenarios of AI Technology in the PE Industry ... 128
8.5 Application Cases of AI Technology in the PE Industry ... 133

About the Authors

Ruihui Xu Ph.D. in Finance is a Senior Research Fellow at the Financial Research Institute of the People's Bank of China. She holds Bachelor and Master degree of mathematics from Xiamen University and the University of Macau, respectively, and completes Ph.D. study in Department of Finance and Business Economics at the University of Macau. During the academic year 2014–2015, she visited the University of California, Berkeley. Her research focuses on macroeconomics, financial markets, and fintech. She has published over 10 academic papers in SCI, SSCI, and Chinese SSCI (CSSSCI) journals. As a co-author, she has published a book named "China's Financial Market Liberalization: Policy and Empirical Analysis".

Dawei Zhao Senior Research Fellow, Ph.D. in Economics, is currently the Deputy Secretary General of the FinTech Research Center of the Financial Research Institute of the People's Bank of China. He holds Bachelor, Master, and Doctorate degrees in Economics all from Central University of Finance and Economics. In 2009, funded by China Scholarship Council, he visited the State University of New York as a visiting scholar. After Dr. Zhao joined the People's Bank of China Financial Research Institute in 2011, he won the First Award of the "Youth Research Project 2019, 2020" of the People's Bank of China, the First Award of the "2017–2018 the PBC FinTech Research Project" by FinTech Committee of the People's Bank of China, and the First Award of the "2018 FinTech Youth Thesis" by FinTech Research Center of National Institution for Finance & Development. With a long-term focus on FinTech and RegTech, Dr. Zhao has published more than 70 academic papers. As the author and co-author, Dr. Zhao has compiled "FinTech and RegTech in China", "Artificial Financial Intelligence in China", "The Era of Artificial Financial Intelligence", "Technology Rebuild Finance: FinTech Utilization and Perspective", "Chained Future: Blockchain Theory and Application", "Development Trends and Supervision of FinTech", "China FinTech Annual Report (2018, 2019, 2020, 2021, 2022)", "Annual Report on China's RegTech Development (2019, 2020, 2021)", and other works.

Abbreviations

AMAC	Asset Management Association of China
AML	Anti-Money Laundering
API	Application Programming Interface
BSE	Beijing Stock Exchange
CAC	Office of the Central Cyberspace Affairs Commission (Cyberspace Administration of China)
CAICT	China Academy of Information and Communications Technology
CBIRC	China Bank Insurance Regulatory Commission
CBRC	China Banking Regulatory Commission
CFT	Counter-terrorist financing
CIRC	China Insurance Regulatory Commission
CNCERT/CC	National Computer Network Emergency Response Technical Team/Coordination Center of China
CSIPFC	China Securities Investor Protection Fund Company
CSRC	China Securities Regulatory Commission
CVC	Corporate venture capital
DLT	Distributed Ledger Technology
ETF	Exchange traded fund
FATF	Financial Action Task Force on Money Laundering
FoF	Fund-of-funds
FSB	Financial Stability Board
GDPR	General Data Protection Regulation
GP	General partner
HKEX	Hong Kong Stock Exchange
IPO	Initial public offerings
LP	Limited partner
M&A	Mergers and Acquisition
MIIT	Ministry of Industry and Information Technology
MOST	Ministry of Science and Technology
MPS	Ministry of Public Security
NCM	Nasdaq Capital Market

NDRC	National Development and Reform Commission
NEEQ	National Equities Exchange and Quotations
NFT	Non-fungible token
NGM	Nasdaq Global Market
NIFA	National Internet Finance Association of China
NIFD	National Institution for Finance & Development
NIPRTC	Northern Industrial Property Rights Trading Center
NLP	Natural language processing
NYSE	New York Stock Exchange
OTC	Over-the-counter market
PBC	People's Bank of China
PE	Private Equity
PRC	People's Republic of China
PSD2	Payment Service Directive 2
RMB	Renminbi
SAC	Securities Association of China
SAFE	State Administration of Foreign Exchange
SAIC	State Administration for Market Regulation
SASAC	State-owned Assets Supervision and Administration Commission of the State Council
SGX	Singapore Stock Exchange
SME	Small-and-Medium Enterprise
SPAC	Special Purpose Acquisition Company
STAR market	Science and Technology Innovation Board
VC	Venture capital

List of Figures

Fig. 3.1 Global and China's fintech investment scale and growth rate. *Note* Global fintech investment data from CB Insights, China's data from FORWORD Business Information 32
Fig. 3.2 Global investment share of fintech applications. *Note* Concerning data inconsistent across reports, this chart calculates the share of different areas. The 2017–2019 data is from KPMG's Pulse of Fintech H1-2020 global, and the 2020–2022 data is from KPMG's Pulse of Fintech H1-2023 global 36
Fig. 3.3 Regional composition of fintech investments. *Note* EMEA = Europe, the Middle East, and Africa. Concerning data inconsistent across reports, this chart calculates the regional share. The 2017–2020 data is from The Pulse of Fintech H1 2021, and the 2021–2022 data is from Fintech Trends H1 2023, since the reports stop releasing data of countries in detail after the second half of 2021 37
Fig. 5.1 Number of PE Punishment Cases across Province in 2022. *Note* Name of provinces or municipal cities (such as Beijing) is the punishment imposed by the local securities regulatory bureau. *Source* CSRC, web news, the authors 71
Fig. 5.2 Key application scenarios for compliance technology 77
Fig. 5.3 Key points of PE investment compliance 77
Fig. 7.1 Cumulative performance of the APAC multi-factor indices for a monthly rebalancing frequency and different levels of AUM *Source* RavenPack (2021) 109
Fig. 8.1 Registrations and growth rate of AI-related companies in China. Qichacha Finance (2023) *Source* 123
Fig. 8.2 Composition of net financial assets of Chinese households (2000–2019). Li and Zhang (2021) *Source* 127

Fig. 9.1 Number of countries with central bank digital currencies (CBDCs) in exploration phases (by Phase Status). *Sources* Finbold.com, Statista.com, Atlanticcouncil.org 142
Fig. 9.2 Blockchain market size in China 2016–2022 (in billion yuan). *Source* Statista 145

List of Tables

Table 3.1 Distribution of startups in the subcategories of the fintech sector 35
Table 3.2 Major stock exchanges' regulations on SPAC listings and mergers and acquisitions 39
Table 5.1 Technology applications in compliance areas 76
Table 8.1 Emerging digital technologies in the asset management industry 129
Table 9.1 Some foreign blockchain equity trading platform projects 152

Chapter 1
Private Equity in the Age of Fintech

Private equity (PE), an essential part of the multi-level capital market in China, is indispensable to enhancing financial support for the real economy in the high-quality development stage. A high-quality and vibrant PE market is conducive to promoting enterprises' innovation, corporate governance, and globalization of firms (Agmon and Messica 2009; Gompers et al. 2016; Aldatmaz and Brown 2020).[1] In recent years, the rapidly developing fintech has altered China's secondary capital market (such as investment decisions and high-frequency trading). However, the application of fintech in the primary market is rare. To fill the gap, this section discusses how fintech could improve the PE market's efficiency and play an essential role in developing a multi-level capital market.

1.1 Current Development of the PE Industry

1.1.1 Definition and Characteristics of PE

PE is an equity investment covering all stages of a company before its initial public offering, including investment in companies in seed, startup, development, expansion, maturity, and pre-IPO stages. According to investment stages, it can be divided into venture capital (VC), development capital, buyout/buy-in fund, mezzanine capital, turnaround, pre-IPO capital (such as bridge finance), and others (such as private investment in public equity, distressed debt, and real estate). In a narrow measure, PE mainly refers to the investment in mature enterprises that have formed a specific scale and generated stable cash flow, which occurs in the late stage of

[1] Aldatmaz and Brown (2020) document an industry spillover effect that positive externalities created by private equity firms are absorbed by other companies within the same industry, raising labor productivity, employment, profitability, and capital expenditures.

R. Xu and D. Zhao, *Digital Transformation of Private Equity in China*, Contributions to Finance and Accounting, https://doi.org/10.1007/978-981-99-8482-4_1

venture capital. M&A funds (merger and acquisition funds) and mezzanine capital account for the most prominent part of the capital scale.

PE has the following major characteristics. First, it has a long duration and poor liquidity, thus investors demand higher returns than those in the public market. Second, without a public market, investors and companies are matched through personal connections, industry associations, or intermediaries. Third, there is a wide range of funding sources, including high-net-worth individuals, venture funds, leveraged buyout funds, strategic investors, pension funds, and insurance companies. Fourth, investment returns are realized mainly by public offering and listing, sale or M&A, and company recapitalization (Cendrowski et al. 2012).

There are four types of PE in China. The first type is specialized independent investment funds with diversified sources of capital, and the second type is investment funds of large financial institutions. The two types of PE are fiduciary, and their investors include pension funds, universities, institutions, high-net-worth individuals, and insurance companies. Interestingly, US investors prefer the first type, believing their investment decisions are more independent, while the parent company may interfere with the second type.

In contrast, European investors prefer the second type of PE, considering its safety due to the parent company's excellent reputation and sufficient capital. The third type is general PE funds which are accredited investors funds. The fourth type is investment funds of large corporations, which serve the corporation's growth strategies and portfolios and are financed by the corporation. The difference in the funding sources affects the PE structure and management style since different funds set different investment objectives and strategies and have different tolerance for risk.

1.1.2 PE in China

As an essential part of the multi-level capital market, PE has played a crucial role in supporting entrepreneurship and innovation, promoting supply-side structural reform, increasing the proportion of direct financing, promoting the growth of enterprises, and sustaining healthy economic development.[2] After more than 30 years of development, the number and scale of active PEs in China have increased by several hundred times. As of July 2022, there are 24,330 PE fund managers and 133,793 PE funds in China, with a scale of 19.97 trillion yuan. However, the proportion of China's PE to GDP is still low, and there is still much room for long-term development and a long way to go to help industrial upgrading and the growth of new economic enterprises.

The rapid expansion of China's PE industry is inextricably linked to the reform dividends of the capital market. China's local PE was born in 1985 when the State Science and Technology Commission and the Ministry of Finance jointly established

[2] PE is believed to be beneficial for the creation of job opportunities and economic growth (Heed 2010).

the China New Technology Venture Capital Corporation, aiming to foster the development of high-tech enterprises in various regions. In 1992, the International Data Group (IDG) entered China and became the first foreign investment institution. In 1995, China implemented the "Administrative Measures on Establishment of Overseas Investment Funds for Chinese Industries" and encouraged foreign investment institutions to enter China. The successful listings of Sohu, NetEase, and Asiainfo in the US have generated considerable returns for the institutions. In 2006, China amended the "Partnership Enterprise Law," which allowed the limited partnership form commonly adopted by international PE funds and vigorously promoted industry development. A series of regulations were introduced to clarify the regulatory system since 2013, including "Notice on Division of Responsibilities for PE Fund Management" and "Measures for Registration of Private Investment Fund Managers and Fund Filing (for Trial Implementation)." The China Securities Regulatory Commission has supervised the PE fund industry since 2013.

In 2015, the PE market experienced explosive growth, driven by abundant liquidity, the rise of emerging technologies (such as mobile Internet, and artificial intelligence), and the inspiration from the government-led "mass entrepreneurship and innovation." In 2017, the annual PE fundraising amount was about 1.8 trillion yuan, and the management scale exceeded 8 trillion yuan. Nevertheless, the rapid growth in this period was highly related to the expansion of shadow banking in China (Ehlers et al. 2018). Long-term funds accounted for only about 25% of the investor structure of domestic Renminbi funds. The PE industry ended its irrational boom and retreated. At the same time, the tightening of asset management regulations in 2018 caused financial deleveraging, shadow banking credit crunched, and banks' off-balance-sheet funding channels to be significantly cut off. In 2018 and 2019, the annual PE fundraising amount fell to 1.3 trillion yuan and 1.2 trillion yuan, respectively. The fundraising amount of early-stage and VC institutions fell more significantly—dropped by 34% and 28% year on year, respectively. In 2020, despite the shock of the covid-19 epidemic, China's PE investment industry improved, and the industry structure was optimized. The growth rate of venture capital funds has remained stable for two consecutive years, and M&A funds have increased their investment in technology-based enterprises in the expansion period (especially in the semiconductor, automobile, and auto parts industries). It is worth noting that the investment growth in the ESG field of China's PE has been significant since 2020.[3] In 2021, the annual investment scale of China's PE hit a 10-year high, reaching 128 billion US dollars. Investment hotspots have shifted to semiconductors, electric vehicles, and renewable energy from traditional online services and e-commerce industries. In 2022, China-based fintechs focused on industry enablement, particularly enabling traditional financial institutions to improve their operations or provide new products and services to their customers (KPMG 2022). In 2023, Fintech firms in China follow the global trend in looking at ways to leverage AI-generated content (AIGC). While China has restricted access to ChatGPT, the tech giants, including

[3] The trend is similar in Asia and countries worldwide (Zaccone and Pedrini 2020; Long and Johnstone 2023).

Baidu, Tencent, and Alibaba, developed their own large language models (KPMG 2023).

The excess earnings and principal return were fair but not quite desired compared to other assets in China,[4] making PE funding less favorable to investors. Chinese PE funds have generated an after-fee internal rate of return (IRR) of about 12.5% in the past 10-year period, but not as high as public funds, real estate, and non-standard high-yield debt based on real estate. Public funds have generated an annualized after-fee return of 14.5% over the past 20 years. Moreover, in terms of return of principal, total exits from PE funds are only equivalent to 16% of the total amount raised. Statics show that more than half of the funds have not entered the exit period, but more importantly, it is due to the limitations of the Renminbi fund exit mechanism and lack of exit channels.

Although the total PE cases and amount have slumped since 2018, the average value of a single investment has increased yearly. The proportion of billion-dollar level cases has grown continuously, with the single amount reaching a 10-year high of 32.1 million US dollars in the first half of 2020. In the evolution of China's PE market from the primary stage to the mature market, competition is accelerating, the survival of the fittest is inevitable, and the head effect and constant strength of the strong have also emerged. In 2019, the top 1% of PE funds in China accounted for 25.5% of the total fundraising in the market, and the top 1% of the enterprises' financing amount accounted for 41.3% of the total investment. The "two-and-eight" effect was highlighted, and the market accelerated differentiation.

In the future, China's PE funds will become more professional and long-term. Managers need to focus more on industry research, and further improve their ability to explore trading opportunities, investment ability, risk control, return to value investing, and invest in valuable enterprises.

---

[4] Some studies examine the relative performance of PE funds versus the public market, and find evidences that PE funds outperformed the S&P 500 net of fees during these specific sample periods (Robinson and Sensoy 2013; Harris et al. 2014). In addition, some studies identify the sources of performance persistence among VC funds. Ewens et al. (2013) find that VC partners' human capital is more important in explaining performance persistence of VC investments than VC firm's organizational capital or from. Nanda et al. (2020) argue that the performance persistence mainly stems from investing in the right places at the right times, and less on the right companies.

1.2 Issues to Be Concerned About High-Quality Development of the PE Market

1.2.1 Clarify the Positioning of the PE Industry Development

In recent years, three major types of investment teams have been integrated and intertwined to promote the development of PE. The first type is professional foreign investment institutions equipped with investment concepts, organization, and practices of developed countries, such as Sequoia, IDG, Softbank, and other investments. The second type originated from listed companies or private enterprises, which focus on specific areas and partially adopt western and Chinese management modes. The third type is funds with national capital characteristics (founded by the state, local government, and state-owned enterprises), which are often more prominent in scale and focus on areas of national strategic importance, such as quantum, satellite, chip, and major equipment. A PE investor must review the investment capability and positioning in the competitive market environment and be able to judge industrial development direction and trends with professional knowledge.

1.2.2 Perform Efficient Risk Management in PE

Efficient risk management is vital to ensure the value of PE. It requires dynamically adjusted risk management measures and good investment strategies. On the one hand, risk management measures should be formulated at different investment stages. In the pre-investment phase, key measures include: selecting the appropriate investment object, focusing on the analysis of the entrepreneurial team, internal management, market situation, core competitiveness, and financial and policy environment. In the investment stage, perform good due diligence, establish an expert advisory group to judge specific projects, and formulate investment agreements to set appropriate investment constraints. In the post-investment stage, pay attention to regular reviews of the target company. In the post-investment phase, focus on regular supervision of the investment object, perform good strategic guidance, resource integration, talent introduction, and assistance in corporate governance. On the other hand, investment institutions should develop good investment strategies, such as segmented, joint, and portfolio investments. Effective investment strategies can mitigate or avoid the risks to a certain extent.

1.2.3 Strengthen the Post-Investment Management

The post-investment management is one of the most essential parts of the PE cycle ("fundraising-investment-management-exit"), but it does not receive enough attention in practice. The post-investment management is critical for gaining income and realizing the value-added of the invested enterprises. In recent years, post-investment management has been providing value-added services. For example, it distinguishes the opportunities and risks of major events, identifies the primary business focus and channels, manages the changes in the core entrepreneurial team, satisfies financing needs on time, and implements option incentives for outstanding talents. Alternatively, post-investment management has transformed from rough investment to exemplary management, which will significantly enhance the value of the investment and reduce the risk.[5]

To strengthen the post-investment management, it is crucial to refine the organization, improve the specialized post-investment management team, and provide effective and reliable suggestions for the business development, financial design and strategic choice of the invested enterprises, and support the enterprises with different management resource at different development stages.

1.2.4 Improve the Exit Mechanism of PE

The smooth exit of PE is essential to realize the return on capital and investment appreciation. It is also a significant link for the next round of fundraising and reinvestment. According to the current practice of China's financial market, the main exit mechanisms include IPO, M&A, and secondary sales. IPO is highly favored in the PE market due to its high return. But M&A has become a major exit channel for PE funds, benefiting from the continuous changes in China's M&A policy. In the past few years, accompanied by the rapid development of science and technology innovation and the PE industry, the exit mechanism has developed into a good multi-channel situation with M&A as the leading channel and IPO issuance and secondary sale as complementary channels.

[5] Bloom et al. (2015) find that PE firms are better managed than government, family, and privately owned firms, and have similar management to publicly listed firms. It holds for firms in both developed and developing countries. And it is correlated to PE's stronger people management practices and monitoring management practices.

1.3 The Combination of Fintech and the PE Industry

In recent years, intelligent technology is gradually changing the social development pattern, industrial structure, and live interaction mode and has constantly generated many innovative enterprises, providing broad space and development opportunities for PE. Meanwhile, in the background of the intelligent era, PE plays an irreplaceable role in promoting long-term capital formation and supporting innovation and entrepreneurship. In the future, PE will play a more significant role in fostering future financial development and serving the real economy.

1.3.1 Key Features of Fintech

Fintech, a portmanteau for "financial technology," refers to integrating technology (such as big data, artificial intelligence, and blockchain) into financial services to improve service quality and efficiency. The PE industry should utilize innovative technologies to enhance operational and compliance capabilities (Guan 2017).

Big data can improve the accuracy of project identification. In the era of big data, decision-making in business, the economy, and various other fields is increasingly based on data and analysis. Financial institutions have developed big data-based risk management systems to effectively prevent financial risks by digging deeper into user data and introducing external public data to judge users' creditworthiness comprehensively. The mandatory disclosure of relevant information by enterprises is not enough to select projects with real investment value, and a solid and adequate extensive data infrastructure is indispensable. Full utilization of internal and external data helps PEs to screen investment projects more objectively and accurately and allocate funds more efficiently.

Artificial intelligence (AI) technology can assist investment decisions. Since 2015, banks, brokerage firms, funds, third-party wealth management institutions, and Internet companies have actively launched robot-advisor products based on artificial intelligence. The products use AI technology to make customer portraits quickly, and analyze the customer's risk appetite, investment horizon, and other preferences. Then the system will recommend suitable investment portfolios to the customer.

Blockchain can enhance the post-investment management of funds. Blockchain technology offers technical advantages such as decentralization, openness, transparency, anonymity, data immutability, and autonomy in information transmission and storage (Choo 2021). Blockchain technology, especially the data immutability feature, has broad applications in the financial market, since it makes the fund flow data immutable and the fund's source and use traceable.

Virtual reality (VR) and augmented reality (AR) technology help to visualize data (Liu 2019). VR technology generates three-dimensional virtual environments using computers or other intelligent computing devices. Users can interact naturally with objects in the virtual world through special input/output devices and get the same feelings as the real world through vision, hearing, touch, and other senses. AR technology, on the other hand, uses computers or other intelligent computing devices to simulate and apply virtual information to the real world, which is perceived by human senses and creates a sensory experience beyond reality. Data visualization help investors understand more intuitively the various social and economic benefits of investment projects and enrich the investment evaluation dimension (Solis 2019).

1.3.2 Advantages of Fintech Applications in the PE Industry

First, fintech applications in the PE industry help meet mass customer asset management needs. Traditional financial institutions generally set thresholds for customer assets when providing asset management services. It excludes mass investors who do not meet the requirement, leaving them less accessible to sound investment advice. Financial managers may have limited time to provide comprehensive services and perfect suggestions even if the asset requirement is met. For example, at the end of July 2021, there were nearly 8,500 mutual funds, and improper asset allocation among the various types of funds may lead to loss. Facing a wide range of products, robo-advisors can synthesize customer needs and provide customers with more effective asset allocation schemes. Even if customers ultimately do not choose the investment schemes offered, they can still be used as an investment reference.

Second, it reduces the cost of wealth management institutions. The low cost of robo-advisors is reflected in low labor and transaction costs. Traditional investment advisors generally set a management fee greater than 1% due to high labor costs, while the current robo-advisor management fee is generally 0–0.5%. As robo-advisors do not need to recruit an offline financial advisor team, the marginal cost will be further reduced with increased financial scale. Its cost advantage over traditional investment advisors is pronounced (Zhao and Zhou 2021). Moreover, as the investment objects of a robo-advisor are mainly exchange-traded funds (ETFs), its expense ratio is significantly lower than that of the active fund. The total expense of ETF is below 0.55%, while the active fund's is above 1%.

Third, it enhances information transparency. Since the traditional investment advisor company and the fund company are selling on a commission basis, the fund company will reward the company with a certain percentage of commission upon successful sales of products, which leads to a high degree of interest correlation between the two companies. In addition, many of the service terms of investment advisors are obscure, and the process of selecting investment targets is also opaque. If the investment advisory company recommends a product with a higher percentage of commission rather than a product with better returns, it will seriously damage the interests of investors. Robo-advisors must fully disclose the selection range of financial products, fees charged, and other aspects so that customers can view investment information anytime and anywhere. In addition, robo-advisors must strictly implement the procedures. They must not mislead customers due to private interests, which reduces moral hazard to a certain extent and increases customers' trust in the product.

Fourth, it provides value-added services such as portfolio rebalancing and tax avoidance. When the asset portfolio deviates from the target investment allocation with market changes, the robo-advisor automatically restores the portfolio proportion to the target investment allocation proportion by buying or selling regularly. Traditional investment advisors usually reallocate assets after a long communication period with clients, and the operation process takes much time and human resources, resulting in increased costs. In contrast, robo-advisors can automatically adjust the allocation proportion based on user questionnaires and market conditions, significantly improving efficiency and reducing costs. Tax avoidance involves selling earlier unrealized investment losses to offset the capital gains tax payable on the investment income, and investing the saved tax to maximize revenue while maintaining certain risks and benefits. The research report of Wealthfront shows that tax avoidance can increase after-tax income by about 1.55% every year.

Fifth, it builds an intelligent risk management system. A large amount of unstructured data can be obtained by digital technology and used for quantitative analysis, risk detection, and early warning of investment objects, thus significantly improving the risk management ability of PE funds. In the post-investment management stage, PE funds can use financial management software to provide small and medium-sized enterprises (SMEs) with effective cash flow management, information collection and accurate analysis, and other services (Zhou 2021). The intelligent risk management system can also offer financial management suggestions for SMEs to improve efficiency and reduce operational risks (Zhao and Wang 2015).

1.3.3 Cases of Fintech Application in the PE Industry

The CreditEase AI platform. CreditEase has applied AI technology in PE. In 2021, it launched the "AI + FOF" system—an AI platform that runs through the entire investment management process of CreditEase Wealth's PE fund-of-funds. It can analyze data from over 80,000 funds of more than 20,000 fund managers and millions of investment objects. The data covers comprehensive aspects, including investment industries, amounts, rounds, the proportion of follow-up financing obtained by the investment objects, and exit returns.

"The interface of the AI + FOF system is like a search engine, which realizes the one-click search functions," said Zhang Jun, Engineering Director of CreditEase's Big Data Innovation Center. The system integrates CreditEase's AI technology accumulated over the past 12 years and can extract valuable data from scattered and disorderly massive information. It then puts the valuable data in a virtual data warehouse, establishes a knowledge graph, learns from it, and then presents it in a structured way.

For example, for general partners (GPs) study, the AI + FOF system can quickly and comprehensively display a GP's data portrait from more than 65 dimensions.

Specifically, the dimensions include the industry trend and distribution, round distribution, currency distribution, geographical distribution of the GP's investment projects, preference for leading or following investment, the proportion of joint investment, proportion of unicorns, proportion of investment projects entering the next round of investment; tracking to each project's financing gap period, relationship mapping with other GPs; fund managers' experience, part-time job situations, and interpersonal networks. It can analyze 10 million pieces of data in real-time every second, and such arithmetic power is beyond the human brain's reach.

The AI system can significantly improve investment efficiency and accuracy and help fund-of-fund managers in all aspects of due diligence, post-investment monitoring, management, and trend analysis of the entire industry.

Nasdaq Linq blockchain platform. The core advantage of blockchain technology is providing an immutable record and a permanently preserved data chain for users, which can precisely eliminate the current pain points of the PE market. The decentralization, encryption, and consensus mechanism features of blockchain can connect the private equity trading market, which lacks credit intermediaries, and help startups issue electronic certificates for private security issuance, improving the transparency of equity trading. Using blockchain-based smart contracts to compile valuation adjustment mechanism (VAM) terms can promote its smooth progress. In the blockchain system, when the original startup enterprise meets the additional financing conditions, the smart contract will automatically transfer the additional investment amount from the investor's account to the financing company's account. Alternatively, when the initial startup fails to meet the additional financing conditions, the smart contract will automatically transfer part of the founder's shares to the investors.

In 2015, the Nasdaq exchange (Nasdaq) in the United States launched the Nasdaq Linq platform in partnership with the blockchain startup Chain.com. Nasdaq Linq enables private securities issuance documented with blockchain technology, a first attempt at using blockchain technology. Issuers can use Nasdaq Linq blockchain ledger technology to complete and record a private securities transaction, browse the issuance of share certificates, confirm the validity of the certificates, and check other information such as asset numbers and price per share. They can also search for certificates in interactive mode, view recent certificates, and check which investors hold the most shares in the enterprise. In addition, startups can also evaluate the shares held by a single investor in the enterprise. Blockchain technology can improve the efficiency of transaction settlement, enable immediate settlement of PE transactions, improve the transparency of the PE market, and enhance the activity and liquidity of the primary market.

1.3.4 *Issues of Digital Technology Application in the PE Industry*

Information technology risks. Using AI technology by PE funds to upgrade business processes will pose a considerable challenge to regulators, causing risk identification, monitoring, and disposal difficulties. It is difficult for regulators to identify high-tech "black boxes" and the hidden risks. Due to the interpretability of algorithms and the fact that technology products and applications do not have the qualification of legal subjects and the ability to bear responsibility, it will be more difficult to delineate the liability subjects, making it difficult to identify risks effectively. Even if the regulators can fully recognize the risks brought by digital technology, there may still be regulatory lag, and the timeliness of post-event risk disposal will be affected. Concerning the high sensitivity of financial data and the data protection environment is still to be improved, further applications of big data and AI technology may not avoid collecting, storing, and analyzing some sensitive information. Such activities are usually difficult to monitor and instantly forewarn by regulators effectively and can only be dealt with after information leakage leads to illegal acts such as network fraud. It causes a severe negative impact on financial consumers' physical and mental health and property safety. Applications of digital technologies have increased the complexity of the PE fund business and increased the difficulty of risk disposal. The potential risks and hazards involve rapid, large-scale, hidden aggregation and opaque management of public funds. Once the risks expose, the difficulty of risk disposal will further increase.

Risk of data leakage. Whether PE funds can ensure data security by increasing the use of digital technology and whether the innovation process brings risks to the entire financial system is an unavoidable problem. PE funds risk data leakage when using digital technology for business innovation. PE funds master a large amount of capital data from the accumulated customer resources and account transaction records. The excessive concentration of data is more likely to lead to data leakage and the risk of violating customers' privacy. Data leakage is common in China, and even information legally required to be protected could be leaked and traded. It is reported that even employees in Alipay, which specializes in digital technology, once download Alipay user data with the content of the data exceeding 20G, and sell to e-commerce companies and data companies many times.

Market monopoly. Fintech is easy to cause market monopoly problems. Judging by traditional standards, the current business model of China's fintech companies is suspected of monopoly. China's Anti-Monopoly Law stipulates that monopolistic behavior includes monopoly agreements by business operators, abuse of dominant market position by operators, and concentration of operators that has or may have the effect of eliminating or restricting competition. Among them, an operator's behaviors of abusing market dominance include: selling goods at a price lower than the cost without justifiable reasons or applying differential treatment to trading counterparts with the same conditions, such as trading prices. When the market share of an operator reaches 50%, or the combined market share of two operators reaches two-thirds, the operator can be presumed to have a dominant market position. China's giant Internet platforms (Alipay, WeChat payment) have a market share of more than 90% in the third-party payment field. All implemented "cross-subsidies" and algorithmic discrimination, which is suspected of monopoly according to the traditional standards.

Institutions with digital technology advantages tend to master a large amount of data. The edges can be amplified by the external characteristics of big data, enabling the institutions to occupy a dominant position in a particular market segment quickly. In this circumstance, many small and weak institutions may lose competitiveness, further exacerbating the market concentration. Ultimately, suppose the "winner-takes-all" attribute of fintech leads to an oligopoly in the PE market. In that case, the market efficiency will be lower, thus violating the original intention of adopting fintech to reduce enterprise financing costs and achieve effective resource allocation.

References

Agmon T, Messica A. Financial foreign direct investment: The role of private equity investments in the globalization of firms from emerging markets. Manag Int Rev. 2009;49:11–26.

Aldatmaz S, Brown GW. Private equity in the global economy: Evidence on industry spillovers. J Corp Finan. 2020;60: 101524.

Bloom N, Sadun R, Van Reenen J. Do private equity owned firms have better management practices? Am Econ Rev. 2015;105(5):442–6. https://doi.org/10.1257/aer.p20151000.

Cendrowski H, Petro LW, Martin JP, Wadecki AA. Private Equity: History, Governance, and Operations. John Wiley & Sons; 2012.

Choo TL. Application of blockchain technology in private equity. World scientific book chapters. In: Lee DKC, Ding D, Guan C, editors. Financial Management in the Digital Economy, chapter 5. World Scientific Publishing Co. Pte. Ltd.; 2021. p. 85–104

Ehlers T, Kong S, Zhu F. Mapping shadow banking in China: structure and dynamics. BIS Working Papers No 701; 2018. https://www.bis.org/publ/work701.pdf

Ewen M, Jones C, Rhodes-Kropf M. The price of diversifiable risk in venture capital and private equity. Rev Financ Stud. 2013;26(8):1854–89.

Gompers P, Kaplan SN, Mukharlyamov V. What do private equity firms say they do? J Financ Econ. 2016;121(3):449–76. https://doi.org/10.1016/j.jfineco.2016.06.003.

Guan XL. The road of financial technology development in private equity industry under the new situation. Tsinghua Financ Rev. 2017;12:90–1. https://doi.org/10.19409/j.cnki.thf-review.2017.12.027.(inChinese).

Harris R, Jenkinson T, Kaplan S. Private equity performance: What do we know? J Finance. 2014;69(5):1851–82.

Heed A. Regulation of private equity. J Bank Regul. 2010;12(1):24–47.

KPMG. The Pulse of Fintech H2; 2022. https://kpmg.com/xx/en/home/campaigns/2023/05/pulse-of-fintech-h2-2022.html

KPMG. The Pulse of Fintech H1; 2023. https://assets.kpmg.com/content/dam/kpmg/xx/pdf/2023/07/global-pulse-of-fintech-h123-report-web.pdf

Liu T. Reshape the micro foundation of green finance with financial technology. Banker. 2019;4:128–30 (in Chinese).

Long FJ, Johnstone S. Applying 'Deep ESG' to Asian private equity. J Sustain Finance Investment. 2023;13(2):943–61.

Nanda R, Sampsa S, Sorenson O. The persistent effect of initial success: Evidence from venture capital. J Financ Econ. 2020;137:231–48.

Robinson D, Sensoy B. Do private equity fund managers earn their fees? Compensation, ownership, and cash flow performance. Rev Financ Stud. 2013;26:2760–97.

Solis J. Data visualization is king. J Private Equity. 2019;22(3):102–7.

Zaccone MC, Pedrini M. ESG factor integration into private equity. Sustainability. 2020;12(14):5725.

Zhao Y, Wang J. Ways of private equity funds to promote the development of small and medium-sized enterprises in the era of internet finance—A case study of private equity funds participating in crowdfunding financing. Bus Econ Res. 2015;34:91–2 (in Chinese).

Zhao DW, Zhou YR. Application of artificial intelligence in commercial banks. Tsinghua Financ Rev. 2021;4:89–92. https://doi.org/10.19409/j.cnki.thf-review.2021.04.024.(inChinese).

Zhou YR. The role and countermeasures of digital inclusive finance in promoting the development of small and micro enterprises. Financ Vertical Horizontal. 2021;1:24–31 (in Chinese).

Chapter 2
Technology Innovation and Private Equity

Development and innovation of science and technology are a source of inexhaustible power for a country and nation to flourish. However, investments in science and technology have distinctive features of long duration, large investment amount, and high risk in early development, which cannot be achieved without long-term capital support and catalytic effect. In recent years, technology innovation mainly focused on frontier areas, with the high interdisciplinary and increased difficulty of breakthrough, which requires tremendous investment and years of investment. The experience and practice of developed countries show that capital markets, especially PE investment funds, can promote science and technology innovation. Meanwhile, technological innovations such as big data, AI, and blockchain have brought opportunities for transforming and upgrading PE investment. According to China's development plans and strategies, developing high technology is critical to national rejuvenation. However, scientific and technological innovation cannot achieve breakthroughs without the impetus of a sound capital market, including PE investment and VC funds.

2.1 Development and Dilemma of PE Investment in a New Stage

The outbreak of the covid-19 epidemic in 2020, overlaid with the economic cycle, led to a severe recession in major economies worldwide, slowing PE investment activity and shifting investors to a wait-and-see mood. In contrast, the PE market in China has risen, as the high and sustained economic growth rate has made China the most active PE market in the world. According to data from the Asset Management Association of China, by the end of 2022, the size of private securities investment funds, PE, and VC funds reached 5.56 trillion yuan, 10.94 trillion yuan, and 2.83 trillion yuan, up more than 100% from the end of 2016, respectively (Asset Management Association of

R. Xu and D. Zhao, *Digital Transformation of Private Equity in China*, Contributions to Finance and Accounting, https://doi.org/10.1007/978-981-99-8482-4_2

China 2021). As an essential part of China's diversified capital market, PE investment has become a necessary force in supporting "mass entrepreneurship and innovation", promoting the development of high-tech industries, guiding the transformation of old and new dynamics, and promoting the structural reform of the supply side.

2.1.1 PE Market Snowballs and Shows a Positive Trend

The trend toward globalization has become more pronounced. In recent years, large foreign investment institutions and fund managers have turned to China for more stable investment returns and to reduce the risks associated with economic cycles. PE investment in China has become globalized, aligning with the rest of the world regarding PE investment structures, management models, and management teams. The trend has accelerated significantly since the outbreak of covid-19 epidemic. Compared to other countries and regions, China has demonstrated a more successful experience in epidemic prevention and control, consolidating its position as a global capital investment center. The PE market is also rising. Regarding market size, China has become the world's second-largest equity investment market, which is expected to continue for a long time.

The PE industry in China has matured considerably. An essential indicator of the maturity of an industry is whether it is in line with the 80/20 rule. In the past few years, the domestic PE market has become highly competitive, and the industry has begun to follow the 80/20 rule, with less than 10% of PE managers managing 75% of the fund size. Benefiting from sophisticated industry regulation and policy stability, China's PE industry has entered a sustainable, stable, and healthy development stage. The entry threshold for PE managers has also increased significantly in recent years. Many investment professionals joined the PE industry and promoted the industry to be more standardized and mature.

The external development environment is increasingly favorable. The government policies impose macro regulation and guidance, can safeguard the external environment, provide legal support for PE investment, and lead the market's direction through direct participation in capital investment.[1] In recent years, China has emphasized recognizing and encouraging PE investment in the science and technology industry. For example, the new Foreign Investment Law, promulgated and implemented in January 2020, clearly states that foreign investors in China's PE market will be equally protected. And the state shall enforce policies to create a stable, transparent, foreseeable, and level-playing market environment. In January 2021, the

[1] It is controversial whether government participation (mixed syndication) bring positive influence as compared with private venture capital (PVC). On the one hand, existing studies find a positive effect of mixed syndication compared to syndication solely among PVCs in Europe (Cumming et al. 2017), and globally (Brander et al. 2015). On the other hand, Zhang (2018) find that start-ups backed by mixed syndication underperform in China, compared to those backed by syndication solely among PVCs. A possible explanations of the underperformance is less complementary resources but higher coordination cost in mixed syndication.

CSRC issued and implemented the "Provisions on Strengthening the Supervision of Private Equity Investment Funds", which stipulate the obligations of related parties of PE funds, probit non-compliant PE investment activities, thus increasing compliance obligations to the PE fund industry. The National Development and Reform Commission and other relevant ministries and commissions have vigorously promoted system construction around PE investment. Local governments have successively introduced many preferential policies for PE investment, such as improving fair tax policies and establishing government-led industry investment funds, which can promote the healthy development of equity-invested enterprises.

The internal governance of PE funds has improved. From the perspective of modern enterprise management, while pursuing performance and scale, an enterprise or institution needs to establish a reasonable equity structure, a compensation system, and an incentive mechanism in line with the market level. Alternatively, good internal governance is fundamental to a company's long-term development. Facing fierce competition, China's PE investment model has evolved from a traditional workshop to an institutionalized operation. The pioneers of China's PEs have taken the lead from the top international PE funds and are committed to expanding their business and improving their management capabilities.[2]

2.1.2 Dilemma of China's PE Industry

Although the scale of China's PE and VC funds is ranked second in the world, high-quality development set new requirements, and the economic and development environment of PEs have changed, there are still some problems to be solved in the PE industry.

The legal system is not yet perfect, and government regulation is inadequate. Since the establishment of the PE market, China has only issued and implemented two rules on PE funds, namely the "Interim Measures for Supervision and Administration of Private Investment Funds" (June 2014) and "Provisions on Strengthening the Supervision of Private Investment Funds" (January 2021). Other relevant regulations include the "Securities Law", "Securities Investment Fund Law", the "Interim Measures for the Management of Venture Capital Enterprises", the "Measures for the Suitability Management of Securities and Futures Investors," and other laws and regulations (Fan 2021). However, there are some problems with the legal provisions. For example, the lack of detailed implementation rules and weak operability substantially reduces the authority and systemic nature of the laws. The role of policies and regulations as the cornerstone of the development of PE investment is not apparent.

Moreover, due to the broad scope of PE investment supervision, the current regulatory responsibilities of each regulatory department lack clarity, including the *National*

[2] This is contrast to the argument of Aizenman and Kendall (2008) that China was the dominant net importer of VC investment during 2003–2007.

Development and Reform Commission (NDRC), China Banking and Insurance Regulatory Commission (CBIRC), China Securities Regulatory Commission (CSRC) and other regulatory agencies. The regulatory strength and accuracy need to be improved in regulating illegal sales of various PE products, "pseudo-PE", and "fake PE". The penetrating supervision of the underlying assets of PE funds needs to be further strengthened.

Investors are growing but still immature, and the market exit channel needs improvement. Compared to narrow domestic investment channels in China, the high return of PE investment attracts many private enterprises, state-owned enterprises, and wealthy individual investors. Nevertheless, investors tend to excessively pursue short-term interests, which often leads to the contradiction between investors' desire for an early exit and the long-term operation of fund management. The exit mechanism of PE funds in developed countries is complete, including public listing, merger and acquisition, repurchase, over-the-counter transaction, liquidation, and property rights transaction. However, in China, there is still a gap in policy guidance in enriching the PE exit mechanism, resulting in relatively few choices of PE exit channels, which restraints the development and growth of the PE market.

The equity trading market is underdeveloped, and capital liquidity is inadequate. PE investment pursues long-term stable equity return and naturally has low liquidity. A well-developed secondary market for PE funds is a good solution to the problem. However, the secondary market of private equity trading in China is still in its infancy. A unified national market has not yet been formed, restricting the circulation of PE investment rights. In addition, the problem of information asymmetry is more prominent in private equity transactions. There is still a lack of credit intermediaries to register private equity investment transactions, and information about the holder and changes cannot be fully registered through authoritative electronic credentials. It often takes a long time to review the authenticity of each link in the transaction process, which will ultimately affect the entire transaction progress.

2.1.3 Technology Innovation Boosts the Development of the PE Industry

Technological innovation and application have brought tremendous changes to the traditional financial sector. The PE market also requires digital transformation and upgrading. The investment and asset management models must also be transformed accordingly to achieve a more efficient capital flow of funds and resource allocation.

AI can serve the management and decision-making of PE investment. Some PEs attach great importance to the innovative application of financial technology and stress the combination of AI technology and business scenarios. The role of AI is mainly reflected in the following three aspects.

First, AI technology can improve the research database. Due to the diversification of PE investment objects, the basic research data of most PEs are purchased through peripheral service institutions. But the purchased basic data cannot be effectively utilized due to the wide variety of business scenarios (Qi et al. 2018). AI can help solve the problem by improving data mining ability, finding the fit to meet the company's business expansion needs, achieving customized development, and mining high-value investment research information from the data.

Second, it improves the efficiency of investment research. The most energy and money-consuming procedure of PE investment is investment research, mainly personnel costs during independent research and field investigation. Applications of AI technology can significantly reduce part of the costs and prevent the procedure from being influenced by adverse factors such as staff changes. Besides, some research tools or data analysis techniques based on AI technology can efficiently support investment decisions, effective screening, and management and risk disposal.

Third, it reduces the management risk of investment institutions. The most effective way to address external compliance and internal operations risks is to carry out comprehensive management through standardized processes and AI-based analysis systems. Utilizing Internet technology, AI technology can detect potential risks of investment and invested enterprises by mining and analyzing industry big data from massive open networks and assist investment institutions in effective risk management and control.

Blockchain technology can improve the transparency of PE transactions. Due to the private nature of PE investment transactions, the information on enterprises is highly non-transparent. In China, the holder information and equity changes in the transaction process cannot be fully recorded or realized through authoritative electronic credentials. And it often takes a long time to review the authenticity and validity of the documents and data for each equity transaction (Wang et al. 2018). The core advantage of blockchain technology is providing immutable records. The decentralization, encryption, and consensus mechanism of blockchain can connect the PE trading markets, which lack credit intermediaries, provide a permanently preserved data chain for users, improve the transparency of equity trading, and enhance the market's liquidity.

Big data helps solve the information asymmetry problem in the PE investment market. The private primary market has problems of information fragmentation, opacity, and high barriers to access, which can easily lead to investment mistakes or loss of investment opportunities. Traditional PE value assessment and due diligence work requires the participation of appraisers, accountants, lawyers, and other cooperation, causing high coordination costs, poor timeliness, long cycle, and relatively simple application scenarios. Big data technology can conduct PE investment evaluation and audit by retrieving additional enterprise data from the Internet and compiling more comprehensive and accurate information (Mao 2019). It improves not only the depth and breadth of the audit but also the quality and efficiency of the audit. Furthermore, the correlation and comparison analysis of data from various aspects help improve the accuracy and objectivity of the audit conclusions.

2.2 Big Data and PE

The integration process of big data technology and various industries has been accelerating, especially in the financial industry. PE funds link professional resources through big data technology to provide automated tools, comprehensive industry data, and compliance information.

2.2.1 Big Data Technology, Industry, and PE Mutually Benefit Each Other

First, big data technology improves PE investment returns. Big data storage and analysis technology can analyze customer behavior, improve business efficiency, strengthen risk management, and ultimately improve investment return. PE fund management companies have accumulated massive business scenario data, and the data analysis and processing require high information processing costs. Applying big data technology, especially specific calculation models and algorithms, can significantly cut data information processing costs and improve profitability. According to a Wall Street Journal report, "PE Funds Turn to Big Data to Find Investments," high-tech and big data tools are increasingly used by professional investors to make decisions about "what to buy" and "how much to invest (Kang 2018; Petersone et al. 2022). Actually, data science has been "lightening the burden" of investment managers over the past few decades. Financial information service providers, including Thomson Reuters and Bloomberg, collect tremendous economic and financial information, provide the original information for private investment institutions to conduct case studies, and offer a pricing basis for specific investments through a series of analytical tools. The application of big data can serve all stages of PE investment, including research, strategic decision-making, and due diligence. With the support of big data, PE investment decision-making can be increasingly rational.

Second, big data technology support digital and rational PE decision-making. Data has become an important production factor. The big data industry is a strategic emerging industry specializing in data generation, collection, storage, processing, analysis, and service and is an important engine to accelerate economic and social development. According to the statistics of IT Orange, the peak investment period of the big data industry occurred between 2015 and 2018, with an annual average of nearly 500 investment events and an investment amount of about 90 billion yuan. The number declined to about 200 investment events per year in the past two years, but the industry prospect is still appealing to PE investment institutions. The "14th Five-Year" period is critical for the transition of China's industrial economy to the digital economy and has put forward new requirements for the big data industry. The "14th Five-Year Plan" focuses on "creating new advantages in the digital economy" and makes the deployment of cultivating and growing new digital sectors such as big data. Since 2021, guidance and supporting policies on the big data industry have been constantly introduced to promote the high-quality development of the big data industry. In addition to the big data industry investment funds established in various regions, PE/VC institutions, which prefer high risk and high return, have become essential in promoting the development and growth of the big data industry. Most big data enterprises listed on the Science and Technology Innovation Board (STAR Market) and the Growth Enterprises Market (GEM) have received PE investments in the past two years.

2.2.2 Big Data Technology Promotes the Development of the PE Industry

First, big data technology improves the accuracy of investment advice to users. Big data technology can unify and filter massive data, automatically classify and summarize the relevant data through a standard storage model, discover the behavioral patterns of customers, and thus lay the foundation of precise marketing strategies. Big data technology draws more accurate conclusions through mathematical calculation, and the advantage is magnified when dealing with large-scale and rapidly growing data. Using specific models and calculation methods to process the massive data can provide relevant suggestions for investment decisions and risk management in a visualized manner, thus enhancing the application of the conclusions.

Second, big data technology enhances PE risk management. Customer information, especially behavioral information, is constantly changing. Continuous monitoring and analysis are required to identify abnormal behavioral details of the customers, particularly for investment management and risk management. Big data technology, particularly storage, analysis, process processing, and cloud computing technologies, can analyze the data and provide real-time suggestions for investment and risk control managers. It dramatically improves the capability of real-time management and effectively enhances the level of risk control of PE funds. The application of big data technology can further help investment managers analyze information and the changes in the valuation of investment objects and strengthen the ability to foresee and prevent risks (Kan 2016).

Third, big data technology facilitates PEs to form a featured value investment system. By utilizing data and analytical advantages, big data technology helps PE fund managers explore more helpful information in the relevant industry environment, thus supporting invested firms to make efficient business and investment decisions and achieve the purpose of enterprise value-added. In the era of big data, extensive and effective mastering of information and use of data helps PE fund managers to explore investment targets and form a value investment system with their characteristics.

PE fund managers also attached importance to data security, which is one of the key issues in developing big data technology. Big data usually contains a high commercial value, but illegal and unauthorized usage may cause customers privacy breaches and economic losses. Therefore, big data security technology development is essential to current big data technology development. Protecting the data security of enterprises and customers is the bottom line to protect economic interests. As a policy response, the Chinese government has successively introduced the "Personal Information Protection Law" and the "Data Security Law," which set strict restrictions on the use of individual data and protect personal information security. PE fund companies have been closely related to big data computing enterprises, paying more attention to applying big data technology, risk management, and data security.

2.3 Mobile Internet Activates PE Business

In the past two decades, driven by the explosive growth and widespread Internet application, financial institutions increasingly provided B-to-C services to their customers by developing mobile applications. Mobile applications are vital for more effective services and enable financial institutions to obtain and accumulate business data. The prevalence of the Internet in remote areas without banking facilities promotes the use of technology-based fintech (Loo 2019), and the widespread use of mobile devices has increased the adoption rate of fintech innovations (Stewart and Jurjens 2018).

Consumption scenarios have changed significantly in the mobile internet era, which demands the digital transformation of the PE industry. In 2020, PE fund investments in the Asia Pacific were dominated by investments in the technology sector, accounting for more than 30% of total deals. The covid-19 epidemic has changed consumer behavior and caused rapid technology penetration, significant preference shifts, and accelerated digital product and service development (KPMG 2021). These trends accelerate, and digital transformation may remain a key theme for the financial sector in the coming years. As pandemic restrictions have been lifted in early 2023 in China, a major hurdle for PE activity has been removed. Although geopolitical and global economic uncertainty continue, the global economy is generally expected to return to relative normality (KPMG 2023). PEs provide more flexible lines of credit than traditional banks, offering various credit products, including direct loans, mezzanine financing, funding loans, and restructuring asset financing. In contrast with tight bank credit availability, this solutions-based approach would speed up capital flow into the PE asset class. As the world's second-largest economy, China has experienced a significant increase in total investable financial assets of individuals and emphasized the development of Internet and digital economy, laying the foundation for developing the Internet wealth management industry.

The Internet accelerates the development of the PE market. Mobile Internet channels such as mobile APPs enable customers to obtain financial services equally and conveniently. It becomes the user entrance, information entrance, and service entrance of inclusive financial services, removes the geographical limitation of financial services, and enhances the breadth and depth of financial services. In addition, with the rise of emerging mobile Internet technologies, information dissemination is more effective, convenient, and less costly. Cloud services are closer to customer needs, inexpensive, and easy to operate. By combining online and offline channels, PE funds can develop products with less cost and higher efficiency, extend the coverage of customer groups, and improve the financial service quality and user experience. Mobile terminals have fast transaction capability, support customized demand, and gain mass investments. Web3 is evolving as a new kind of Internet, with open protocols and standards that allow for new avenues of value transfer, data sharing, and application development across platforms. Bain & Company's web3 and digital asset database tracks nearly 5,000 firms that have cumulatively raised more than $94 billion, most of it over the past three years. In 2022, private investors injected between $20 billion and $30 billion into web3-related companies during the year. And that number doesn't include the significant internal investments made by corporations and financial institutions (Bain and Company 2023). The upward trend of PE deals in the Internet sector will probably be maintained and extended to related sectors.

2.4 AI Assists in Efficient Decision-Making

AI technology is based on a modern computer system that simulates human cognitive and reasoning mechanisms, uses mathematical theories and methods to obtain external information, independently processes and makes decisions on information, and outputs answers to questions (Chang 2021). The rapid iterative development of AI technology promotes the maturity of simulating human functions, bringing a profound transformative impact on various aspects of PE investment, such as service channels, service methods, risk management, credit financing, and investment decisions.

In the past decade, the financial market experienced the PC and mobile Internet eras and is now entering the era of AI. The influence and application of AI are a significant concern in the PE industry. Traditional technical indicators and data analysis may fail to predict price changes in the PE industry, as it echoes multiple factors, rapid data changes, and incomplete information. With AI technology, deep learning and reinforcement learning functions enable a computer to learn automatically from complex and irregular data, develop rules to solve problems, and adaptively optimize the rules.

The main application of AI technology in PE investment is data-based and algorithm-based. Compared with big data technology, the core breakthrough of AI technology lies in deep learning, intelligent analysis, and intelligent decision-making. AI can be applied in PE research, arbitrage and hedging, financial forecasting, intelligent timing, and algorithmic trading. AI technology enables machines to obtain investment information, collate data, conduct quantitative analysis, write research reports and risk tips, and assist investors in investment research. The rapid and intelligent analysis of massive data and information can realize the whole portfolio management process from information acquisition to reporting completion.

With more efficient algorithm models and more professional industry cognition, the analysis ability across different financial fields can be formed. The time for data processing on complex financial problems can be shortened, significantly saving the workforce and improving decision-making efficiency.

The AI platform can assist the fund-of-fund manager in many aspects, including conducting due diligence, post-investment monitoring and management, and trend analysis of the whole industry, greatly enhancing investment efficiency and accuracy. On the one hand, machines have a natural advantage in dealing with massive amounts of information, such as collecting a large amount of information, conducting data analysis, and reporting writing. Natural language processing technology can analyze text information and look for the inherent patterns of market changes. Based on the collected historical market data, AI can analyze and make predictions about the growth of companies, thus assisting in investment decisions. In addition, AI can automatically generate many documents with fixed formats, such as prospectuses, research reports, due diligence reports, and investment intention letters, based on the collected information, thus improving efficiency and reducing repetitive and time-consuming tasks.

On the other hand, AI assists in PE research, investment, advisor, and customer service. AI can perform functions such as intelligent recommendation, improve the efficiency of investment research and enhance the interaction experience. Machine learning methods can efficiently assist investment decisions, and voice semantic processing can provide intelligent customer service with lower service costs and better customer experience (Guan 2017). Some financial institutions and Internet finance companies have already used AI technologies (such as natural language processing, voice recognition, and vocal recognition) to provide technical support for remote customer service, business consultation, and processing. It sends users timely responses and reduces the pressure of manual services and operating costs (Ma and Wei 2018).

Some PE funds have been explored in robo-advisor. By adopting AI and big data technologies, robo-advisor can replicate the model of excellent fund managers to optimize asset management strategies, provide users with customized investment decision references, and dynamically update asset allocation suggestions. Compared with subjective investment decisions, robo-advisor has several main features. First, its objective quality makes the analysis and prediction more reliable and transparent. Second, the faster strain speed and more immense computing power make possible judgments under more complex conditions, with more trading targets and a larger scale of funds. Third, it can continuously optimize trading and investment capabilities through deep learning.

Robo-advisors surpass humans in investment allocation and trade execution capabilities and help investors overcome emotional weaknesses. Investors, even experienced ones, are inevitably affected by negative emotions such as fear, greed, and anxiety. On the contrary, AI is rational in making investment decisions and reacts faster toward unexpected events, which helps to effectively control the withdrawal of the net value of PE products. In the future, applications of robo-advisor will be further extended in the PE industry, as accompanied by continuous iterative innovation and development of AI neural network and decision tree technology.

In China, the application of AI technology in PE investment is in the exploratory stage. For example, Goldenwise Capital launched a robo-advisor product called "Whale Finance", which is tailored for Chinese users to make overseas investments. The product takes a proactive approach to quantitative investment. It also makes timely adjustments based on changes in market conditions to deliver better investment performance.

In the future, with the rapid expansion of the PE fund scale, a new era of AI investment is coming.

2.5 Blockchain Increases Business Trust

Blockchain technology, a distributed database technology, originated in the field of digital cryptocurrency and has been developing rapidly in recent years. Blockchain technology has the feature of decentralization. With no centralized management agency in the blockchain network, trust must be shared with all nodes in the network. Meanwhile, the characteristics of immutable certificates and smart contracts make blockchain technology widely used in payment and settlement, asset management, debt financing, consumer finance, and other fields.

Blockchain technology has unique advantages in improving the efficiency and security of PE transactions. First, some problems of PE transactions can be solved with blockchain's decentralization, information immutability, and distributed bookkeeping features, including bottleneck of transaction efficiency, transaction time lag, fraud, and operational risks. Second, blockchain technology can effectively solve technical issues such as miscellaneous files, data loss, and complex processes in PE transactions and reduce violations such as underhand operations. Third, the distributed ledger and other functions can optimize the over-the-counter (OTC) market (Zhong 2019). The OTC market is relatively decentralized, with low requirements for real-time liquidity, easy-to-correct transaction errors, and a high tolerance for global risks. The application of blockchain technology can promote the construction of private equity trading platforms, including regional equity exchange markets, inter-institutional markets, and other OTC markets, and facilitate the improvement of the equity market in the multi-level capital market.

Blockchain technology has the following advantages when applied to various equity trading and circulation aspects. For fundraising and trading, it can optimize the equity registration and transfer process and enhance transfer efficiency. First, the distributed ledger can ensure that the shared information is traceable and easy to audit so that the equity transferor and transferee can promptly obtain and match the transfer information. Second, smart contracts can set the conditions for the transfer, simplify the review process, improve efficiency and transparency, and thus reduce operating costs. For clearing and settlement, smart contracts can be embedded with blockchain technology to build a unified clearing and settlement model. First, buyers and sellers are automatically matched with smart contracts, and the transaction is quickly and accurately publicized on the blockchain. Second, consistency can be guaranteed through transaction signatures, consensus algorithms, and cross-chain technology, which automatically completes operations such as account matching and reduces capital clearing operations and supervision costs (Yao 2018). Third, as blockchain data is irrevocable and copied to each node within a short time, the time frame for settlement can be significantly shortened, and the risk of the counterparty and capital occupation can be reduced. For registration and authorization, decentralization and de-intermediation can be achieved through technical means such as zero-knowledge proof, homomorphic encryption, secure multi-party computation, ring signature, and group signature. It can further enhance the efficiency and transparency of registration and authorization, protect the privacy of transaction identity and content and safeguard the asset rights and interests of equity owners.

The application of blockchain in PE trading platforms covers the following aspects. (1) Data storage. By establishing a data flow platform based on the decentralization feature of blockchain, the PE trading platform can track the whole process of data transactions and avoid large-scale data loss or leakage caused by attacks on centralized institutions and mishandling of authority. (2) Data management. Blockchain keeps transaction records and realizes equity assets' confirmation, authorization, and real-time monitoring. (3) Transaction process. Compared to the complex clearing rules and high costs of the traditional centralized clearing system, blockchain technology ensures instantaneous transaction verification and realizes automatic clearing and settlement of equity transactions, making equity transactions more convenient and secure.

The structure of a blockchain PE trading platform generally contains two layers. The bottom layer is a blockchain P2P network, which creates trading accounts, records transactions, and forms a decentralized distributed ledger through the interconnection between accounts. The top layer is used to store basic information of trading users and use the stored information to realize the registration, purchase, and transfer of PE funds. For the purchase, sale, or transfer of equity assets, the platform can invoke the underlying blockchain and executes smart contracts to record the information of the purchase, sale, or transfer of assets into the counterparty's blockchain account, conduct real-time settlement, and record the changes of account balances and equity owners. During the transaction process, the issuance, settlement, and delivery of transaction instructions are all carried out on the blockchain platform, and all blockchain nodes can be queried. In addition, each node has a copy of the blockchain information, and the loss of any node does not affect other nodes and the entire network, thus ensuring the security of the blockchain trading platform.

There have been many successful cases of applying blockchain technology to PE transactions. In 2015, the NASDAQ Stock Exchange launched Linq, a PE trading platform jointly developed with the blockchain company Chain. With Linq, customers can view the history of securities issuance and transfer securities. It saves the equity paper certificate and worksheets generated during the financing process for PE investors and shareholders of private companies, solves the problems of data errors or human tampering that may exist when conducting equity transactions manually, and significantly improves the efficiency of transactions. Based on blockchain technology, the platform enhances trust between different parties. In December 2015, the Chain became its first Linq user, and companies, including ChangeTip and PeerNova also use the Linq platform. In February 2017, Northern Trust officially launched a private equity ecosystem based on blockchain technology, which was developed by Northern Trust and IBM. When required, the blockchain network provides real-time data to fund managers, investors, and regulators. It also brings significant advantages to traders by shortening the listing time of new high-tech PE funds. In addition, global financial institutions and companies are laying out blockchain equity trading platform projects such as Equibit, Bitshares, and Overstock. Many stock exchanges or financial institutions invest in the R&D and experiment of blockchain equity trading platforms.

In China, PE funds also actively explore the innovation and deep integration of blockchain and PE business. Northern Industrial Property Rights Trading Center and Tai Cloud Technology, the first blockchain company listed on the National Equities Exchange and Quotations, jointly developed the blockchain equity registration system TERS, the first application in the field of blockchain equity registration in China. In January 2018, ShareX, a blockchain-based equity management trading platform, and Potential Stock, an equity transfer platform, entered strategic cooperation. December 2020 witnessed the launch of a blockchain-based PE fund management platform invested by Yangzijiang Investment Fund Management Company. The platform realizes all critical transaction and management information through blockchain technology. Microservice architecture performs vital business operations online (such as fundraising, investment, management, and exit), collects data rapidly, and configures external disclosure statements flexibly.

Applying blockchain technology in PE investment has bright prospects but also faces some challenges and risks. There are risks arising from the technology's immaturity, such as the security and immutability of blockchain and compliance risks. Blockchain's effectiveness in promoting the development of PEs has yet to be further tested by the regulatory authorities and the industry. And its large-scale application will also face a series of technical limitations.

References

Aizenman J, Kendall J. The internationalization of venture capital and private equity. National Bureau of Economic Research Working paper No. w14344; 2008

Asset Management Association of China. Overview of private equity fund registration and filing in 2021; 2022. https://www.amac.org.cn/researchstatistics/report/zgsmjjhysjbg/202201/P020220106409073144772.pdf

Bain & Company. Global Private Equity Report 2023: Navigating a Shifting Tide; 2023. https://www.bain.com/insights/topics/global-private-equity-report/

Brander JA, Du Q, Hellmann T. The effects of government-sponsored venture capital: international evidence. Rev Finance. 2015;19(2):571–618. https://doi.org/10.1093/rof/rfu009.

Cumming DJ, Grilli L, Murtinu S. Governmental and independent venture capital investments in Europe: A firm-level performance analysis. J Corp Finan. 2017;42:439–59. https://doi.org/10.1016/j.jcorpfin.2014.10.016.

Fan YX. Analysis of the exit mechanism of private equity investment funds in China. Bus Econ. 2021;8:79–81. https://doi.org/10.19905/j.cnki.syjj1982.2021.08.029.(inChinese).

Guan XL. The development path of financial technology in the private equity industry under the new situation. Tsinghua Financ Rev. 2017;12:90–1. https://doi.org/10.19409/j.cnki.thf-review.2017.12.027.(inChinese).

Kan JY. Research on the development status and countermeasures of domestic private equity investment funds. Southwest Finance. 2016;1:47–51 (in Chinese).

Kang J. Private equity turns to big data to find deals. Wall Street J 2018.

KPMG. Looking ahead: Private Equity trends for 2021, Jan 2021; 2021. https://kpmg.com/cn/en/home/insights/2021/01/looking-ahead-private-equity-trends-for-2021.html

KPMG. Asset Management and Private Equity 2023 Outlook, 31 Jan 2023; 2023. https://kpmg.com/cn/en/home/insights/2023/01/asset-management-and-private-equity-2023-outlook.html

Loo MKL. Enhancing Financial inclusion in ASEAN: Identifying the best growth markets for fintech. J Risk Financ Manage. 2019;12(4):1–21.

Ma SL, Wei FY. Application of artificial intelligence technology in the financial field: Main difficulties and countermeasures. Southern Finance. 2018;3:78–84 (in Chinese).

Mao QX. The application of enterprise value assessment in private equity investment practice. Natl Circ Econ. 2019;36:59–60. https://doi.org/10.16834/j.cnki.issn1009-5292.2019.36.027.(inChinese).

Petersone S, Tan A, Allmendinger R, Roy S, Hales J. A data-driven framework for identifying investment opportunities in private equity. arXiv e-prints; 2022. https://doi.org/10.48550/arXiv.2204.01852

Qi Y, Jin J, Zhang TY. Evaluation of private equity investment projects in the context of 'Artificial Intelligence.' Bus Account. 2018;10:7–11 (in Chinese).

Stewart H, Jurjens J. Data security and consumer trust in FinTech innovation in Germany. Inform Comput Secur. 2018;26(1):109–28.

Wang JS, Han CZ, Han KY. The application of blockchain technology in China's equity trading. China's Circ Econ. 2018;2:83–90. https://doi.org/10.14089/j.cnki.cn11-3664/f.2018.02.010.(inChinese).

Yao Q. Similarities and differences between distributed ledgers and traditional ledgers and their practical significance. Tsinghua Financ Rev. 2018;6:64–8. https://doi.org/10.19409/j.cnki.thf-review.2018.06.025.(inChinese).

Zhang Y. Gain or pain? New evidence on mixed syndication between governmental and private venture capital firms in China. Small Bus Econ. 2018;51(4):995–1031.

Zhong GC. Research on the application prospect and supervision of blockchain in private equity trading platform. Hainan Finance. 2019;4:73–81 (in Chinese).

Chapter 3
Private Equity Investment in Fintech

Fintech has empowered PE, and PE has accelerated fintech development. A study by the International Monetary Fund shows that market valuations of publicly-traded fintech companies have quadrupled since the global financial crisis, outpacing many other sectors (He et al. 2017). According to the *2023 Chinese Fintech CEO Survey Report* jointly published by the National Internet Finance Association of China (NIFA) and KPMG, PE is the most dominant investor in fintech, accounting for 53% and 46% in 2020 and 2021, and 39% and 36% in 2022 and 2023, respectively, while the proportion of traditional financial institutions is on the rise, from 10% in 2020 to 19% in 2023. A developed capital market can facilitate the exit of PE investment, making PE participates in fintech more actively. Existing studies show that PE investment is conducive to promoting fintech innovation.

3.1 The Importance of PE Investment in Fintech

3.1.1 PE Investment Model in Fintech

The assets of fintech companies, especially startup fintech companies, are mainly intangible assets such as intellectual property. Startups in the fintech sector tend to use equity for financing to avoid high leverages. However, traditional financial institutions focus on collateral, loan guarantees, and financial indicators such as past operating income, net profit, and net assets. They are constrained by regulatory requirements, making it challenging to meet the financing needs of the emerging industry. PE investment emphasizes the future growth of enterprises, particularly innovative enterprises.

Venture capital, traditional financial institutions, and fintech companies have great potential to cooperate in developing fintech. Venture capital has keen market insight and efficient capital allocation capabilities, traditional financial institutions have

R. Xu and D. Zhao, *Digital Transformation of Private Equity in China*, Contributions to Finance and Accounting, https://doi.org/10.1007/978-981-99-8482-4_3

strong incentives to implement strategic transformation against China's economic transformation, and fintech companies have innovative technology and effective and flexible teams. Interaction between the three can create positive synergy and promote technological innovation.

Venture capital (VC), corporate venture capital (CVC), and private equity (PE) are the three primary modes of private investment in the fintech sector. Investment institutions and professional investors usually initiate VCs to invest in innovative companies, taking potentially high risks and seeking excess returns. CVC is generally set up by enterprises and directly invests in fintech startups as part of the enterprises' long-term growth strategy. The enterprises typically provide operational, marketing, and partnership network support to their fintech startups, and foster disruptive technologies (Rossi et al. 2020). In recent years, there has been a significant increase in corporate venture capital investments, such as Comcast Ventures, Google Ventures, Intel Capital, Johnson & Johnson Innovation, and Microsoft Ventures (Chemmanur et al. 2014). For innovative companies, corporate venture capital investment funds have a longer investment horizon and are better partners than VC (Chemmanur et al. 2014).

PEs make equity investments in unlisted fintech companies by setting up PE funds or fund-of-funds (FoF), with exit strategies such as stock listing, merger, acquisition, buybacks, and liquidations. In addition, some traditional financial institutions also set up joint ventures with technology companies to gain competitive advantages in fintech fields that are highly related to their primary business. With the help of shareholders, such companies have a comparative advantage in financing from the capital market.

PE investment is conducive to nurturing innovative fintech companies and promoting capital formation. Staged financing improves the efficiency of capital utilization and creates greater value. Angel investment can provide startup capital, resources, and management experience and help identify the development direction. VCs facilitate the enterprise to rapidly expand the market, enhance competitiveness and become bigger and stronger, laying the foundation for subsequent financing. When the product and business are stable, PE provides the capital and experience to implement strong corporate governance and reform the profit model, preparing the enterprise for an initial public offering.

A developed capital market can boost the availability of venture capital, which is more favorable for fintech development (Haddad and Hornuf 2019). The developed capital markets promote fintech financing through the following channels. First, fintech startups have more extensive access to funding from traditional financial institutions. Second, active stock markets facilitate the exit of VC through IPOs, create a positive incentive for VC, and stimulate entrepreneurial activity (Black and Gilson 1999). Since the global financial crisis in 2008, banking regulations have tightened, and global small and micro enterprises have faced a financing gap from the traditional financial system (European Central Bank 2013; Schindele and Szczesny 2016). These factors have magnified the importance of alternative funding sources for fintech development.

3.1.2 PE Promotes Technology Innovation

Empirical evidence from Europe and the United States has shown that VC and PE investment can promote innovation. With data from 20 manufacturing industries in the United States from 1965 to 1992, Kortum and Lerner (2000) find that the impact of VC on technology patents is positive and significant, with a magnitude larger than that of traditional R&D; its contribution to industrial innovation was about 8% during 1983–1992. Based on data from 10 manufacturing industries in 21 European countries from 1991 to 2005, Popov and Roosenboom (2012) show that VC investment contributes 10.2% of industrial innovation (number of patents granted). Moreover, the role of VC in promoting innovation is more pronounced in countries with lower barriers to entrepreneurship, more favorable tax and regulatory environments, and lower capital gains taxes. Arqué-Castells (2012) used data from 233 venture-backed firms in Spain and found that firms' patent applications increased significantly after VC fund investment, especially in the first two years after receiving a venture investment. Bertoni et al. (2010) compared 33 Italian VC-backed firms and 318 firms without VC investment and found that VC positively impacts the subsequent patenting activity of VC-backed firms. Meanwhile, corporate VC can also enhance the innovative behavior of parent companies (Ernst et al. 2005; Keil et al. 2008).

For PE investment, Wright et al. (2001) argue that it promotes revitalization and strategic innovation. Lerner et al. (2011) analyze a sample of 6398 patents from 472 firms granted from 1984 through May 2007 and find that firms pursue more influential innovations, as measured by patent citations, in the years following PE investment, which implies that PE investments are associated with a beneficial refocusing of firms innovative portfolios. In a 407 UK PE deals study, Amess et al. (2016) found a 6% increase in quality-adjusted patent inventories three years after the deal.

The mechanism of the positive impacts includes the following. First, PE can improve the incentives and governance of startups by providing resources such as capital, market, and entrepreneurial expertise (Large and Muegge 2008; Faria and Barbosa 2014). Gompers et al. (2016) surveyed 885 institutional venture capitalists at 681 firms and found that strategic guidance (87%) accounted for the highest percentage, followed by connections with investors in future rounds (72%), connections with potential clients (69%), and operational guidance (65%).

Second, PE creates value by helping the firm form a scale effect, increase revenues, improve incentives and governance, facilitate high-value exits or sales, make additional acquisitions and replacements, and reduce costs. Surveys show that companies with PE investments are more likely to adopt innovation strategies, such as entering into licensing agreements, selling technology rights, and participating in collaborative R&D agreements (Link et al. 2014). A study of 30 German equity funds by Maas et al. (2020) shows that some equity funds are more likely to emphasize innovation when identifying investment targets, as evidenced by being involved in the monitoring and managing of their innovation activities.

3.2 Overview of PE Investment in Fintech

3.2.1 Global Fintech and PE

The size of fintech is challenging to ascertain because of the varying definitions of fintech (Thakor 2020). For example, Buchak et al. (2018) paper views fintech as also including technology-assisted products provided by banks (e.g., online lending), but Thakor (2020) argues that banks should be excluded from the definition of fintech. Data from different statistical agencies vary widely, and some agencies adjust statistics scope over time. A typical example is the much-cited KPMG report, *The Pulse of Fintech*. For example, the size of global fintech investment (VC, PE, and M&A) in 2018 was $111.8 billion in *The Pulse of Fintech 2018* (KPMG 2018), published in 2019, was $150.4 billion in *The Pulse of Fintech H1 2020* (KPMG 2020a), and $145.9 billion in *The Pulse of Fintech H2 2020* (KPMG 2020b). Given this, we utilize various data sources to analyze trends and structural features.

The fintech investment surged from 2015 to 2018, and its growth rate became lower in 2019 (Fig. 3.1). In 2020, fintech investment was hampered by the social isolation related to the covid-19 epidemic. Conversely, social isolation accelerated digitalization and increased the demand for fintech in related industries. As a result, the scale of fintech investment remains stable.

The world and China share the same trend. According to CB Insights, global fintech investment (including VC, PE, and M&A) increased from $3.2 billion in 2012 to $55.3 billion in 2018, fell to $42.1 billion in 2020, and hit a historical peak

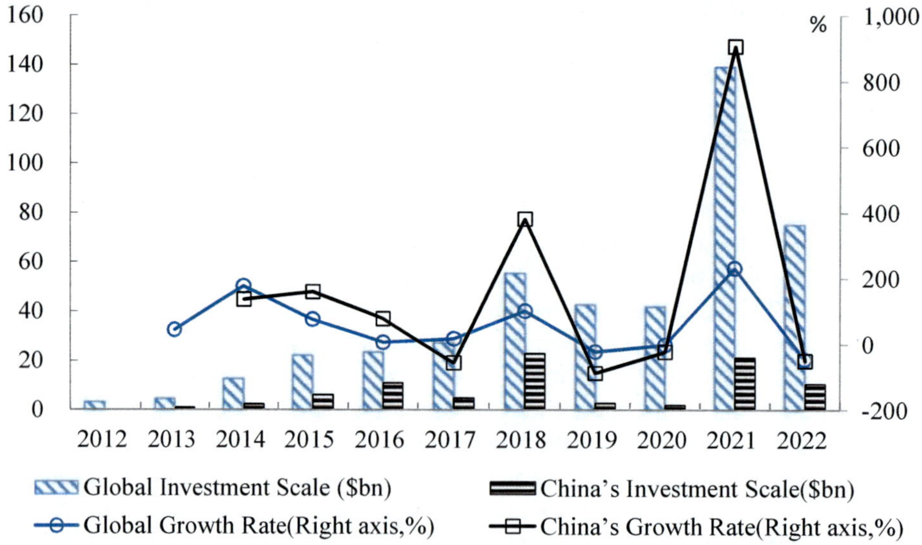

Fig. 3.1 Global and China's fintech investment scale and growth rate. *Note* Global fintech investment data from CB Insights, China's data from FORWORD Business Information

of $139 billion in 2021, followed by a drop of 46% in 2022 to $75.2 billion. According to FORWORD Business Information, fintech investment in China was 6.089 billion yuan in 2013, soared to 158.111 billion yuan in 2018, then declined sharply to 13.826 billion yuan in 2020. Fintech investment in China surged to a record high at 135.591 billion yuan in 2021, and decreased to 73.939 billion yuan in 2022, as driven by the popularity of the metaverse concept. The cumulative investment amount of global fintech investment from 2012 to 2022 reached $448.7 billion, and China's fintech investment from 2013 to 2022 reached 568.6 billion yuan.

According to the KPMG reports, the surge of fintech investment in 2018 stems not only from fintech business model innovation, mega M&A deals, and an increase in cross-border M&A, but also the increasing need for companies to leverage artificial intelligence (AI), machine learning and other technologies for compliance management. The mega M&A deals mainly include Vantiv's acquisition of Worldpay for $128.6 billion in the first quarter, Ant Finance's $14 billion financing in the second quarter, and Refinitiv's $17 billion PE investment in the third quarter. Against the backdrop of Payment Service Directive 2 (PSD2), General Data Protection Regulation (GDPR), and other laws and regulations that have strengthened regulation of the fintech sector, funding has accelerated to crucial technology areas such as big data.

Currently, fintech has become an essential part of financial services. According to the Centre for Finance, Technology and Entrepreneurship, the ratio of the market capitalization of the fintech industry to the banking industry has grown from less than 3% in 2010 to more than 30%. Specifically, the 100 largest commercial banks have a market capitalization of about $7.1 billion, and the 100 largest fintech companies have a market capitalization of approximately $2.8 billion.

In 2020, global fintech investment remained large, mainly due to the epidemic highlighting the importance of digital innovation and fintech. In the first half of 2020, the epidemic caused a disruption in cross-border M&A and a slowdown in fintech investment. In contrast, in the second half of 2020, fintech investment rebounded significantly. According to KPMG's *Pulse of Fintech* at the second half of 2020, fintech investment in the second half of 2020 was $71.9 billion (compared to $87 billion in the *Fintech Report—1H 2021*), more than double the amount in the first half of the year. Specifically, enterprises increased fintech investment and accelerated transformation, and big tech companies expanded their businesses through mergers and acquisitions.

In 2022, while global fintech investment dropped, the total investment remained at a high level compared to years before 2021. Investment in seed and early-stage deals surged, and will benefit the fintech ecosystem in the long-term. The outlook for fintech investment remains positive provided the ongoing transformation of financial services worldwide (KPMG 2023).

3.2.2 *PE Investments in the Fintech Subcategories and Different Regions*

Chemmanur et al. (2020) researched the funding patterns of fintech companies based on data from the Venture Scanner database.[1] Table 3.1 shows the number of startups and investors and the total amount of funds raised in 16 subcategories of fintech as of January 2020. The largest category was consumer lending, which raised $48.34 billion, with the largest share at 12 percent. Typical companies in the consumer lending category include SoFi, a P2P lending platform, and CommonBond, a fintech lender. Among them, CommonBond services focus on originating student loans, lending through an online platform, making efficient decisions, and securitizing student loans, thus keeping interest rates low and competitive.

Payments-related categories are more diverse, involving consumer payments, payment backend and infrastructure, and POS payments, corresponding to the second, third, and sixth largest financing amounts, respectively, with over $80 billion combined fundraising. Typical companies include India's mobile payment platform MobiKwik, the US-based Stripe, and iZettle, which Paypal acquired in September 2018.

The commercial lending category is in fourth place in financing amount, with cumulative fundraising of $26.73 billion and 8% of the number of companies. Typical companies in this category are Atlanta-based Kabbage, which provides financing for small and medium-sized businesses, and LendInvest, an online investment platform focusing on short-term bridge loans.

Fintech companies in the personal finance category raised a cumulative $8.14 billion, with 8.9% of the companies. A typical company is Credit Karma, founded in 2007 and headquartered in San Francisco. Its online services were launched in 2008 and became available through a mobile app in 2012.

Investment subcategories include retail and institutional investments, with more than $9 billion raised. Typical firms in the retail investing category include smart advisers Wealthfront and Betterment and the micro-investing platform Acorns. Typical companies in the institutional investing category include San Diego-based alternative investment platform Artivest.

Crowdfunding is the fintech subcategory that has received the least amount of funding and the fewest number of companies. Typical companies include Kickstarter and Indiegogo.

The financing stages of fintech companies are divided into seed, VC, and PE stages. The seed stage funding usually comes from angel investors or private lending. The VC stage includes Series A, B, and C equity investments. The PE stage financing comes from PE firms. As displayed in Chemmanur et al. (2020), the year with the largest share for seed-stage funding is 2013. Until 2018, fintech financing is dominated by VC-stage financing. In 2019, there is slightly more PE stage financing

[1] Venture Scanner focuses on collecting detailed data on the funding and exits of startups in the technology industry. The dataset covers startups founded since the 1980s, with the majority of fintech companies founded in 2014 and beyond.

Table 3.1 Distribution of startups in the subcategories of the fintech sector

Subcategory name	Number of companies	Number of investors	Amount raised (US$ billion)	Number of companies as a percentage	Typical company
Consumer lending	382	1308	483.4	11.8	SoFi, CommonBond
Consumer payments	216	732	377.7	6.7	MobiKwik, Obopay
Payments backend and infrastructure	261	780	359.0	8.1	Stripe, BlueSnap
Business lending	266	1021	267.3	8.2	LendInvest, Kabbage
Small and medium business tools	331	993	159.8	10.2	AvidXchange
Point of sale payments	206	661	113.1	6.4	iZettle
Consumer and commercial banking	102	393	94.3	3.2	Monzo
Personal finance	288	813	81.4	8.9	Credit Karma
Banking infrastructure	198	577	58.1	6.1	Symphony
Retail investing	201	596	53.0	6.2	Wealthfront
Financial transaction security	122	514	43.8	3.8	Kount
Institutional investing	228	513	38.5	7.1	Artivest
International money transfer	90	378	36.8	2.8	Wise
Equity financing	153	357	24.5	4.7	Seedrs
Financial research and data	97	251	18.7	3.0	Credit Benchmark
Crowdfunding	90	232	9.1	2.8	Kickstarter
Total	3231	10,119	2218.5	100	

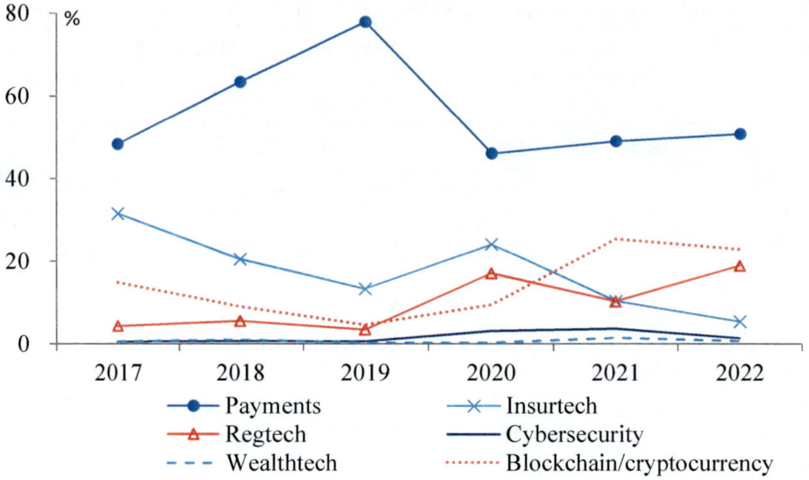

Fig. 3.2 Global investment share of fintech applications. *Note* Concerning data inconsistent across reports, this chart calculates the share of different areas. The 2017–2019 data is from KPMG's Pulse of Fintech H1-2020 global, and the 2020–2022 data is from KPMG's Pulse of Fintech H1-2023 global

than VC stage financing, which may mean that the fintech industry is gradually maturing.

By sector, payment technology and insurtech account for the largest share but have declined significantly since 2020, but regtech follows an inverse trend. The development of payment technology and insurtech is highly related to the traditional financial system. Traditional financial institutions actively build mobile apps to provide consumers convenient services and customized products. The share of blockchain/cryptocurrencies dropped in 2019 and then picked up. The share of wealth technology and cybersecurity technology tends to increase over time, related to the development of AI technology and the tightening of cybersecurity regulation (Fig. 3.2).

By region, the Americas saw the most fintech investment, dominated by the United States. In the second half of 2020, fintech M&A in the U.S. drove a rebound in global fintech investment. The U.S. led nine of the top 10 fintech M&A deals, with the largest deal being Charles Schwab's $22 billion acquisition of TD Ameritrade, followed by Credit Karma ($7.1 billion), Vertafore ($5.3 billion), Iberia Bank ($2.5 billion), and Avaloq ($2.2 billion), among others.

The continued sound of Europe's fintech ecosystem is conducive to developing large-scale and networked advantages. On the one hand, the governments and regulators of major European economies (such as the UK, Germany, and France) encourage the development of fintech. For example, the Bank of England encourages the healthy development of fintech through tools such as the Fintech Accelerator and the Fintech Hub, aiming to build a more efficient and resilient financial system (Bank of England 2019). Spain announced a regulatory sandbox arrangement in the second half of 2020 to promote the development of fintech. On the other hand, some European

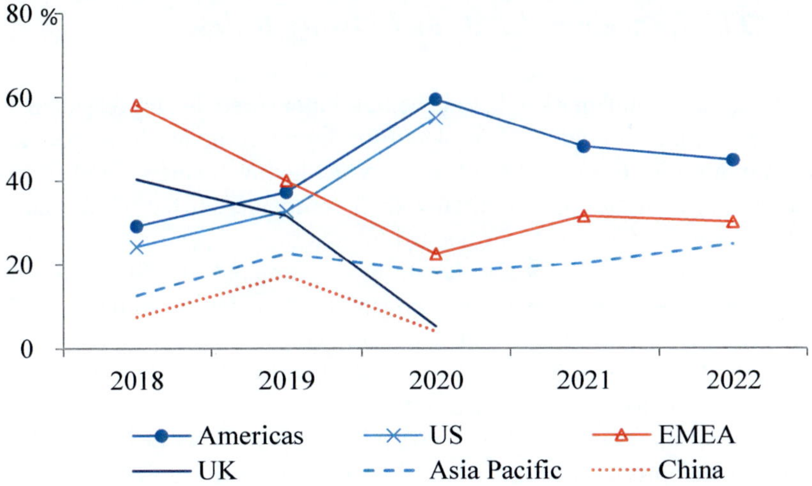

Fig. 3.3 Regional composition of fintech investments. *Note* EMEA = Europe, the Middle East, and Africa. Concerning data inconsistent across reports, this chart calculates the regional share. The 2017–2020 data is from The Pulse of Fintech H1 2021, and the 2021–2022 data is from Fintech Trends H1 2023, since the reports stop releasing data of countries in detail after the second half of 2021

regulatory initiatives have boosted the development of fintech, especially regtech. PSD2, which came into effect in 2018, requires banks to be equipped with the necessary APIs to provide data securely, facilitating the development of open banking and driving related fintech investments. Regtech investments have also increased in Europe following the GDPR since companies increased relevant investments to meet regulatory requirements.

In the Asia–Pacific area, China accounted for a primary share before 2018. Since 2019, China's share has declined significantly, while Southeast Asian countries (such as Indonesia and India) have picked up larger shares of fintech investment (Fig. 3.3).

3.3 Fintech Investments Through Special Purpose Acquisition Companies

A favorable financing environment, including IPOs and Special Purpose Acquisition Company (SPAC), facilitates PE exits and promotes global fintech investment.

3.3.1 The Concept of SPAC and Listing Rules

A SPAC is a capital market listing vehicle sponsored by professional investors and raises capital through IPO, to acquire a target company in a specific field or industry within a proposed period, thereby achieving financing and listing of the target company. SPACs are essentially shell companies. If the SPAC cannot find a target company and complete the acquisition within the specified time, it will return money to the investors. If the acquisition is completed, the SPAC and the target company will merge to form a new company (a "transferee company"), which will become the successor to SPAC as a listed company.

Compared with traditional IPO, the advantages of SPAC listing are mainly reflected in three aspects. First, from the sponsor's perspective, SPAC listings are more convenient, easier to exit, and have a higher possibility of success, lower cost, and substantial profits. Second, from the investor's perspective, SPACs offer the opportunity to invest in unlisted companies (usually enjoyed by PE investors). The right to redeem shares allows SPAC investors to minimize investment losses. Third, from the target company's perspective, a SPAC offers a shorter preparation time for IPO, greater price and trading certainty, and more flexible deal structuring. In addition, compared with "back-door Listing," SPAC companies are newly established. They have no business, a clear shareholding structure, no historical debt problems, and no "back-door Price" to be paid by the target company's shareholders to the SPAC.

In recent years, SPAC IPO filings have been steadily growing in popularity over the last decade. For the U.S., 2020 was a significant year for SPACs, with a dramatic increase in the number of IPOs, and the number of SPAC listings exceeded traditional IPO listings for the first time. According to SPAC Analytics, in 2020, SPACs had raised capital in 248 IPOs with $83.386 billion. In 2021, SPAC IPOs recorded a historical peak in the U.S., raising $162.503 billion in 613 IPOs. However, in 2022, the proceeds of SPAC IPOs became significantly lower than the last two years, although it surpassed 2017 and 2018 levels. There were 86 SPAC IPOs in 2022, raising approximately 13.431 billion. The drop in new SPAC IPO filings is likely related to the new accounting rules for SPACs introduced by the U.S. Securities and Exchange Commission (SEC) in April 2021.

Against the backdrop of a significant spike in the number of SPAC listings and capital raised in the U.S. in 2020, major international exchanges have been conducting studies on the SPAC listing (Schumacher 2019). The UK's newly revised SPAC rules and guidelines were enacted on 10 August 2021. The Singapore Exchange launched its Main Board listing rules for SPACs on 2 September 2021, effective on 3 September 2021, and became the first exchange in Asia to allow SPAC listings. The Hong Kong Stock Exchange (HKEX) released a consultation paper on SPAC on 17 September 2021 for a consultation period until 31 October. The HKEX concluded in December 2021 to create the SPAC. An overview of the specific requirements for SPAC listings and subsequent M&A by the stock exchanges in Hong Kong, China, Singapore, and the United States is shown in Table 3.2.

Table 3.2 Major stock exchanges' regulations on SPAC listings and mergers and acquisitions

	Hong Kong stock exchange (HKEX)	Singapore stock exchange (SGX)	New York stock exchange (NYSE)	Nasdaq global market (NGM)	Nasdaq capital market (NCM)
SPAC capital raising size/ market capitalization requirements	Over HKD 1 billion	Market capitalization greater than S$150 million	Market capitalization greater than $100 million	Market capitalization greater than $75 million	Market capitalization greater than $50 million
Sponsor qualifications	Must meet suitability and eligibility requirements, and at least one SPAC sponsor must be a SFC licensed company	Promoter track record and management team expertise	Initiator experience and track record	–	–
Investor Qualification	Professional investors only	No request made			
Minimum number of public shares held	The transferee company must have at least 100 shareholders	At least 300 public shareholders hold at least 25% of the issued shares	400	400	300
Minimum price per share/unit	HK$10	S$5	4 USD		
Whether to allow different rights for the same stock	–	Not allowed	There are no regulations, but they are usually divided into two categories: promoter and investor shares		
Minimum investment share of the promoter	At least one promoter holds at least 10% of the promoter's shares	Depending on the market value of SPAC, the share can be 2.5% to 3.5%	–		
Promoter's commission share limit*	10%	20%	No related regulations		
Time from IPO to M&A completion	36 months, extendable by up to 6 months	24 months, extendable up to 12 months	36 months, but generally agreed at 18–24 months		

(continued)

Table 3.2 (continued)

	Hong Kong stock exchange (HKEX)	Singapore stock exchange (SGX)	New York stock exchange (NYSE)	Nasdaq global market (NGM)	Nasdaq capital market (NCM)
Minimum percentage of proceeds that must be deposited in a trustee account	100%	90%	90%, but the market practice is 100%		
SPAC M&A transaction approval criteria	The successor company must comply with the relevant exchange regulations regarding IPOs				
Shareholder meeting approval requirements for SPAC M&A transactions	The approval of a majority of SPAC shareholders, excluding the promoters and other shareholders with significant interests, is required	Subject to the approval of a majority of SPAC shareholders and subject to the bylaws			
Independent third party investment	Independent third-party investments must represent at least 15% to 25% of the expected market value of the successor company	No related regulations			
Redemption rights holders	All Shareholders	Independent Shareholders	All shareholders		
Lock-in period	12 months	6 Months	No regulation. Market practice is 6–12 months after completion of the acquisition		

*Note** This is the interest in shares (including warrants or other convertible securities) acquired by the founding shareholders and management team for nominal or nil consideration
Source Yang and Luo (2021)

3.3.2 *Overview of Fintech Investments Through SPAC*

Fintech investments through SPAC mainly occur in the U.S., but the target companies invested in cover a global scope, involving payment technology, insurtech, digital banking, and other fintech applications.

1. Payment technology. On 30 March 2021, Paysafe Group Holdings Limited, a London-based online payment services platform, completed a merger with Foley Trasimene Acquisition Corp. II, a SPAC company. The combined company operates under the name Paysafe Limited. The transaction involves $1.45 billion of Paysafe common stock and warrants traded on the New York Stock Exchange. On 29 June 2021, Payoneer, a cross-border payments provider founded in 2005, and FTAC Olympus Acquisition Corp., a SPAC company, completed a business combination that formed a new entity Payoneer Global Inc. listed on the NASDAQ exchange.
2. Insurtech. On 6 October 2020, health insurer Clover Health Investments announced a merger agreement with SPAC firm Social Capital Hedosophia Holdings Corp. III for $828 million, raising its market capitalization to $3.7. On 24 November 2020, INSU Acquisition Corp. II announced a combination agreement with Metromile, a digital insurance provider founded in 2011, and its market capitalization would be $956 million.
3. Wealth technologies. On 1 June 2021, SoFi Technologies, an online personal finance company founded in 2011 and headquartered in San Francisco, merged with SPAC company Social Capital Hedosophia Holdings Corp. for $2.4 billion in funding.
4. Cryptocurrency. A Norwegian cryptocurrency firm, Arcane Crypto, went public with a $33 million reverse takeover of Swedish firm Vertical Ventures. After the merger, Arcane Crypto was listed on Nasdaq First North, issuing more than 6.6 billion new shares.
5. Other cases. On 2 December 2021, Singaporean app company Grabs completed a merger with the U.S. SPAC company Altimeter Growth Corp in a deal worth $40 billion.

3.4 Cases of PE Investment in Fintech

3.4.1 *Foreign Cases*

Small and medium-sized companies dominate the national and regional fintech industry. Many fintech companies have made breakthroughs in specific segments and continue to expand business boundaries and partner networks to strengthen their competitive edge in obtaining different stages of private equity investment. PE also exits through M&A and IPO of fintech companies to realize profits.

Case 1: Credit Karma

Founded in 2007 and based in San Francisco, financial technology platform Credit Karma launched its online services in 2008 and began offering them through a mobile app in 2012. Some of its services are free, including providing individual consumers with free credit scores and credit reports, tax preparation services, and information on various financial products. It makes a profit through targeted advertising and referring users to partner lenders.

As its business expanded and its competitive edge became more prominent, Credit Karma attracted many PE investors and a soaring amount of funding. In January 2007, Credit Karma closed a seed round of financing with exclusive participation from Archer Venture Capital. On 15 October 2008, Credit Karma closed a $500,000 angel financing with Pathfinder. In November 2009, Credit Karma closed a Series A round of funding for $2.5 million led by QED Investors. Credit Karma launched a new product, WaytoSave, in February 2010 to help users get good deals with a good credit score and a new credit score platform in January 2013 to allow users to monitor their credit scores daily. In April 2013, Credit Karma raised $30 million in series B funding from Ribbit Capital and Susquehanna Growth Equity. At the time, Credit Karma's revenue had grown 40 times since its Series A round, and it had 10 million users. In March 2014, Credit Karma completed a Series C round of $85 million led by Google Capital, with half of the remaining funding from Tiger Fund, Ribbit Capital, and Susquehanna Growth Equity. At the time, Credit Karma's user number had grown to 21 million. In September 2014, Credit Karma raised $75 million in Series D funding, led by SV Angel and followed by Founders Fund, Tiger Global Management, QED Investors, Felicis Ventures, and others. In June 2015, Credit Karma completed a Series E round of funding for $175 million, co-invested by Tiger Global Management, Viking Global Investors, and Valinor Management.

After completing its Series E round of funding, Credit Karma strengthened its competitive advantage through acquisitions. In December 2015, Credit Karma acquired Snowball, a mobile notification app developer. In December 2016, it acquired AFJC Corporation, a shareholder of OnePriceTaxes.com, to strengthen its tax-related business. In March 2018, it acquired a private finance company, Penny. In May 2019, it acquired a UK Noddle credit scoring service customer from TransUnion.

In February 2020, U.S. software developer Intuit announced the acquisition of Credit Karma for $7 billion, consisting of approximately $3.4 billion in cash and 13.3 million shares of Intuit stock and equity awards worth roughly $4.7 billion. Credit Karma operates as a separate division of Intuit.

Case 2: SoFi Technologies

SoFi Technologies, an online personal finance company, was founded in August 2011 and is headquartered in San Francisco, California. It focuses on loan refinancing for low-risk students and graduates and has since expanded into mortgage refinancing, personal loans, credit cards, investment services, and banking business, and focuses on lending to financially responsible individuals. SoFi Relay's Credit Score Monitoring & Budgeting Tool allows users to track funds in banks, credit cards, investments, loan balances, and transactions and set financial goals through a single user interface. TransUnion provides free credit score tracking and weekly updating. In addition, SoFi is involved in the cryptocurrency business. In February 2019, SoFi announced it would cooperate with Coinbase to offer cryptocurrency trading, including bitcoin, ethereum, and litecoin.

PE funds have helped SoFi to expand its scale and into new business areas. In September 2012, SoFi closed a Series A round of financing for $77.2 million with Baseline Ventures, DCM, and others. In October 2013, SoFi announced that it had raised $500 million in debt and equity to fund and refinance student loans. The funding comprised $90 million in equity, $151 million in debt, and a $200 million bank line of credit, with the remainder coming from alumni and community investors. In April 2014, SoFi closed a Series C round of funding for $80 million from Discovery Capital Management, Peter Thiel Wicklow Capital, and other institutional investors. In February 2015, SoFi closed a Series D round of funding for $200 million led by Third Point Management and followed by Institutional Venture Partners and Wellington Management. In September 2015, SoFi completed a Series E round of funding of $1 billion led by Silver Lake, followed by SoftBank, DCM Ventures, RPM Ventures, and Third Point Ventures. In February 2017, SoFi raised $500 million in Series F financing, led by Silver Lake and followed by Softbank, DCM Ventures, RPM Ventures, and Third Point Ventures. In May 2019, SoFi closed a Series G round of funding for $500 million led by Qatar Investment Authority, followed by GGV Capital and Pegasus Tech Ventures. With PE investment, SoFi continues to expand its business scope and strengthen its core competitiveness. In April 2020, SoFi acquired the payment company Galileo (based in Salt Lake City) for $1.2 billion and the 8 Securities, a Hong Kong-based investment app.

In May 2021, SoFi was listed on the NYSE through a SPAC. SoFi was merged into SPAC company Social Capital Hedosophia Holdings Corp V. The transaction valued SoFi at $6 billion.

Case 3: Revolut

Fintech unicorn Revolut, founded in 2015 and based in London, United Kingdom, offers digital bank accounts and other financial services. In December 2018, Revolut was granted a specialized European Union banking license by the European Central Bank (ECB). It is authorized to accept deposits and offer consumer credit, but it does not provide investment services. In 2021, Revolut was granted a full banking license by the ECB. Operating with an electronic money institution license in the United Kingdom, Revolut applied for a UK banking license in January 2021.

On 14 July 2016, Revolut completed Series A funding, led by Balderton Capital, followed by Index Ventures, Seedcamp, Point Nine, Venrex, and eight other institutions. On 20 July 2016, Revolut received 1 million pounds through equity crowdfunding. On 8 June 2017, it obtained debt financing from TriplePoint Capital. On 11 July 2017, it finished the Series B round of funding, securing $66 million, led by Index Ventures and Balderton Capital, Ribbit Capital, and Greyhound Capital. On 30 July 2017, it raised $5.3 million through equity crowdfunding. On 26 April 2018, it completed Series C funding for $250 million, led by DST Global, followed by

Index Ventures, Global Founders Capital, Draper Esprit, Ribbit Capital, and other institutions. On 27 March 2019, it received debt financing from Future Fifty. On 17 February 2020, completed Series D financing for $500 million, led by TCV, followed by DST Global, Ribbit Capital, Lakestar, and GP Bullhound. On 24 July 2020, it finished Series D + round financing with an exclusive $80 million investment from TSG Consumer Partners. In July 2021, it closed a Series E financing round with $800 million from Softbank Vision Fund and Tiger Global Management.

Case 4: Klarna

Founded in Stockholm, Sweden, in 2005, Klarna is committed to providing global merchants access to high-conversion overseas local payment methods. In December 2007, it closed Series A financing of $2.2 million from Investment AB Öresund. In May 2010, it closed Series B financing of $9 million from Sequoia Capital. In December 2011, it closed Series C financing of $155 million from DST Global and General Atlantic. In August 2015, it received a strategic investment of $80 million, invested by Wellcome Trust, Northzone. In March 2017, it received a strategic investment of SEK 46 million from Creandum Investment. In July 2017, it received a PE investment of $250 million from Permira. In October 2018, it received a strategic investment of $20 million from H&M. In April 2019, it received a PE investment of $93 million from Sequoia Capital, Northzone, H&M, CO: LAB, Otiva, and Permira. In August 2019, it received a strategic investment of $460 million, led by Dragoneer Investment Group, followed by Black Rock, IPGL, MerianChrysalis, and Institutional Venture Partners. In January 2020, it received a strategic investment of $200 million from the Commonwealth Bank of Australia. In March 2020, it received a strategic investment from Ant Financial Services Group.

Case 5: Nubank

Nubank, a Brazilian fintech platform founded in 2013, offers customers international credit cards with no annual fees, free digital accounts, and rewards programs. In July 2013, it finished seed round funding of $2 billion from Sequoia Capital and Kaszek Ventures. In September 2014, Sequoia Capital, QED Investors, Kaszek Ventures, and Nicolas Berggnien raised $14.3 million in Series A financing. In June 2015, it completed a Series B round of funding of $30 million from Sequoia Capital, QED Investors, Tiger Global Management, and Kaszek Ventures. In January 2016, it closed a Series C round of financing for $52 million from Sequoia Capital, Founders Fund, Tiger Global Management, and Kaszek Ventures. In December 2016, it closed a Series D round of financing for $80 million from Sequoia Capital, Founders Fund, Redpoint Ventures, QED Investors, DST Global, and Tiger Global Management. In March 2018, it completed Series E financing of $150 million from Founders Fund, Redpoint Ventures, QED Investors, DST Global, Tlirive Capital, Dragoneer Investment Group, and Ribbit Capital. In July 2019, it closed Series F for $400 million from Sequoia Capital, DST Global, Thrive Capital, Dragoneer Investment Group, Ribbit Capital, Tencent Holdings, and TCV. In January 2021, it completed a Series G round of financing for $400 million from Sequoia Capital, Ribbit Capital, Tencent, Invesco, Dragoneer, Whale Rock Capital Management, Whale Rock, and

Singapore's GIC. In June 2021, it completed Series G financing for $750 million from Berkshire Hathaway and Sands Capital Ventures.

3.4.2 China Cases

The traditional financial system and a few big technology companies mainly influence the market structure of China's fintech industry. Traditional financial institutions represented by commercial banks set up technology subsidiaries. Technology giants represented by Baidu, Alibaba, and Tencent (BAT for short) invest massively in fintech startups at home and abroad. Regarding China's fintech application areas, the payment technology sector has the highest industry concentration. BAT companies hold more than 80% of the market share; the insurance technology sector is dominated by traditional insurance institutions (Xu and Xu 2020). The "winner-takes-all" phenomenon in fintech has inhibited investment in areas with high concentration, such as payment technology. There are still active investments in less concentrated domestic fintech sectors but on a smaller scale, such as B2B services, regtech, and wealthtech (KPMG 2020b). Investments and M&A globally by Alibaba and Tencent, among others, have helped strengthen China's competitiveness in technology areas such as cloud computing, blockchain, and artificial intelligence.

In 2020, regulatory measures such as setting caps on private lending rates, antitrust, and data privacy protection were implemented, and investors have postponed their fintech investments decision under uncertainty. At the same time, some fintech companies focus on empowering traditional financial institutions with fintech rather than providing products to the consumer directly (KPMG 2020b).

Case 1: Traditional Financial Institutions Set up Fintech Subsidiaries

To promote digital transformation, some banks have set up fintech subsidiaries. Fintech subsidiaries mainly serve the parent company's banking business, providing IT solutions and technology products to peer banks. In 2015, Industrial Bank Group established Industrial Digital Financial Services (Shanghai) Co., Ltd with a registered capital of 350 million yuan, the first fintech subsidiary of commercial banks. Till April 2021, China's commercial banks have established 12 fintech subsidiaries. For example, the China Construction Bank's Jianxin fintech LLC (2018, with a registered capital of 1.6 billion yuan), ICBC's ICBC Technology Co., Ltd (2019, 600 million yuan), Bank of China's BOC fintech LLC (2019, 600 million yuan), Agricultural Bank's Agribank fintech Limited Liability Company (2020, 600 million yuan), Everbright Bank's Everbright Technology Limited (2016, 150 million yuan), and China Merchants Bank's Zhaoyin Yunchuang Information Technology Company Limited (150 million yuan) (Chen and Yan 2021).

On 21 August 2020, the Securities Association of China released a "*Research Report on Promoting the Development of Digital Transformation of the Securities Industry*," encouraging eligible securities companies to establish or acquire fintech subsidiaries to promote innovation. In this regard, some securities companies have actively increased investment in intelligence and digitalization to enhance their fintech capabilities. Till April 2021, there were two fintech subsidiaries of securities companies in China. Shanxi Securities' wholly-owned fintech subsidiary Shanzhi Technology (Shenzhen) Co., Ltd (established in 2020 with a registered capital of RMB 200 million) and CICC's joint venture with Tencent Digital to establish a fintech subsidiary JinTeng Technology Information (Shenzhen) Co.

On 1 February 2021, the China Banking Regulatory Commission implemented "*Internet Insurance Business Supervision Measures*" to encourage insurance companies to embrace new technologies such as big data and blockchain. According to incomplete statistics from 01FUNDS, as of early April 2021, the insurance industry has established 27 fintech subsidiaries, of which two have been listed on stock exchanges, namely Shanghai Lujiazui International Financial Assets Exchange Co. of Ping An of China and Wanda Information Co. of China Life, respectively.

Case 2: Fintech Giants Make Fintech Investments at Home and Abroad

Domestically, the fintech giants represented by BAT have invested extensively in various fields of fintech. Baidu established Du Xiaoman (formerly Baidu Finance), Alibaba established Ant Financial Services Group, Tencent established Tencent Financial Technology (FiT), and Jingdong established Jingdong Technology, among others. In HuRun Report "Global Unicon 2020", the unicorn companies whose shareholders are Alibaba include WeLab and Akulaku, which are engaged in consumer finance, while those whose shareholders are Tencent include WeZhong Bank and Lianeasy Finance.

Meanwhile, the fintech giants have increasingly invested globally in recent years in areas such as digital banking, robo-advisor, payments, and insurtech. In 2018, Ant Financial raised $14 billion through VC to fund its global expansion. In December 2020, a wholly-owned subsidiary of Ant Financial obtained a digital wholesale banking (DWB) license granted by the Monetary Authority of Singapore.

In October 2018, Tencent invested $180 million in Brazil's Nubank (valued at $4 billion) for a stake of about 5%. Tencent continues to invest in Nubank in its Series F and G funding rounds. Tencent has participated in the Series C and D funding rounds of Argentine digital bank Ualá since 2019, investing $150 million and $350 million, respectively, along with SoftBank. In addition, Tencent participated in the Series B financing of Indian digital bank NiYOSolutions and invested in German digital bank N26, among others. In 2020, Alibaba and Jingdong raised $11 billion and $3.9 billion in secondary listings on the Hong Kong Stock Exchange.

Case 3: Financing for Fintech Startups

Lufax.[2] Shanghai Lujiazui International Financial Assets Market Co., Ltd (Lufax), a Ping An Group of China member company, was established in September 2011 with a registered capital of 837 million yuan. On 13 March 2015, Lufax received $485 million in Series A financing from Ping An Innovation Investment Fund. On 18 January 2016, Lufax received a series B financing of $1.216 billion. The investors

[2] https://www.lufax.com/.

were China Minsheng Bank, Tencent Investment, Minsheng Commercial Bank International Holdings Co., LTD., Bank of China Investment, and Guotai Junan Securities. On 3 December 2018, Lufax received $1.33 billion in Series C financing from Macquarie Capital, LionRock Capital, SBI Holdings, Hermitage Capital, JPMorgan Chase, UBS, Spring Capital, Qatar Investment Authority, Hedosophia, Goldman Sachs, and UOB. On 30 October 2020, Lufax was listed on the NYSE.

Wecash. Wecash is a big data service evaluator specializing in credit decision-making. Through identity identification, combined with personal social behavior and information, Wecash performs online credit scores. Wecash was founded in November 2013. On 1 July 2014, it received 40 million yuan in Series A financing from IDG capital. On 3 March 2015, it received $20 million Series B financing from SIG Haina Asia VC and IDG Capital. On 5 April 2017, it received $80 million Series C financing from Lead Bambu Capital, Guangyuan Investment, China Merchants VC, Hongdao and SIG Haina Asia VC. On 2 March 2018, it received a 6.4 billion yen strategic investment. On 20 March 2018, it received $160 million in Series D financing from SEA Group, Link Capital, Sagamore, ORIX China, Jiufu, Guangyuan Investment, Hongdao Capital, and SIG Ventures.

MediTrust Health.[3] It is a health insurance technology company dedicated to helping patients solve their medical payment problems through innovative payment methods and helping patients manage their medical expenses more efficiently. It focuses on medical payment services in new specialty drugs, chronic drugs, rare drugs, and devices. On 11 April 2018, it obtained Angel round financing, and the investors were STO Capital, Shangyao cloud health, and Yuanyi capital. On 8 April 2019, it received Series A financing from BioTrack Capital and SAIF Investment Fund. On 10 March 2020, it received strategic funding from China RE Group. On 23 November 2020, it received Series B financing from Sinovation Ventures, Huaxing Growth Capital, Shanghai Biomedical Industry Fund, Northern Light VC, BioTrack Capital, and SAIF Investment Fund. On 5 March 2021, it raised 1 billion yuan in Series B + financing, led by Ant Technology Group Corporation, Shanghai Biomedical Fund, and Innovation Works, and followed by Huaxing Growth Capital, Northern Light VC, Boyuan Capital, Marathon Venture Partners, and SAIF Investment. On 8 August 2021, it received over 1 billion yuan in Series C financing, led by Boyu Capital and Janchor Partners Pan-Asian Master Fund, followed by Lilly Asia Ventures, Lake Bleu Capital, BOC Investment, AIHC Capital Management Limited, Everbright Holdings, New Alliance Capital, Boston Capital B Capital Group, CICC Capital, Shanghai Biomedical Industry Equity Investment Fund Partnership (Limited Partnership), Sinovation Ventures (Beijing) Enterprise Management Co. Ltd., Huaxing Growth Capital, Marathon Venture Partners.

[3] https://www.meditrusthealth.com/.

Xuncetech.[4] Shenzhen Xunce Technology Limited was founded in 2016. Big data technology provides one-stop comprehensive data management services for institutional and large individual investors, including compliance risk control monitoring and real-time net worth monitoring. On 12 April 2017, it received Series A financing from YF Capital, South China VC, Resource Investment, Sinovation Ventures, Hongtai Capital Holdings Co. Ltd., Starwin Capital, Chuangfuzhi Capital, Runliangtai Fund, and Stark Investment. On 12 September 2017, it received round angel financing from YF Capital, Sinovation Ventures, and Hongtai Fund. On 12 April 2019, it received Series A + financing from Goldman Sachs, YF Capital, and South China VC. On 22 June 2020, it received Series B financing from Yuxin Capital, Wealth Forest Asset, Tencent Investment, NewMargin Capital, GBA Fund Investment Limited, and Madison Square Investment Limited.

XforcePlus.[5] Shanghai Yunli Information Technology Limited (XforcePlus) was founded in June 2015, focusing on developing and applying industry solutions in the enterprise SaaS (cloud computing software services). It is a professional supply chain information collaboration provider and VAT invoice management cloud platform solutions. On 28 February 2017, XforcePlus received a Pre-A financing round with investors Feng Yuanhong Capital, Eastern bell Capital, and PGA Capital. On 21 November 2017, it received Series A financing from Hillhouse Capital. On 4 September 2018, XforcePlus received Series A + financing; the investor is Danhua Capital. On 19 February 2019, it received Series B financing from IDG Capital, Jolly Capital, and Hillhouse Capital. On 10 October 2019, it received $100 million in Series C financing from Hillhouse Capital, Temasek Capital, and Eastern bell Capital. On 1 June 2021, it received about $200 million in Series C + financing from Dragoneer Investment Group, MSA Capital, Huatai Investment, and Taihe Capital.

Wiseco Technology.[6] Wiseco Technology uses big data, artificial intelligence, and cloud computing technologies to provide services for financial institutions, including customer acquisition, risk management, intelligent collection, and technology system services. It is featured with no involvement in credit business or data transactions. Wiseco has formed strategic cooperation with the FICO company in the research and development of big data algorithms and artificial intelligence technology. On 5 July 2018, it received a 100 million yuan Angel round of financing from Huagai Capital. On 30 July 2018, it received a 100 million yuan Pre-A round of financing from Name Boya Capital, IPINYOU Interactive, Huagai Capital, and Santai Holding. On 30 May 2019, it received 650 million yuan Series A financing from Huachuang Capital, Sino-Ocean Capital, Name Boya Capital, HD Capital, and Creen Pine Capital.

Caogen Investment.[7] It is a leading integrated Internet financial service platform in China, founded in 2013. It provides professional, comprehensive, safe, and effective

---

[4] https://www.xuncetech.com/.

[5] https://www.xforceplus.com/.

[6] https://www.wisecotech.com/.

[7] https://www.cgtz.com/.

investment and wealth management services for small and micro enterprises and individual investors. On 29 January 2015, it received Series A financing from Shunwei Capital. On 6 June 2016, it received 1 billion yuan in Series B financing from SFUND. On 21 February 2017, it received 100 million yuan in Series C financing from Huawen Media. On 4 June 2018, it received 2.3 billion yuan Series D financing from Huawen Media, SFUND, Geo-Jade Petroleum Corporation, and Shunwei Capital.

References

Amess K, Stiebale J, Wright M. The impact of private equity on firms' patenting activity. Eur Econ Rev. 2016;86:147–60. https://doi.org/10.1016/j.euroecorev.2015.08.013.

Arqué-Castells P. How venture capitalists spur invention in Spain: evidence from patent trajectories. Res Policy. 2012;41(5):897–912. https://doi.org/10.1016/j.respol.2012.01.008.

Bank of England. Embracing the promise of fintech, Quarterly Bulletin 2019; Q1. https://www.bankofengland.co.uk/quarterly-bulletin/2019/2019-q1/embracing-the-promise-of-fintech

Bertoni F, Croce A, D'Adda D. Venture capital investments and patenting activity of high-tech start-ups: a micro-econometric firm-level analysis. Ventur Cap. 2010;12(4):307–26. https://doi.org/10.1080/13691066.2010.486157.

Black B, Gilson R. Does venture capital require an active stock market? J Appl Corp Financ. 1999;11:36–48. https://doi.org/10.1111/j.1745-6622.1999.tb00512.x.

Buchak G, Matvos G, Piskorski T, Seru A. Fintech, regulatory arbitrage, and the rise of shadow banks. J Financ Econ. 2018;130(3):453–83. https://doi.org/10.1016/j.jfineco.2018.03.011.

Chemmanur T, Loutskina E, Tian X. Venture capital, value creation, and innovation. Rev Financ Stud. 2014;27(8):2434–73. https://doi.org/10.1093/rfs/hhu033.

Chemmanur TJ, Imerman MB, Rajaiya H, Yu Q. Recent developments in the fintech industry. J Financ Manage Markets Inst. 2020. https://doi.org/10.1142/S2282717X20400022.

Chen YN, Yan XM. Technology subsidiary of China's licensed financial institutions. 01ThinkTank 2021. https://new.qq.com/omn/20210422/20210422A0AFXD00.html (in Chinese)

Ernst H, Witt P, Brachtendorf G. Corporate venture capital as a strategy for external innovation: An exploratory empirical study. R&D Manage. 2005;35(3):233–42. https://doi.org/10.1111/j.1467-9310.2005.00386.x.

European Central Bank. Survey on the access to finance of small and medium-sized enterprises in the Euro Area. 2013. Available at: www.ecb.europa.eu/stats/money/surveys/sme/html/index.en.html

Faria AP, Barbosa N. Does venture capital really foster innovation? Econ Lett. 2014;122(2):129–31. https://doi.org/10.1016/j.econlet.2013.11.014.

Gompers P, Kaplan SN, Mukharlyamov V. What do private equity firms say they do? J Financ Econ. 2016;121(3):449–76. https://doi.org/10.1016/j.jfineco.2016.06.003.

Haddad C, Hornuf L. The emergence of the global fintech market: economic and technological determinants. Small Bus Econ. 2019;53:81–105. https://doi.org/10.1007/s11187-018-9991-x.

He D, Leckow RB, Haksar V, Griffoli TM, Jenkinson N, Kashima M, Khiaonarong T, Rochon C, Tourpe H. Fintech and financial services: Initial considerations. Staff Discussion Notes No. 17/05; 2017. Available at: https://www.imf.org/en/Publications/Staff-Discussion-Notes/Issues/2017/06/16/Fintech-and-Financial-Services-Initial-Considerations-44985

Keil T, Maula M, Schildt H, Zahra SA. The effect of governance mode and relatedness of external business development activities on innovative performance. Strategic Manage J 2008; 29(8): 895–907. https://doi.org/10.1002/smj.672

Kortum S, Lerner J. Assessing the contribution of venture capital to innovation. Rand J Econ. 2000;31(4):674–92. https://doi.org/10.2307/2696354.

KPMG. The Pulse of Fintech 2018, 2019–2–13; 2018. https://home.kpmg/xx/en/home/industries/financial-services/pulse-of-fintech.html.

KPMG. The Pulse of Fintech H1 2020, 2020–9; 2020a. https://home.kpmg/xx/en/home/industries/financial-services/pulse-of-fintech.html.

KPMG. The Pulse of Fintech H2 2020, 2021–8; 2020b. https://kpmg.com/xx/en/home/campaigns/2021/08/pulse-of-fintech-h2-2020.html.

KPMG. The Pulse of Fintech H1 2023, 2023–7; 2023. https://assets.kpmg.com/content/dam/kpmg/xx/pdf/2023/07/global-pulse-of-fintech-h123-report-web.pdf.

Large D, Muegge S. Venture capitalists' non-financial value-added: An evaluation of the evidence and implications for research. Ventur Cap. 2008;10(1):21–53. https://doi.org/10.1080/13691060701605488.

Lerner J, Sorensen M, Strömberg P. Private equity and long-run investment. The case of innovation. J Financ 2011; 66(2):445–77. https://doi.org/10.1111/j.1540-6261.2010.01639.x

Link AN, Ruhm CJ, Siegel DS. Private equity and the innovation strategies of entrepreneurial firms: Empirical evidence from the small business innovation research program. Manag Decis Econ. 2014;35(2):103–13. https://doi.org/10.1002/mde.v35.2.

Maas C, Steinhagen P, Proksch D, Pinkwart A. The role of innovation in venture capital and private equity investments in different investment phases. Ventur Cap. 2020;22(1):105–26. https://doi.org/10.1080/13691066.2018.1526864.

Popov A, Roosenboom P. Venture capital and patented innovation. Evidence from Europe. Econ Policy. 2012; 27(71):447–82. https://doi.org/10.1111/j.1468-0327.2012.00290.x

Rossi M, Festa G, Devalle A, Mueller J. When corporations get disruptive, the disruptive get corporate: Financing disruptive technologies through corporate venture capital. J Bus Res. 2020;118:378–88.

Schindele A, Szczesny A. The impact of Basel II on the debt costs of German SMEs. J Bus Econ. 2016;86:197–227. https://doi.org/10.1007/s11573-015-0775-3.

Schumacher B. A new development in private equity: The rise and progression of special purpose acquisition companies in Europe and Asia. Nw J Int'l L Bus. 2019;40:391.

Thakor AV. Fintech and banking: What do we know? J Financ Intermediation. 2020;41: 100833. https://doi.org/10.1016/j.jfi.2019.100833.

Wright M, Hoskisson RE, Busenitz L. Firm rebirth. Buyouts as facilitators of strategic growth and entrepreneurship. Acad Manage Executive. 2001; 15(1):111–25. https://doi.org/10.1016/j.jfineco.2016.06.003

Xu Z, Xu RH. Chapter 7: regulating FinTech for sustainable development in China. In: Amstad M, Huang B, Morgan PJ, Shirai S, editors. FinTech in Asia: policies and practices. Tokyo, Japan: Asian Development Bank Institute Press; 2020.

Yang MH, Luo JY. Hong Kong stock exchange SPAC consulting review, Hong Kong, the United States, Singapore SPAC regulatory comparison, published in Ryan Capital WeChat Official Account, September 21, 2021. https://www.hkmipo.com/2021/09/21/9bde5d6a50/

Chapter 4
Technology Applications in Private Equity Regulation

China's PE industry entered the initial development stage in the early 1990s by establishing several investment fund companies.[1] The PE industry has made significant progress and remarkable achievements after more than 30 years of development, together with China's advancing capital market reform. The PE industry is essential in promoting the development of China's multi-level capital market, serving the real economy, and enriching investment channels. Meanwhile, China has established a regulation framework[2] consisting of national regulatory departments, financial bureaus at local government level, and self-regulatory organizations run by industry associations (Long 2019). The framework efficiently safeguards the healthy and orderly development of China's PE industry. Although China's PE industry continues to develop and regulation improves,[3] the long-existing issues, such as incomplete registration and filing, illegal business practices, and illegal fundraising, have become the shackles restricting the future high-quality development of China's PE industry.

Differing regulatory environments and how PE firms have evolved largely caused the differences between PE in the West and China (Yong 2012). Traditional approaches, including self-regulation, industry co-regulation, and the resort to regulation, are important in protecting the stakeholders of the funds and the portfolio

[1] It refers to Wuhan Securities Investment Fund, Shenzhen Nanshan Venture Capital and other companies established in 1991.

[2] The China's fintech regulation framework, just like that the regulation framework of PE, is embedded in the existing financial regulatory framework. The regulators of fintech include the PBC, China Securities Regulatory Commission (CSRC), China Bank Insurance Regulatory Commission (CBIRC, replaced by National Administration of Financial Regulation in May 2023), Financial Stability and Development Committee, National Internet Finance Association (responsible for industry self-regulation) (Xu and Xu 2020).

[3] In China, foreign PE firms entered the market before China's local PE industry was developed, which led to different laws and regulations faced by foreign and local PE firms. In recent years, China exert great effort to regulate foreign and local firms and level the playing field (Yue and Zhang 2010; Bradford and McKinzie 2020).

R. Xu and D. Zhao, *Digital Transformation of Private Equity in China*, Contributions to Finance and Accounting, https://doi.org/10.1007/978-981-99-8482-4_4

companies (McCahery and Vermeulen 2012). With data of 100 Dutch institutional investors' domestic and international asset private equity allocations, Cumming and Johan (2007) find evidence that a perceived comparative dearth of regulations of private equity funds impedes institutional investor participation in private equity funds, particularly concerning the lack of transparency. PE should be regulated to prevent systemic financial instability and (Thomsen 2009; Heed 2010).

Currently, the integration of technology and the financial industry is deepening. Digital technology represented by the Internet, big data, cloud computing, AI, and blockchain has provided new impetus for the development of the PE industry but also brought unknown risks and posed new challenges to the regulation of the PE industry. In this regard, this chapter discusses "how to build a technological and digital regulatory system for the PE industry. How can digital technology be used to improve the PE industry's regulatory means and tools? The answers to the questions are of great theoretical significance and practical value for further improving PE supervision in China.

4.1 Regulatory Framework of China's PE Industry

The primary laws and regulations of China's PE industry include the *Securities Investment Fund Law of the People's Republic of China* (hereinafter referred to as the "*Securities Investment Fund Law*"),[4] the *State Council's Opinions on Further Promoting the Healthy Development of the Capital Market* (hereinafter referred to as "*the Opinions*"), and the *Interim Measures for the Supervision and Administration of Private Investment Funds* (hereinafter referred to as the "*PE Fund Supervision Measures*"). The regulatory authorities and responsibilities are as follows. The China Securities Regulatory Commission is responsible for industry supervision, the Asset Management Association of China is responsible for industry self-regulatory management, and local financial bureaus are responsible for risk disposal of the local PE industry.

In general, the *State Council's Opinions on Further Promoting the Healthy Development of the Capital Market* emphasizes that "the further promotion of the healthy development of the capital market and the improvement of the multi-level capital market system are of great importance to accelerate the improvement of a modern market system, broaden the investing and financing channels for enterprises and residents, optimize the allocation of resources and promote economic transformation and upgrading." It put forward guidance and suggestions on preventing and resolving the risks and creating a good development environment for the PE industry. The *Securities Investment Fund Law* and the *PE Fund Supervision Measures* put forward clear requirements for industry supervision and self-regulatory management of the PE industry.

---

[4] It is published on the CSRC website. http://www.csrc.gov.cn/csrc/c101939/c1045353/content.shtml.

4.1.1 China Securities Regulatory Commission: Industry Supervision

The *Securities Investment Fund Law* empowers the **China Securities Regulatory Commission (CSRC)** to perform regulatory duties in the supervision and administration of the securities market. The CSRC and its dispatched institutions undertake the following responsibilities related to the PE industry.

(1) Formulate policies and regulations regarding the supervision and administration of securities investment fund business, and exercise the power of examination, approval, or registration.
(2) Handle fund filing.
(3) Supervise fund management companies, fund custodian institutions, and other institutions with securities investment fund business, investigate and penalize the activities violating the relevant securities laws and regulations.
(4) Formulate and implement measures on the qualifications and code of conduct of senior management for the relevant institutions, and guide the Securities Association of China and the Futures Associations of China in administrating the personnel qualifications engaged in securities businesses.
(5) Supervise and inspect the disclosure of fund information.
(6) Guide and supervise the activities of fund associations.
(7) Other duties stipulated by laws and administrative regulations.

The CSRC and its dispatched agencies are empowered to take the following measures in performing their duties under the law and relevant regulations.

(1) Conduct on-site inspections of fund management companies, fund custodian institutions, and fund service providers, and request them to report relevant business information.
(2) Enter the places where violations of securities laws and regulations occur to investigate and collect evidence.
(3) Interview the parties, entities, and individuals related to the investigated incident and request clarification on matters related to the incident under investigation
(4) Access and copy information on the investigated incident, including property right registration, communication records, and other related information.
(5) Access and copy documents and materials of the parties, entities, and individuals related to the investigated incident, including the securities transaction records, registration, and transfer records, financial accounting data, and other relevant documents and materials. Seal documents and materials that may be transferred, concealed, or destroyed when necessary.
(6) Query the parties, entities, and individuals related to the investigated incident about funds, securities, and bank accounts. With the approval of the primary person in charge of the CSRC, freeze or seize the illegal funds, securities, and other property which have been or may be transferred or concealed as proved by evidence and relevant documents and materials which have been or may be concealed, forged, or destroyed.

(7) During the investigation of violations of securities laws and regulations (such as manipulation of the securities market and insider trading), with the approval of the primary person in charge of the CSRC, restrict the parties related to the investigated incident from trading securities for not more than 15 trading days. It may be extended for another 15 trading days if the case circumstances are complicated.

4.1.2 The Asset Management Association of China: Industry Self-Regulation

The Asset Management Association of China (AMAC) is a self-regulatory organization of the securities investment fund sector. Fund management companies and fund custodian institutions shall join the AMAC, and fund service providers may join fund associations. The AMAC issued some self-regulatory rules, such as the Charter of the AMAC, the Management Measures for Members of the AMAC, and the Implementation Measures for Disciplinary Actions of the AMAC (for trial implementation). The AMAC performs the following duties.

(1) Educating and organizing members to comply with laws and administrative regulations concerning securities investment and safeguard investors' legitimate rights and interests.
(2) Safeguard the legitimate rights and interests of members following the law and reflect the suggestions and demands of members.
(3) Develop and implement industry self-regulatory rules, supervise and inspect the practice of members and their employees, and take disciplinary action against those who violate the association's self-disciplinary rules or the bylaws.
(4) Develop the sector's practice standards and business rules and organize fund practitioners' examinations, qualification management, and business training for fund employees.
(5) Provide member services, organize exchanges regarding the sector, promote innovation in the sector, and conduct sector publicity and investor education.
(6) Conduct mediation for fund business disputes between members or between a member and its clients.
(7) Handle registration and filing for non-publicly offered funds following the law.
(8) Other functions prescribed by the bylaws of the association.

4.1.3 Local Financial Bureaus: Current Supervision Status and Future Trend

According to decisions of the National Financial Work Conference 2017, local financial authorities conduct prudential supervision over locally registered financial institutions of certain types. The local financial bureaus have embarked on supervising the PE industry through on-site inspection and risk disposal and play an increasingly important role in preventing risks in the PE industry and regulating the development of the PE industry.

In December 2021, the People's Bank of China issued the "*Regulations on Local Financial Supervision and Administration (Draft for Comments)*,"[5] aiming to clarify the responsibilities of the central and local governments, set up a unified regulatory framework, improve the local financial regulatory system and enhance the effectiveness of local financial supervision. It proposed that: "the local market supervision and administration department shall, together with the local financial bureau, strictly manage the commercial registration of newly established investment companies. Investment companies that engage in PE funds, proxy sales of various financial products, financial investment advisory, and other financial services shall obtain a business license or complete registration and filing following the provisions of the financial supervision and regulation department of the State Council. The local financial bureau shall clean up or rectify the investment companies that fail to obtain the business license or complete the registration and filing process within a prescribed time limit." In the future, after the *Regulations on Local Financial Supervision and Administration* are implemented, local financial bureaus will be more involved in the supervision of the PE industry, playing an irreplaceable role in the regulatory system of the PE industry.

In July 2023, the State Council released the *Regulation on the Supervision and Administration of Private Equity Investment Funds*, China's first regulation covering the supervision and administration of PE funds, which will take effect on September 1, 2023. It is expected to facilitate the industry's high-quality development, advance China's technological innovation, and better serve the real economy. The regulation delineates the bottom line of supervision to control risks from the outset. According to the CSRC, differentiated supervision will be adopted according to fund managers' business type, asset management scale, compliance, risk control, and capability to serve investors. Based on the new regulation, the CSRC will further optimize its management of PE funds' fundraising, investment, capital operations and information disclosure practices. The new regulation also rolls out strict punishment for violations such as misappropriation and misuse of fund capital. It clearly states that the PE industry should serve the real economy and promote technological innovation.

4.2 Risk Issues in the Development of China's PE Industry

After more than 30 years of development, China's PE industry has developed remarkably. According to the CSRC, as of May 2023, 22,000 PE fund managers were registered with the Asset Management Association of China, with 153,000 funds under management, totaling 21 trillion yuan ($2.9 trillion).

[5] The notice and draft are published on the PBC's website. http://www.pbc.gov.cn/rmyh/105208/4436903/index.html.

With the rapid development, the role of China"s PE industry has been increasingly prominent in enhancing the proportion of direct financing, promoting the formation of innovative capital, and supporting technological innovation and industrial restructuring (AMAC 2022). However, some issues and shackles still constrain the high-quality development of China's PE industry. For example, some fund management companies **do not standardize** the review of qualified investors, and the reported fundraising method does not match the actual situation, illegal use of investor funds, and inadequate information disclosure. Some fund management companies promise to guarantee the principal and return to investors in a disguised way, and information is not updated or not timely updated, products are not filed promptly following the provisions, failure to cooperate with self-regulatory inspection, and other illegal business practices.

4.2.1 Some Institutions Do not Standardize the Review of Qualified Investors

Some institutions violate the relevant provisions of the *PE Fund Supervision Measures* and the *Administrative Measures on Private Investment Fundraising*. Typical practices include: advertising and promoting PE fund products to unspecified targets through Internet channels (some institutions even raise funds directly from non-qualified investors). There is no specific object program on the fund's website and no access restriction. It enables investors to browse information about the PE funds prohibited from being publicly advertised, including the net value of funds, and information on products that have not been filed. The websites set links to subscribe to PE funds, enabling investors to purchase the products without restrictions. Some institutions did not standardize fundraising solicitation materials, did not identify potential risks to investors, and failed to conduct qualified investor reviews as required. Some institutions violated requirements on investor suitability management, failed to carry out effective risk ratings on PE funds, and failed to recommend PE fund products to investors whose risk identification and risk-bearing ability matched the risk ratings.

4.2.2 Some Reported Fundraising Method Does not Match the Actual

For fundraising, the fund management companies must provide the documents and information for the registration and filing and ensure the authenticity, accuracy, and completeness of the documents and information provided. In practice, some institutions have changed the subject and method of fundraising, which is inconsistent with the reported information. In addition, some institutions even entrust unqualified institutions to raise funds. Some institutions entrust related parties to raise funds, but the related parties neither have the qualification for fund sales business nor are they members of the AMAC.

4.2.3 Some Institutions Use Investor Funds Illegally

In practice, some institutions fail to use investors' funds in accordance with the signed and filed agreements. First, some institutions illegally used the funds deposited by subsequent investors in the fundraising account and did not use the funds according to the agreed purpose. Instead, the funds are used to pay the principal and income of previous investors. Second, some institutions invested investors' funds in other PE fund projects managed by the company, and the relevant transaction pricing lacks a reasonable basis. In addition, some PE funds did not conduct reasonable valuation when opening subscriptions, redemptions, or rolling issuance. They were priced separately from the actual yields of the underlying assets.

4.2.4 Some Institutions Have Inadequate Information Disclosure

To ensure smooth fundraising, PE fund managers naturally have the motivation to conceal negative information, resulting in inevitable information asymmetry between the managers and investors and inadequate information disclosure. First, some institutions did not disclose information about possible conflicts of interest to investors. For example, some institutions increase capital to related parties or enterprises of the same actual controller but do not promptly disclose the risks of related party transactions to investors, which may mislead investors in their decision-making. Second, some private equity funds failed to timely disclose important information that may affect investors' rights and interests, such as arbitration, litigation, and other related situations of institutions. As argued by Heed (2010), PE aimed at alternative assets, which makes the market opaque to outsiders, and the lack of standardised methodologies for disclosure and performance reporting limits the availability of a lender to monitor a borrower's credit quality. Studies show that asymmetric information is one of the driving factors of positive announcement effects of private equity placements (Renneboog et al. 2007). PE firms try to reduce agency problems by minimizing information asymmetries (Brown et al. 2020).

4.2.5 Some Institutions Promise to Guarantee the Principal and Return to Investors in a Disguised Way

The *PE Fund Supervision Measures* stipulate that "PE fund managers and PE fund sales institutions shall not promise investors principal investment against loss or commitment minimum return." The *Administrative Measures on Private Investment Fundraising* prohibits illegal financial activities such as unlawful marketing and promotion, false advertising, or illegal guarantees for principals and returns. When promoting PE funds, the fundraising institution and its employees are prohibited from promising investors no loss of capital or a minimum return in any way, including advertising "expected return", "predicted investment performance," and other relevant content. They must not exaggerate the positive side of the funds and use words that may mislead investors, such as "safe", "guaranteed", "commitment", "insured", "hedged", "high yield" and "no risk". In practice, some institutions disguise their promises to investors by signing a balance replenishment agreement with investors and using the funds of subsequent investors to pay the balance replenishment of early investors.[6]

4.2.6 Some Information is not Updated or not Timely Updated

The PE fund managers shall report to the AMAC and update information promptly following the regulations when there are significant changes in the basic information of PE fund managers and the employees, the investment, and the leverage of the funds under management. Timely information disclosure is necessary to protect investors' right to know, alleviate information asymmetry between PE fund managers and investors, and help investors make correct investment decisions. Some institutions delay updating information changes in related parties, arbitration, and litigation to ensure smooth fundraising (Guo 2022). Some institutions even intentionally conceal the administrative supervision measures taken by the regulator. Some institutions file with the AMAC after the fundraising is completed or after a long time.

In addition to the abovementioned issues, other types of illegal operations exist. For example, the PE fund managers fail to cooperate with the AMAC to complete the self-discipline inspection and make arrangements to ensure the safety of PE fund property and the dispute resolution mechanism for products that have not been entrusted. Concerning the risk issues, using technology to enrich the tools and means

[6] Return misreporting of PE and VC fund managers is well documented in literature. With a sample of 997 buyout funds and 1,074 venture funds from Burgiss database, Brown et al. (2019) find that some underperforming managers manipulate reported returns during fundraising, and those managers are less likely to raise a next fund. With data of VC funds headquartered in the U.S. from PitchBook, Smith et al. (2022) find that fund managers can manipulate returns by inflating NAVs and by reporting selectively, and selective reporting by GPs overstates VC fund returns by 4 percentage points.

of PE investment supervision will help effectively deal with various risks in the PE industry (Shan and Zhao 2022).

4.3 Policy Suggestions for Establishing a Digital Regulatory System in the PE Industry

To promote the industry's healthy and sustainable development, further improving the laws, regulations, and self-regulatory guidelines and fully implementing the regulatory measures is necessary. Especially in the wave of rapid technology evolution, improving the effectiveness of PE investment supervision and enriching the tools and means with technology is necessary.

4.3.1 The Main Tasks

To improve the financial regulatory system and prevent systemic financial risks, it is of great practical significance to strengthen the digital regulatory system of the PE industry. Supervisors can utilize supervisory technology (suptech) to support supervision, and promote efficient and proactive monitoring of risk and compliance at financial institutions (Broeders and Prenio 2018). Promoting the application of regulatory technology is the main task of optimizing investment supervision in the future.

China has the foundation and conditions to launch the digital construction of the PE investment supervision system. First, the construction of regulatory informatization has achieved satisfactory results. The central regulatory information platform has provided a data basis for digital construction. Moreover, regulators and industry self-regulatory organizations have also carried out exploration and forward-looking research on big data and machine learning. Second, the constant maturity and implementation of big data, cloud computing, and other technologies have provided a technical basis for digital construction. The successful application of big data and AI algorithms offer advanced examples of digital construction (Yang 2021; Hu 2022).

The main tasks of constructing China's digital PE investment supervision system should include the following aspects.[7]

First, the ability of macro-prudential supervision to prevent systemic financial risks should be enhanced. Technology is a double-edged sword. Applications of AI

[7] Financial Services Authority (2006) identified risks posed by the PE market, including excessive leverage, unclear ownership of economic risk, market abuse, conflicts of interest, market access, market opacity, and overall capital market efficiency. To strengthen oversight of PE, the FSA exert efforts in improving its data collection, and enhance regulatory reporting requirements for PE firms to incorporate information on committed capital in addition to the existing requirements.

and other new technologies in the PE industry inevitably make the risk transmission path more complex, the flow of funds more frequent, and illegal and irregular behavior more hidden. It requires the regulatory authorities to be more rational and effective in using technology to form predictions and responses in advance, improve the identification and monitoring of new market operations, and maintain the stable operation of the financial market.

Second, micro-prudential supervision should be promoted to enhance market entities' healthy and orderly development. A digital supervision system of the PE industry can improve the prudential supervision of China's regulatory authorities, optimizing the rule formulation and making the evaluation system more objective. In particular, using big data, AI, and other advanced technologies can provide timely and effective detection and analysis of abnormal trading, insider trading, market manipulation, disclosure information falsification, and other behaviors. It provides more efficient PE industry supervision and promotes healthy and orderly development.

Third, the means of supervision and adequate protection of financial consumers' legitimate rights and interests should be enriched. On the one hand, a digital supervision system of the PE industry can improve the effectiveness of risk warnings. Compared with traditional means, it can provide capital market dynamic reports more quickly and comprehensively and promptly detect market changes and issues. On the other hand, new technologies can continuously enrich regulatory measures, improve regulatory capacity, and enhance regulatory effectiveness. Cross-market monitoring information can be shared to crack down on unqualified institutions, punish illegal business activities, and effectively protect small and medium-sized investors' legitimate rights and interests.

Forth, it should improve the efficiency of supervision and provide scientific decision support for the regulatory authorities. The combination of information technology and supervision can effectively enhance the supervision and monitoring capacity and business service capability. Meanwhile, new technologies can also be used to optimize and transform the existing process of supervision, promote the reform of the financial regulatory model, enhance the deep integration of technology and business, and further strengthen the ability of inspection and law enforcement, providing more comprehensive, scientific and objective decision-making support for the regulatory authorities.

4.3.2 The Principles and Objectives

The digital construction of China's supervision system of the PE industry should follow the general principle of "technology-led, demand-driven; co-construction and sharing, multi-party collaboration; Coordinated planning, continuous promotion; capacity improvement, mechanism innovation".

"Technology-led, demand-driven" refers to the use of advanced technological means to lead the supervision, promote the innovation of the regulatory model, and thoroughly analyze and grasp the actual needs and pain points of various regulatory authorities and related parties. "Co-construction and sharing, multi-party collaboration" means that regulatory authorities and related parties jointly build a big data platform, support each other in digital construction, and apply the digital system to solve practical problems in PE investment supervision. "Coordinated planning, continuous promotion" means that under the unified leadership and organization of the Financial Stability Development Committee of the State Council, the CSRC shall take the lead and coordinate with related authorities and parties in planning all aspects of the digital construction and continuously advance the construction and application of the system in phases and at different levels. "Capacity improvement, mechanism innovation" refers to the formation of a new set of the regulatory system, mechanisms, and capacity for supervising the PE industry through the construction of a big data platform and diversified analysis centers, promoting the innovation of the regulatory model, improving the efficiency of PE investment in serving the real economy, and realizing the full coverage of financial risk regulation in the capital market.

The digital construction of a regulatory system of the PE industry should follow the above-mentioned principles, realize the integration of various data resources with overall planning, better serve the daily supervision of PE investment, comprehensively improve the intelligent level of PE investment supervision, and promote the change of PE investment regulation concept and model. Meanwhile, digital construction should also consider security and scalability so that the collection and use of information data and the application of new technologies can be realized in a secure technical system and fully consider the needs of the rapid development of the capital market.

Moreover, digital construction should be based on the actual situation of China's PE industry and focus on the following three goals. First, improve the construction of various infrastructure and central regulatory information platforms, realize the interconnection of business processes and the comprehensive sharing of data, and form a complete and full process support for the supervision of PE investment. Second, actively apply big data, cloud computing, and other technological means to conduct real-time data collection, calculation, and analysis, realize real-time monitoring of market operation, and strengthen the ability to identify abnormal trading and detect and timely handle various violations of laws and regulations as soon as possible. Third, explore the use of AI technology, including machine learning, deep learning algorithms, data mining, and other means to provide intelligent applications and services for the supervision of PE investment, optimize various types of regulatory work models, such as ex ante examination, interim monitoring and ex post inspection and punishment, improve the ability to proactively identify problems, enhance the intelligence level in the supervision of PE investment, and promote innovation in PE investment supervision model.

4.3.3 A General Framework of a Digital PE Investment Regulatory System

The core of the digital construction of China's PE investment **regulatory system** is to build an efficient regulatory big data platform and comprehensively use electronic early warning, statistical analysis, data mining, and other technologies to conduct real-time monitoring and historical analysis, and investigation. It can assist regulators in conducting panoramic analysis of PE investment market subjects and real-time monitoring and surveillance of the market situation, timely detect suspected insider trading, market manipulation, and other illegal behaviors, perform regulatory duties, and maintain the order of PE market transactions.

First, build a logically integrated big data platform for PE investment supervision. The regulatory big data platform is the core of digital construction. The platform should carry the transaction, disclosure, and regulatory data from the relevant regulatory systems, integrate and unify external data resources, and provide data support for regulatory decision-making. The big data platform can use virtualization or container technology to achieve unified management of computing, memory, storage, and network resources, build a proprietary cloud platform, and use the distributed architecture to realize the collection, storage, calculation, and management of massive data. Meanwhile, it can be an auxiliary tool for regulatory decision-making by introducing general algorithms and models such as deep learning and graph analysis and tools such as voice recognition and image recognition.

Second, set up multiple flexible and intelligent data analysis centers. The CSRC can lead to a unified plan for building multiple data analysis centers according to regulatory needs. Each analysis center can use the massive data in the big data platform to conduct targeted data analysis and processing according to regulatory requirements.

Finally, provide a variety of standard and professional analysis services. Each analysis center can provide one or more specific regulatory business analysis services. Meanwhile, the CSRC can give standardizations on delivering services, such as panoramic portrait services and financial analysis services. Specific analysis centers can be assigned to develop specialized services that require special data, unique algorithms, or knowledge of specific areas.

4.3.4 Additional Suggestions for Building a Digital PE Investment Regulatory System

With the general framework of building a digital PE investment regulatory system, the development of a comprehensive platform and introduction of big data, cloud computing, artificial intelligence, blockchain, and other technological means into the whole process of PE investment supervision will significantly improve the capacity and efficiency of PE investment supervision.

(1) Use technology to integrate resources, build a comprehensive platform, and improve the supervision capacity of the PE investment market

Make full use of AI, big data, and other technologies in data collection and integration, real-time monitoring, analysis and prediction, and model construction. Establish a comprehensive platform for PE investment supervision that integrates information sharing, information disclosure, risk monitoring, and other functions. Facilitate coordination among regulators and self-regulatory organizations, create synergy, and eliminate regulatory overlaps and gaps.

First, build an information-sharing platform for the PE industry. With the Internet and big data technology, the information-sharing platform of the PE industry can collect and integrate the scattered industry information and solve the problem of "information islands". For PE fund managers, the information-sharing platform can provide information inquiry and reporting services and reduce the costs of information acquisition and compliance. For regulators, it can provide industry statistics, monitoring information, and other information services conducive to regulating and optimizing the PE industry environment, thus improving the efficiency of PE supervision and investor protection.

Second, improve the information disclosure platform of the PE market. To reduce the information disclosure cost of PE fund managers and the search cost of investors, we propose building an extensible business reporting language system integrated with the existing system. The production, collection, transmission, release, analysis, and utilization of information should be based on unified technical specifications. This approach can efficiently reduce the cost of information exchange, improve the accuracy and utilization of information, and realize the openness and transparency of information with minimum costs. It significantly reduces information asymmetry and improves the market's ability to identify credit risks.

Third, establish a risk monitoring platform for the PE industry. With AI and big data technology, a coherent information system across various markets and regulatory business lines can be established to realize real-time monitoring across markets and accounts. Meanwhile, machine learning and data mining can be used to develop transaction monitoring models to effectively identify new types of trading behavior, improve the ability to detect violations, and enhance the information level of PE investment supervision.

Fourth, establish an information reporting platform for the PE investment industry. The information reporting platform can be built to collect the industry reporting information and all kinds of public opinions, which can be gathered, mined, and transferred to the regulatory authorities and self-regulatory organizations for processing promptly. On the one hand, it can support the regulatory authorities and self-regulatory organizations to collect clues about violations of laws and regulations and investigate and deal with the violations. On the other hand, early detection and handling of problems can protect investors' rights and interests from infringing, thus enhancing investor protection's efficacy.

(2) "Portrait" the PE fund managers manage the whole process of fundraising, and facilitate real-time decision-making for investors

Use big data technology to collect the information of PE fund managers and related parties through multiple channels and in multiple dimensions, then clean, integrate, analyze and model the information. Use models to verify the information, remove the false and retain the true. Build a "portrait" of PE fund managers, given the authenticity and reliability of the information. Based on it, build a dynamic scoring system for PE fund managers' credit level and risk status. Before fundraising, analyze and determine the credit and risk characteristics of PE fund managers with data mining and statistical analysis methods, and evaluate their credit level and business ability to obtain credit scores. The credit score can be an important reference for investors, helping them effectively identify the PE fund manager's malicious concealment of information unfavorable to fundraising. In the post-investment stage, AI and big data technology can monitor the PE fund manager's operation in real-time. After the fund project's completion, the fund managers' credit score shall be adjusted according to the performance. According to the rules, the credit score of those who strictly abide by the contract and operate in good faith shall be raised, and the credit score of those in breach of contract and suspected of malicious fraud shall be lowered.

(3) **"Portrait" of investors improves investor suitability management**

Big data technology can be used to "profile" and "stratify" investors to standardize the suitability management of investors and safeguard the legitimate rights and interests. PE investors vary in a professional level, asset allocation portfolio, risk tolerance, and PE funds vary in risk levels. The healthy development of the PE investment market requires investors' risk tolerance and professional level match with PE fund products. Therefore, it is necessary to manage the suitability of PE investors and provide different investors with PE products that match their risk tolerance. High-risk PE products can only be sold to investors with more PE investment experience, and their financial assets and average annual income exceed a certain threshold. Investors who do not meet the requirements can only invest in low-risk PE products.

(4) **Bring the whole process of PE investment on blockchain to solve problems such as information asymmetry and default disposal difficulties**

The features of blockchain technology, including open and transparent information and immutability, are highly compatible with the inherent requirements for the orderly development of the PE industry. Bringing the whole process of PE investment on blockchain may be an essential technological solution for the pain points of PE industry development.

First, blockchain technology can effectively solve the information asymmetry problem of PE investment, improve fundraising efficiency and reduce costs. On the one hand, blockchain technology can ensure the openness and transparency of information for PE fund managers and the fundraising process (Zhong 2019). Investors can also obtain unified information sources through blockchain, a reference basis for investment decisions. On the other hand, data's immutability can alleviate the information asymmetry problem in fundraising. The operation behavior of each node on the chain is fully recorded, and all notes will form a "consensus" after joint verification to ensure the authenticity and reliability of the information. In addition, it can significantly improve fundraising efficiency and reduce costs. Redundant verification of a large number of fundraising-related documents will be diminished, and the supervision and audit within the department and the inspection of the project duration can be automatically monitored and controlled through the electronic system in real-time.

Second, blockchain makes smart contracts from virtual to real, ensuring a more effective PE fund default prevention mechanism, stronger post-default reimbursement measures, and less damage to stakeholders' interests. First, PE investment nested in smart contracts can reduce the default risk of PE funds. Investors can attach a string of codes to the funds invested in the PE fund to specify the purpose of the funds. When the funds are not used for the specified purpose as agreed, they will be frozen, and the default information of the PE fund will be recorded and made public on the chain, increasing the default cost of the PE fund and reducing the risk of default. Second, smart contracts can improve the enforcement of default disposal and protect investors' rights and interests. When a PE fund defaults, the smart contract can automatically identify, value, and enforce the contract according to the established rules, dispose of the PE fund's assets or margin promptly, and compensate for the loss of investors.

(5) Use technology to improve further the risks monitoring and early warning mechanism of PE investment

Environment changes impose higher requirements on PE market risk monitoring and prevention. The global economic situation has changed dramatically, and the trend of a financial pattern is uncertain. Meanwhile, there are still illegal business practices in China, including nonstandard review of qualified investors, inconsistent fundraising methods, unlawful use of investors' funds, inadequate information disclosure, disguised commitment to investors to protect principal and earnings, information not updated or updated promptly, products not filed as required, and failure to cooperate with a self- regulatory inspection. The above issues may lead to violent fluctuations in China's PE industry and systemic financial risks. Using technology to improve further the PE market's risk monitoring and early warning mechanism and build a solid financial security line of defense is imminent.

The risk monitoring and early warning mechanism can be promoted from both systematic and specific risk levels to establish a hierarchical risk monitoring and early warning system. One of the crucial tasks is to build systematic and targeted monitoring and early warning indicator system that aligns with the reality of China's PE industry. The selection of the indicators should be based on foreign experience and fit China's reality, covering systematic risk, credit risk, interest rate risk, and other risks. In addition, another important task to improve the risk monitoring and early warning mechanism is to formulate various risk response methods, including administrative instructions and risk management tools.

References

Bradford H, McKinzie R. Private equity in China: The impact of regulatory systems on private equity firms; 2020

Broeders D, Prenio J. Innovative technology in financial supervision (suptech)-the experience of early users. BIS Financial Stability Institute Insights on policy implementation No 9; 2018. https://www.bis.org/fsi/publ/insights9.htm

Brown G, Gredil O, Kaplan SN. Do private equity funds manipulate returns? J Financ Econ. 2019;132:267–97.

Brown G, Harris B, Jenkinson T, Kaplan S, Robinson D. Private equity: accomplishments and challenges. J Appl Corp Financ. 2020;32(3):8–20. https://doi.org/10.1111/jacf.12415.

Cumming D, Johan S. Regulatory harmonization and the development of private equity markets. J Bank Finance. 2007;31(10):3218–50.

Financial Services Authority. Private equity: a discussion of risk and regulatory engagement; 2006. https://www.treasurers.org/ACTmedia/dp06_06.pdf

Guo BS. Research on risk prevention and control strategies of private equity investment funds based on the perspective of risk control. Enterprise Reform Manage. 2022;20:99–101. https://doi.org/10.13768/j.cnki.cn11-3793/f.2022.1135.(inChinese).

Heed A. Regulation of private equity. J Bank Regul. 2010;12(1):24–47.

Hu M. Application and enlightenment of fintech in the private equity investment industry in the United Kingdom and the United States. Finance. 2022;3:89–94 (in Chinese).

Long JP. Improving China's private equity regulatory system: Orientation, framework and countermeasures. Southern Finance. 2019; 2019(5). (in Chinese)

McCahery JA, Vermeulen EP. Private equity regulation: a comparative analysis. J Manage Gov. 2012;16:197–233.

Renneboog L, Simons T, Wright M. Why do public firms go private in the UK? The impact of private equity investors, incentive realignment and undervaluation. J Corp Finance. 2007; 13(4): 591–628. https://doi.org/10.1016/j.jcorpfin.2007.04.005

Shan CY, Zhao DW. Research on the application of Regtech in private equity investment management. Financ Develop Rev. 2022;4:37–48. https://doi.org/10.19895/j.cnki.fdr.2022.04.001.(inChinese).

Smith EE, Smith JK, Smith RL. Bias in the reporting of venture capital performance: The disciplinary role of FOIA. Rev Corp Finance. 2022;2(3):493–525. https://doi.org/10.1561/114.00000022.

Thomsen S. Should private equity be regulated? Eur Bus Organ Law Rev. 2009;10(1):97–114.

Xu Z, Xu RH. Chapter 7: regulating FinTech for sustainable development in China. In: Amstad M, Huang B, Morgan PJ, Shirai S, editors. FinTech in Asia: policies and practices. Tokyo, Japan: Asian Development Bank Institute Press; 2020

Yang R. Research on high-quality post-investment management of state-owned private equity enabled by blockchain technology. Reform Opening up. 2021;14:17–22. https://doi.org/10.16653/j.cnki.32-1034/f.2021.014.003.(inChinese).

Yong KP. Private Equity in China: Challenges and Opportunities. John Wiley & Sons Singapore Pte. Ltd.; 2012

Zhong GC. Research on the application prospect and supervision of blockchain in private equity trading platform. Hainan Finance. 2019;04:73–81 (in Chinese).

Chapter 5
Technology Applications in Private Equity Compliance Management

With the transformation and development of China's economy and the multi-level capital market, PE investment has become increasingly prominent. As a tool connecting capital and asset, PE investment benefits both investment objects and the economy. For the investment objects, it provides capital support for the operation of enterprises, improves corporate governance structure, and promotes the sustainable development of enterprises. For the economy, it encourages the development of new industries through capital allocation, advances industrial transformation and upgrading, and plays an essential role in optimizing economic structure. China's PE investment has achieved rapid development, with the number of investment institutions rising, the scale of capital management increasing, and the industry competition becoming more and more intense.

In the rapid development of the PE industry, non-compliance behaviors have continued to occur frequently, causing losses and adverse effects to investors and PE fund managers. Typical non-compliance behaviors include illegal operations, disguised debt, PE disguised as public offerings, the standards of qualified investors unmet, dereliction of duty in PE fund management, and loss of registration and filing information. The PE industry regulation has been stepped up to resolve the accumulation of risks. Since the end of 2019, many rules and guidelines have been introduced for the PE industry. The regulators have clarified the tightening regulatory condition, enhanced the regulatory content, and imposed higher compliance requirements for the PE industry. In such circumstances, the compliance costs of PE institutions have further increased, and the competition in the PE investment fund industry has become increasingly fierce.

Application scenarios of technology in financial institutions' compliance continue to emerge, and new technologies such as blockchain, big data, and AI provide solutions for financial institutions to improve compliance capabilities. With interconnection between the institutions and the regulators in a digital way, the institutions can

R. Xu and D. Zhao, *Digital Transformation of Private Equity in China*, Contributions to Finance and Accounting, https://doi.org/10.1007/978-981-99-8482-4_5

obtain digital regulatory requirements from the regulators, which are accurately translated into internal constraints to ensure real-time institutional and business compliance. Meanwhile, the institutions can submit data to the regulators in real-time to dynamically form various compliance reports, reducing manual intervention and improving accuracy (Su 2020).

In the trend of closer integration of technology and finance, technology's application and evolution have become powerful tools to meet regulatory requirements and solve compliance problems. After entering the era of strong supervision, what are the applications of technology in PE investment compliance management in the whole process from the establishment to liquidation? How can technology effectively avoid compliance risks and reduce compliance costs? What are compliance technology's operation mechanisms and development trends in the PE industry? This chapter provides an in-depth analysis of these issues.

5.1 The Origins of Technology Application in PE Compliance Management

5.1.1 Service Transformation During the Expansion of the PE Industry

1. **The PE industry is growing rapidly along with economic growth**

PE investment in China has a late start but fast growth. It dates back to 1984 when China introduced the concept of venture capital. Along with the development of China's economy and the emergence of high-quality enterprises, PE investment has continued to grow. Its investment and management capabilities have been continuously improved.

2. **PE investment plays a vital role in promoting economic transformation and development**

In the process of "fundraising—investment—operation and management—exit," PE investment can bring the enterprise a stable source of capital and additional values such as successful management experience, advanced management technology, diversified sales market, and professional knowledge and skills. PE investment can influence the industrial structure from the capital to output by making forward-looking investments at critical stages of new economic development. In detail, venture capital investment cultivates new industries, restructuring funds, and acquisition funds can realize industrial restructuring and upgrading and eliminate backward sectors. The market-oriented capital allocation can optimize the organizational structure, lead industrial transformation and upgrading, and ultimately influence the macroeconomic structure. In summary, PE investment has become a strong driver for developing a new economy and transforming the traditional economy.

3. **PE investment is crucial in promoting financial structural reform**

As an alternative source of financing, PE investment can increase the proportion of direct financing, thus improving the current financing system centered on indirect financing by banks. The efficient direct allocation of capital can help promote establishing and improving the multi-level capital market. PE investment funds can directly and effectively serve the real economy by realizing a virtuous circle between capital and industry, which is the proper meaning of financial reform.

4. **PE investment has a bright future with China's economic transformation**

The transformation and upgrading of China's economic structure have a long way to go, and PE investment as a vital capital force still has broad development space. Since 2016, the State Council and various ministries and commissions have proposed increasing the direct investment proportion. Various policies have been implemented continuously, providing development opportunities for the PE industry. In addition, the expansion of the middle class in China has also laid a wealth foundation for fundraising.

5.1.2 Compliance Operations Become a Pain Point, and the Cost of PE Investment Further Increases

1. **Compliance guidance has been issued successively, and industry development has gradually standardized**

In June 2013, the regulatory responsibility of PE investment funds was transferred to the CSRC. In August 2014, the CSRC promulgated the *Interim Measures for the Supervision and Administration of Private Investment Funds*, which laid the foundation of the current regulatory framework for PE investment funds. Since then, the AMAC has issued many detailed rules and guidelines under the authorization of the CSRC. The regulatory framework has gradually matured, and the regulatory content has become increasingly perfect. Since 2018, regulators have intensively issued many rules and guidelines, including the "*Notice on the Filing of Private Investment Funds*," the "*Notice on the Filing of Private Investment Funds (2019 Edition)*", the "*Implementation Rules on the Integrity of Fund Management Institutions and their Staff*," and "*Notice on the Publication of the List of Application Materials for the Filing of PE Investment Funds*." The regulations and guidelines for PE investment funds have been stepped up, imposing higher requirements for compliance.

In 2021, PE compliance guidance continued to be upgraded. On January 8, the CSRC officially issued "*Certain Provisions on Strengthening the Supervision of Private Investment Funds*," the first regulatory document related to the PE industry in the form of a departmental regulatory document after the issuance of the "*Interim Measures for the Supervision and Administration of Private Investment Funds*" by the CSRC in 2014. On February 9, the AMAC issued the "*Notice on Strengthening the Self-Regulatory Management of PE Information Reporting and Optimizing Industry Services*" to further strengthen the information submission of PE funds and promote the data quality of the industry. On June 9, the AMAC issued the "*Notice on Matters Related to Strengthening the Qualification Registration of Practitioners of Private Fund Managers*," requiring that the total number of employees of institutions applying for registration as private fund managers should not be less than 5, and those general employees should not work part-time. The threshold for registration and operation has been significantly raised. The standardization and normalization of compliance supervision have made PE investment standardized. In July 2023, the State Council released the *Regulation on the Supervision and Administration of Private Equity Investment Funds*, China's first regulation covering the supervision and administration of PE funds, which will take effect on September 1, 2023. The regulation delineates the bottom line of supervision to control risks from the outset and rolls out strict punishment for violations such as misappropriation and misuse of fund capital.

2. **PE regulation continues to upgrade, and strict supervision has become the norm**

Compliance and risk control of the PE industry lagged behind its rapid development and have gradually become the pain point. In addition to issuing regulations and self-regulatory rules, the CSRC and the AMAC have also launched several supporting self-inspections and special inspections. The scope and strength of inspections have been continuously expanded. The local securities regulatory bureaus have carried out risk self-inspection for PE managers, requiring PE managers to submit self-inspection reports and other relevant materials. In addition to the regular PE risk census, regulators across the country also conduct PE inspections, including in Beijing and Shanghai.

As a result, the violator institutions take administrative supervision measures or are filed for inspection. Their clues of suspected violations are transferred to the public security department or local government. The relevant violations and regulatory measures taken are recorded in the integrity archives of the capital market. The AMAC imposed on-site and off-site self-regulatory penalties on non-compliant PE fund managers and their practitioners. It provides punitive measures in conjunction with inspections, including cancellation of membership of PE fund managers, revocation of PE manager registration, suspension of fund product filing, and correction within a certain period. The number of institutions subject to punishment shows a significant upward trend (Tu 2019). In 2022, 24 provinces, cities, and regions have issued PE regulatory inspection notices and material lists, and 229 violation penalties have been reported on the websites of local securities regulatory bureaus (Fig. 5.1). By sorting out the violations, we find that the violations heavily concentrated in registration and filing, fundraising and promotion, disclose information, and investor suitability management. The violations with the most inspections and penalties in 2022 centered on fundraising (104 violations).

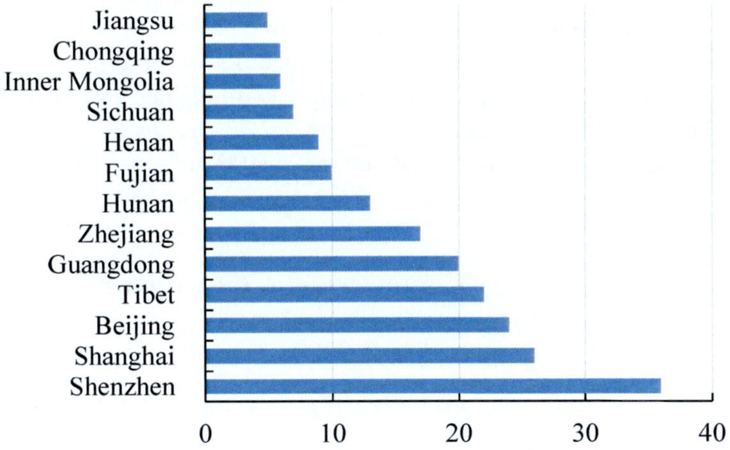

Fig. 5.1 Number of PE Punishment Cases across Province in 2022. *Note* Name of provinces or municipal cities (such as Beijing) is the punishment imposed by the local securities regulatory bureau. *Source* CSRC, web news, the authors

3. **Operating costs increase, and competition in the industry has intensified**

With the gradual strengthening of regulatory requirements, the compliance costs of PE investment are also increasing. It is mainly manifested in two aspects. On the one hand, the resources invested in meeting the compliance requirements include human resources, capital investment, and time cost. It is worth noting that labor compliance costs play a major part in compliance costs of the financial sector. According to survey estimates from the Securities Industry Association (2006) in the U.S. financial sector, 93.9% of regulatory compliance costs are labor related and 3.3% are physical capital-related. On the other hand, the penalties due to violations bring direct capital loss and reputation loss. Take the operating cost as an example. On February 5, 2016, the AMAC issued the "*Announcement on Further Standardizing the Registration of Private Fund Managers*," which tightened the lenient PE fund registration policy, raised the entry threshold, and standardized the management and operation of private funds. The operating cost of PE funds has increased significantly after introducing the new regulations. An estimation indicates that a compliant PE fund company's annual operating expenses are about 1.52 million yuan. The actual expenditure will be higher if calculated with the medium price level in the first-tier cities. On July 1, 2017, the CSRC implemented the "*Administrative Measures for Securities and Futures Investor Suitability Management*," resulting in increased operating costs. Only 20 PE fund companies were filed within three months after implementing the new rules.

The "3 + 3" PE investment advisory model[1] increases the "intellectual cost" of PE fund operation. According to a survey by Xueqiu, the annual compliance cost

[1] "3 + 3": the private fund manager needs at least three staff members with traceable performance of no less than three years, and the performance needs to be proved by the corresponding product report or other supporting materials issued by the trustee, auditor or other third-party institutions.

of a PE fund manager in Beijing, Shanghai, and Shenzhen is estimated to range from 1.85 million to 2.5 million yuan (calculated according to the cost of Grade B office buildings) (Xueqiu 2018). Suppose the compliance cost is about 2 million yuan annually, and the management fee ratio is 2%. The scale and survival line of a PE fund manager's operation scale should reach 100 million yuan.

5.1.3 With Technology Empowerment, Compliance Technology Provides Solutions

1. **Compliance management is increasingly strengthened**

In June 2021, the AMAC and industry organizations and law firms compiled and published the "*PE Investment Fund Industry Compliance Management Handbook (2021)*". The handbook reorganizes the existing laws, regulations, and self-regulatory rules of PE funds by institutions' compliance and integrity management workflow. It helps PE fund managers enhance their awareness of compliance management and strengthen business operation regulation. Currently, the AMAC has published lists for PE investment to provide clear compliance guidelines for PE fund registration and filing and promote convenience. The lists include "*Application Materials List for Private Investment Fund Filing (Non-Securities)*," "*Application Materials List for PE Fund Filing (Major Changes and Liquidation)*," and "*Application Materials List for PE Fund Manager Registration (Non-Securities)*."

As the supervision is strengthened, PE fund management companies have also made greater efforts in compliance. Measures include strengthening communication with regulatory authorities, actively learning the latest regulatory policies and requirements, improving internal control, and strengthening compliance management information construction. The measures help investment institutions to comply effectively and reduce operational risks. Fund managers use technological solutions to facilitate compliance with and monitoring regulatory requirements (Colaert 2017).

2. **The regulators promote the construction of information platforms**

Regulators have further strengthened the infrastructure of the PE industry, built information reporting and monitoring systems, and continuously promoted the informatization and digitalization of the PE supervision system. Since April 5, 2017, PE institutions have been required to register and file their products on the "Asset Management Business Electronic Registration System" (AMBERS),[2] whose function is constantly improved. On January 7, 2021, the AMAC upgraded the AMBERS system and launched the "Material Matters Report" functional module for fund managers to submit major PE fund events, a sub-module of the product record module in the AMBERS system. On February 5, the AMBERS system was launched with a trial run of the annual financial monitoring report module for PE funds, which focuses

[2] https://ambers.amac.org.cn/cas/login?service.

on the financial status of funds, indicating that regulators are increasingly concerned about the financial compliance of PE funds. On December 14, the AMAC issued the "*Notice on Facilitating the Filing of Executive Information by Applicants for Registration and PE Fund Managers,*" launched a practitioner management platform, and introduced the information reuse function of the AMBERS to make the information filing more standardized, simplified, and convenient.

3. **Compliance technology becomes an inevitable option**

In practice, PE investment institutions have a wide range of operating links and dense and messy compliance points. How to conduct business in compliance is the manager's main concern. Increasing manpower is not a good solution for compliance problems since it reduces the efficiency of finance, operation, and human resources increases the cost of fund management, and aggravates the non-standardization of information, which is not beneficial to the development and effective supervision of the PE industry. Technology empowerment has become an inevitable choice for high-quality compliance (Colaert 2017; Jin 2021). Compliance technology provides powerful technological enablement for data privacy protection, automated regulatory data processing, violation identification and early warning, and attribution of responsibility for data violations (Zhou 2022; Fu 2023). In particular, as regulatory technology has been used to reduce regulatory gaps, strengthen policy effectiveness and prevent financial risks, the PE industry should also support applying compliance technology to enhance its operational capabilities and compliance efficiency.

5.2 Development of Compliance Technology

5.2.1 The Foundation of Compliance Technology Has Been Continuously Consolidated

Before the term compliance technology emerged, financial institutions had already used technology to improve risk management and compliance effectiveness. In the 1980s, large financial institutions started to apply financial engineering technologies and Value-at-Risk (VaR) systems. In the 1990s, along with the development of financial technology and financial globalization, financial institutions applied technology to the compliance field. They started setting up compliance, legal, and risk management departments. In the twenty-first century, compliance technology has entered a new stage of development, with efficient data management and business compliance as the core foundation to support financial risk prevention.

CompTech, as a branch of RegTech, is mainly applied in the compliance of financial institutions to improve risk control and reduce compliance costs (Shan and Zhao 2019; Tao and Wan 2019). Current compliance technology uses next-generation technologies such as cloud computing, AI, and application programming interfaces (APIs) in traditional compliance operations, significantly improving compliance efficiency and reducing compliance costs. Information technology has dramatically increased the amount of data in the financial industry, which provide sufficient sample data for learning and analysis. The innovation of algorithms and models improves the operation efficiency of information systems. The upgrading of hardware has made the financial infrastructure more stable. The combination and synergy of data, algorithms, and hardware provide a solid foundation for developing compliance technology.

Financial institutions take the lead in developing compliance technology to meet compliance needs. The growing number of regulatory alerts about financial risks has further accelerated the development and adoption of compliance technology. In 2022, the number of regulatory events monitored by Thomson Reuters Regulatory Intelligence (TRRI) was 61,228, which involved 1,374 regulators in 190 countries (TRRI 2023). Since the global financial crisis, global financial institutions have paid more than $340 billion in fines (KPMG 2020) and continue to face regulatory penalties related to failures in market conduct, anti-money laundering, regulatory reporting, and information and consumer protection. In addition, the cost of remediation can be several times greater than the fines.

Compliance technology is gradually growing, and the number of compliance technology startups is increasing, enhancing the compliance business capabilities of financial institutions. According to FinTech Global, global compliance technology investments grew exponentially from $1.5 billion in 2017 to nearly $8 billion in 2020, achieving a compound annual growth rate of 74.7%.

5.2.2 The Importance of Compliance Technology Application is Highlighted

The application of compliance technology has apparent benefits for regulators, financial institutions, and consumers. The regulators benefit in the following aspects. First, it reduces systemic risk by improving financial institutions' compliance efficiency, and reducing risks to the financial system. Second, it strengthens supervision. Financial institutions' automatic and timely reporting of business data helps regulators respond quickly to changing circumstances. Third, it improves efficiency by resolving regulatory reporting inconsistencies.

For financial institutions, compliance technology provides significant competitive advantages. First, it enhances risk management. Compliance technology uses automated solution technology to reduce human error and enables rapid analysis through big data technology, while relatively simplified predictive analysis can more effectively prevent potential problems. Second, it reduces costs. According to Hendrikse (2020), a typical European bank serving 10 million customers could save up to 40% or €10 million annually and avoid growing fines by the regulator by implementing technology to improve the "Know Your Customer" (KYC) processes. Third, it helps to attract and retain customers. Compliance technology can help improve the user experience, provide more efficient and fast services, and make compliance inspection more effective, thus gaining a competitive advantage for users.

For consumers, compliance technology improves the user experience. Financial institutions can spend more time managing customer relationships and provide better financial services by reducing the time spent on administrative-related work, such as compliance with entry requirements and information disclosure. Meanwhile, customer assessment and risk assessment based on big data promote financial inclusion and improve the accessibility of financial services.

5.2.3 Compliance Technology Has Rich Application Scenarios

Compliance technology applies some modern information technologies, including AI, machine learning, big data, cloud computing, blockchain, biometric technology, encryption technology, natural language processing, and API. Cloud computing and application programming interfaces are the most critical essential technologies, while others can be classified as emerging technologies. (See Table 5.1 for details).

The application scenarios of compliance technology cover data management, customer identification, transaction monitoring, risk management, law and regulation tracking, automated regulatory reporting, private placement issuance, and information disclosure (Xu and Liu 2019). Among them, regulatory compliance management, transaction monitoring, and risk management are the key areas of concern for institutions (see Fig. 5.2 for details).

5.3 PE Investment Compliance System[3]

The compliance risk control of PE investment funds includes compliance with registration and filing and information reporting, standardization of internal management and operation, compliance with fundraising, the effectiveness of suitability management, the compliance of investment operation, implementation of the "*Interim Provisions on the Operation of Private Asset Management Business of Securities and Futures Institutions*," the integrity of information disclosure, the effectiveness of risk control, and other aspects. It includes the compliance requirements for PE fund managers and product operation (see Fig. 5.3). PE investment funds have a complex history of regulatory evolution and diversified investment fields and methods, and their compliance management involves the responsibilities of multiple government departments. With the gradual improvement of laws, regulations, and

[3] This subsection refers to AMAC (2021).

Table 5.1 Technology applications in compliance areas

Classification	Key technologies	Advantages
Basic technologies	Cloud computing	It enables financial institutions to operate at a lower cost without purchasing and maintaining equipment and has greater flexibility in generating, storing, managing, and using data while enhancing data security and advanced data protection. It allows users to access applications anytime, from any location, and on any device
	API	It facilitates the exchange of information and execution of instructions between different computer systems
Emerging technologies	AI	It helps to realize the automation, autonomous detection, and insight generation of business processes and attracts customers and employees through daily communication. It facilitates large-scale real-time analysis and interpretation of data and provides timely prediction and alerts for more comprehensive risk monitoring
	Machine learning	It continuously improves and performs more accurate and predictive analysis from larger, more complex data sets
	Natural language processing	It is a branch of AI that allows the system to recognize and interpret meanings from human language and create two-way communication between the system and users
	Optical character recognition (OCR)	It identifies and converts text from various documents into digital data. It can extract information in large quantities from a wide range of sources and convert the information into a format that can be used by machine learning, natural language processing, and other technologies that benefit from datasets
	Internet of things	It can collect, interpret, and use more real-world data and increase productivity through monitoring and controlling a wider range of processes
	Distributed ledger	It is a modern database system using blockchain technology. It is usually used to record asset transactions and provide secure, immutable, and auditable information tracking on assets
	Biometric technology	It uses the unique biometrics of individuals to verify their identity, improve the security of authentication and provide a better user experience in a more convenient process

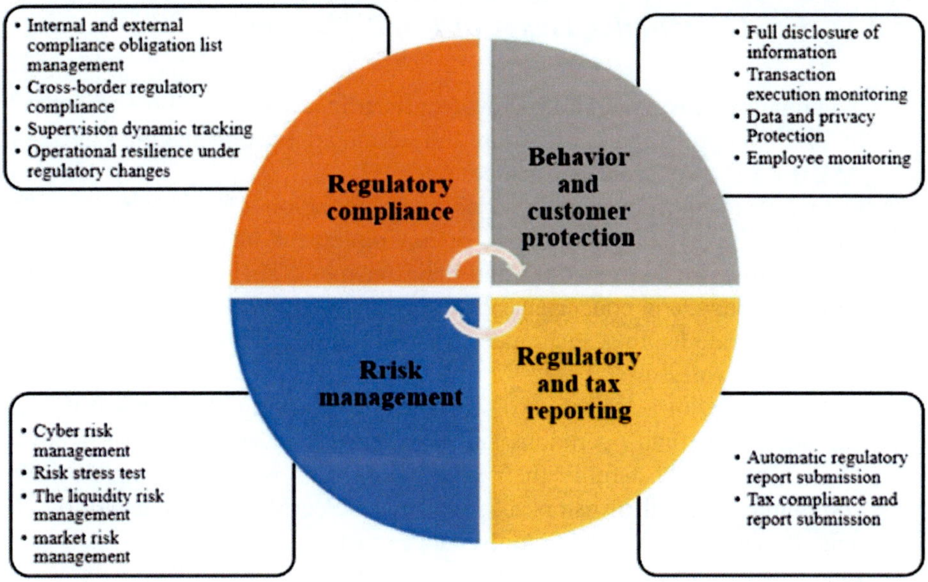

Fig. 5.2 Key application scenarios for compliance technology

self-regulatory rules, the PE investment industry gradually established a multi-dimensional, all-round and standardized development matrix, covering the entire life cycle of "fundraising-investment-management-exist."

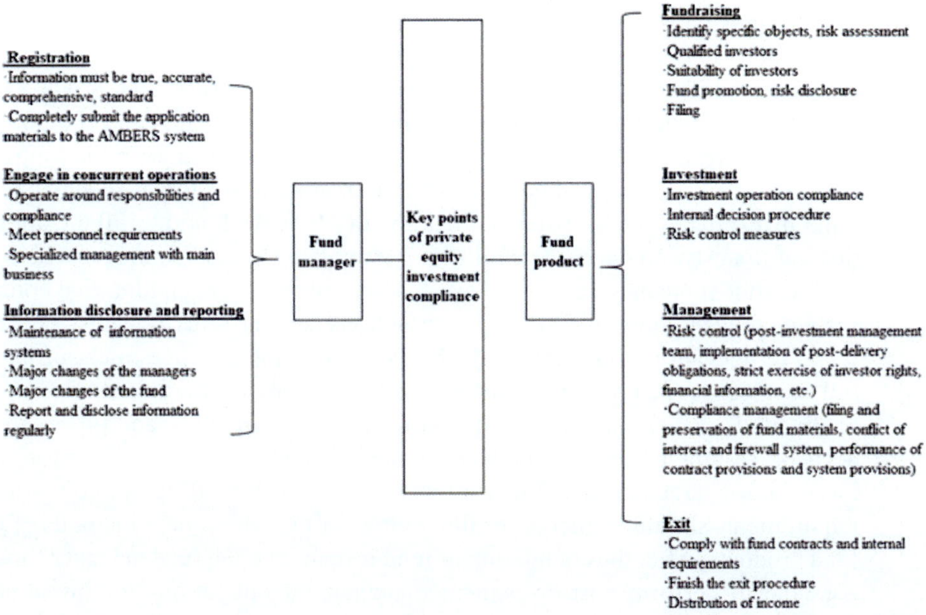

Fig. 5.3 Key points of PE investment compliance

5.3.1 Key Compliance Issues of Fund Managers

1. Compliance with registration. Provide authentic, accurate, comprehensive, standardized materials and information, and submit application materials through the AMBERS system prudently and completely.
2. Compliance with engaging in concurrent operations. Fund managers should comply with external regulatory rules, implement internal stipulations, and realize professional operations and main business. They should not directly or indirectly engage in concurrent operations that may conflict with the PE funds, such as private lending, guarantees, crowdfunding, P2P/P2B, financial leasing, and other businesses.
3. Compliance with information disclosure and reporting. To improve the transparency of PE fund operations and fully protect investors' right-to-know, PE fund managers must fulfill their information disclosure obligations by timely communication with investors and reporting to the AMAC through multiple channels. It covers the information of changes in major events of the manager, the fund, regular reporting, disclosure, and other information. The main channels include the AMBER, the Private Fund Information Disclosure Backup System, and Practitioner Information Management System.

5.3.2 Key Compliance Issues of Fund Products

1. Fundraising. There are many compliance requirements involved in fundraising. The PE fund managers and fund sales institutions must raise funds from qualified investors in a non-public way and meet the suitability requirement. In detail, it includes identifying specific targets and risks tolerance assessment, product risk classification, investor suitability matching and management, fund promotion, risk disclosure, and the opening of fundraising accounts for filing. On the contrary, raising funds from unspecified persons or unqualified investors is illegal.
2. Fund Investment. The investment operation of the fund should fulfill the obligations of honesty, prudence, and diligence, establish a sound control mechanism for investment business, a scientific risk assessment system and internal control system, prevent improper related transactions and benefit transmission, and preserve relevant information properly. When looking for investment projects, full consideration should be given to the restrictions on the investment scope of PE funds. When making investment decisions, a scientific and professional decision-making process should be formulated according to industry sectors and investment characteristics. When implementing projects, different compliance requirements should be met according to the various investment methods of the fund products. After the completion of fund investment, the fund manager should continue to perform post-investment management obligations for investment projects.

3. Fund operation. In the post-investment stage, a special post-investment management team and the process should be established to strengthen risk control and continue to perform the obligation of information disclosure and reporting following regulations. The fund materials should be properly archived and preserved.
4. Fund exit. PE funds must comply with the fund contract and internal requirements to initiate the project exit process. Upon exit completion, the funds must be distributed to the exit proceeds according to relevant regulations. This process has many common compliance points, such as the initiation of the pre-exit procedure, payment of taxes, change of registration procedures, determination of distributable proceeds, and order of proceeds distribution. Ensuring that each step in the exit process is legal and compliant is necessary.

5.4 The Practice of Technology Application in PE Compliance Management

Compliance technology can help fund managers conduct compliance management on the fund establishment, fundraising, filing, and liquidation process. Compliance technology has been applied in the "fundraising-investment-management-exit" cycle of PE investment to reduce operational risks associated with compliance obligations (Packin 2018; Shan and Zhao 2019). On the one hand, it helps PE institutions to realize automated data submission and report generation, reducing compliance costs. On the other hand, it can track the dynamic changes of regulatory policies in real-time, grasp the core regulations and empower enterprises to quickly meet the regulatory requirements, reduce the risk of violations and avoid unnecessary regulatory penalties by preset compliance control reminders. The critical role of compliance technology cannot be separated from the development of modern information technology such as AI, big data, and cloud computing. Big data brings extensive data resources and realizes data precipitation. Cloud computing provides solutions to problems related to data storage and big data. AI can solve the problems of unstructured data, high granularity, and colossal quantity and attain effective processing and analysis of business data and transaction data.

5.4.1 An Investment Management System Provides A Comprehensive Solution for Compliance Operations

The PE investment management system is a centralized embodiment of technology application in PE compliance management. The current management system uses AI, machine learning, and other technologies to solve the problems of PE fund management companies in internal management, customer management, marketing, operation, risk control, and compliance. It provides a set of comprehensive system solutions for PE fund management companies. It is a trend in the PE industry to introduce an asset management system and empower PE investment management using technology. The ultimate goal of standardized management, automatic early warning, and compliance guidelines can be achieved by applying technology.

1. **Controllable process to achieve standardized management**

The investment management system takes investors, funds, and projects as the primary management line, covering the whole business chain of fundraising, investment, post-investment management, and exit of investment companies. It connects limited partners (LP), channels, management companies, fund management, investment managers, and partners so that all categories of projects operate according to the process with minimum risk, improve compliance efficiency, reduce investment risks, and help investors and risk control personnel to conduct all-round standardized management of the project investment process. Meanwhile, it provides important reminders and alerts for information disclosure dates to avoid errors and omissions in the filing.

For example, eFront Invest, a smart investment management system developed by Intel Leagle, provides diversified investment management for LPs and enables LPs to fully control the funds or projects they invest in, including performance evaluation and portfolio management. Plan the investment process for the general partners (GP), from fund operation to investor relationship management, and provide investment lifecycle management. Through pre-investment transaction and project database management, the project and project data can be efficiently managed, and project information can be analyzed penetratingly. Automatic data processing and standardized approval process management can be realized through online operations. Post-investment compliance management can be realized through financial and operational data management, investment events, critical terms management, supervision, and compliance rule construction. Standardized exit is achieved through multi-dimensional investment tools and performance compensation management.

2. **Data integration and intelligent risk warning**

For the risk control personnel, the management system supports comprehensive compliance management of business operations. It provides intelligent risk monitoring and automatic early warning according to the requirements of AMAC and relevant laws and regulations and realizes the whole process management of risk disposal. By setting compliance rules, it can trigger notifications for risks associated with inconsistent information reporting, regulatory penalties, judicial filings, business operations, senior managers, shareholders, and related parties intelligently and completely generate trigger result reports, timely follow up on the warning information and makes corrections for processing.

For the post-investment personnel, it sends timely risk warnings and improves the management efficiency of the projects. For example, the equity investment management solution of ActionSoft realizes the penetrating management of investors, funds, and projects through intelligent integration of industrial and commercial data, public opinion monitoring, investment research, and other data, and realizes risk control management through customer rating and risk factor assessment (Hou 2018).

5.4.2 Electronic Contracts Normalize Contract Signing

It is a general trend for PE investors to sign electronic contracts. In August 2018, the electronic contract management system built by China Securities Internet System Co., Ltd.[4] was officially launched to provide the whole process service of online signing and management of electronic contracts for all parties of PE funds, promoting China's PE funds to enter the era of electronic contracts. In October 2020, the AMAC issued the "*Administrative Measures for the Electronic Contracts Business of Private Investment Funds (for trial implementation) (draft for comments)*," which stresses the necessity of developing electronic contracts and standardizes the meaning, basic business scope, and legal effect, rights and obligations of each party, data confidentiality, and storage of electronic contracts for PE funds.

Electronic contracts realize process standardization and online trace, which improves operational efficiency and helps standardize the signing of PE fund contracts. First, it ensures that the contracting parties have the conditions for compliance operation. A digital certificate is issued only if the PE fund managers and PE fund custodians meet the requirements and pass the access threshold following regulatory requirements. Investors also need to pass real-name authentication to ensure the authenticity of their identities. Second, the electronic signing system provides an overall identity authentication mechanism to provide technical tools to review users' signing qualifications compliance. Third, it ensures data integrity and accuracy. During the signing process, the contracting parties adopt a secure communication mechanism through the platform to ensure the security of data transmission. The default minimum visible principle of the contracting parties' data effectively protects the data privacy of the parties. In addition, the platform uses high-strength encryption for the data generated during the signing process for secure storage. It ensures all data's integrity, accuracy, and immutability through blockchain technology (O'Shields 2017). It can issue a completion certificate report upon request of the contracting parties in case of disputes (Clack et al. 2017), effectively preventing the chaos of signing a "yin-yang contract."

5.4.3 Electronic Database Serves Suitability Management

The core of suitability management is to strengthen PE fund managers' responsibility for selling suitable products to investors by referring to investors' risk tolerance and product risk, full disclosure of risks, and matching opinions (Chen 2019).

[4] https://www.interotc.com.cn/zzbj/.

1. **Electronic template information promotes compliance with investor suitability determination**

The determination of investor suitability has been the focus of regulatory penalties. The main steps of investor suitability management include user authentication, confirmation of specific objects and matching of product risks, filling in the AMAC information form, uploading and reviewing asset certificates, confirmation of risk disclosure, submission of purchase applications, signing of fund contracts, automatic control of the cooling-off period, and mobile intelligent return visit. These processes are mainly completed offline by manual filling, scanning, and transmission and may lead to low efficiency and high compliance risks.

Establishing a complete set of system automation systems and databases can embed numerous system templates perfectly and precisely into the compliance fundraising process. The process can be completed 100% online through technology and network applications, and the corresponding nine electronic certificates can be retained to provide third-party credentials for compliance. For example, the fundraising platform of Haifeng Fund services & Technology standardized the template of the basic information form for investors to fill in online and automatically generated the certificates saved in the cloud and downloaded instantly, following the requirements of the AMAC for suitability identification.

2. **Integration of information in databases facilitates dynamic assessment of investors**

PE fund managers in suitability management often overlook the dynamic assessment of investors. The "*Guidelines on the Implementation of Investor Suitability Management for Fundraising Institutions (for Trial Implementation)*" stipulate that fundraising institutions shall establish an investor assessment database, build information files for investors and conduct a dynamic assessment of investors' risk levels. Fundraising institutions shall fully use the existing information and the results of existing assessments to avoid the repeated collection of investor information and improve assessment efficiency.

"Dynamic assessment" does not mean that the assessment method is constantly changing but that the old information must still be kept and cannot be directly overwritten by new information. In investor database construction, the administrator generally uses electronic documents and filing cabinets to save the material online and offline. However, offline preservation is faced with problems such as the cumbersome process of paper document changes, high cost, preservation difficulties, heavy workload of manual records, error-prone, and additional human expenditure.

The digital dynamic assessment database provides technical solutions. For example, iPrivateBuy (CBS) provides a powerful investor database-building function for managers, which covers investors' information related to compliance requirements, risk assessment, qualification, contracts, and return visits, truly realizing a complete "online archive" for investors. In addition, iPrivateBuy (CBS) can perfectly realize dynamic assessment and preservation. It records all information changes, transaction records, data addition of investors, and marks in detail in the system's backend. Meanwhile, the system provides a one-click export function. When required by supervision, relevant certificates can be directly exported, sorted out, and submitted to improve compliance efficiency.

3. **Electronic return visit**

A return visit is an essential step of suitability compliance after establishing the fund, mainly to confirm the suitability match between investors and the subscribed PE fund products and whether the match situation has changed. The abnormal conditions found during the return visit should be tracked and checked continuously, and the existence of hidden risks should be promptly investigated and regularly summarized. The form of the return visit should be chosen to leave traces.

The investor database can be used to realize electronic return visits and meet compliance requirements. First, screening and spot check. A random inspection and return visit can be conducted on ordinary investors and investors whose risks do not match. Second, flexible configuration. The database can be configured to meet the compliance requirements of the standard suitability return visit template but also for personalized configuration. Third, automatic trace. When the suitability return visit is completed with electronic return visit forms, the return visit form will be kept in the database management background for archiving to leave a trace automatically.

4. **Professional data extraction generates compliance reports**

The PE industry has some difficulties in data governance. For example, the complexity of the data structure work, the short time and large volume of data governance and report collation, and the variable disclosure requirements of the regulation. The financial and operational data received every quarter must be stored and managed for internal management, and the data maintenance workload is enormous. Professional database management can enhance the efficiency of data processing and reduce the error rate of manual maintenance. For regulatory compliance, a professional data governance platform can generate internal reports with different frequencies and various analytical reports and charts required by regulatory departments, improving efficiency and reducing compliance risks.

First, it ensures data security. Various forms of data can be collected, including GP reports, investment agreements, and financial reports. External data can be accessed as an aid, including industrial, commercial, and judicial data and macroeconomic and market data. Data is sent directly from the client to the data governance platform for unified closed-loop management to ensure data safety. In addition, it realizes checklist reminders, preliminary screening of data, task distribution, progress management, data trace, data review, and export.

Second, it ensures efficient data processing. Data integrity can be guaranteed through complete data processing control, including double entry, cross-checking, and third-party data review and verification. Two people enter the same information, and the probability of the same erroneous data is extremely low. Targeted third-party data verification can further improve data quality while ensuring timeliness.

Third, it promotes data visualization. The value of the data can be explored in various ways and from different computing angles by using the constant calibration of computing models and engines. The data can be utilized to automatically generate regular reports, irregular reports, and other forms of reports to meet the requirements of internal management and regulatory compliance.

5.4.4 Intelligent Matching for Compliance Fundraising

Compliance technology can identify specific targets through intelligent information collection and risk tolerance assessment. It can also intelligently recommend matching funds based on the assessment results and ensure that product information is only displayed for targeted objects.

1. **Intelligent due diligence of specific objects**

First, intelligent recommendation. Based on big data and AI algorithms, intelligent due diligence can conduct keyword segmentation and inverted indexing of a huge database of questions and assessments, automatically recommend the suitable question set and assessment criteria when creating a new project, draw up a due diligence plan based on a full understanding of the target enterprise, and constantly supplement and improve it. With a PE database and data mining technology, banks, securities companies, and other PE-related institutions can synchronize the dynamic information of the institution to determine whether to cooperate.

Second, generate due diligence reports. Due diligence includes a lengthy process, including preparation, formulation of investigation procedures, review of financial statements, contracts, and other important information, analysis of information, and production of a due diligence report. AI can convert most of the basic system information into data. The data analyzed by the intelligent system can be presented in Excel or a third-party system, and data on key indicators can be extracted to generate a due diligence report. Intelligent due diligence saves time, cuts costs, reduces human errors and needs for manual review, and improves work efficiency. Third, continuous evolution. The question base and evaluation base of PE investment institutions' intelligent systems are constantly updated according to the project's industry changes and investment characteristics. The recommendation algorithms are also continuously evolving in the project practice.

2. **Intelligent matching of investors and products**

For the risk tolerance assessment of investors, fundraising institutions can personalize the risk assessment to meet regulatory compliance requirements. Technology can be used to ensure the effectiveness of assessment methods, quickly obtain the risk assessment results with intelligent model calculations, and provide immediate feedback to investors.

For the risk level assessment of fund products, fundraising institutions use a combination of qualitative and quantitative methods. They set assessment factors and weights in models, verify and improve through practice, establish a corresponding relationship between the assessment score and the risk level of fund products, and establish a long-term mechanism for risk evaluation.

For the intelligent matching of fund products and services, the institutions assess users' risk tolerance based on data and match them with suitable fund products and services. Improve producing intelligent matching through continuous data enrichment, iteration, and algorithm improvement. Automatically adjust the classification of investors and the risk ratings of products or services according to information changes.

3. **Compliance matching displays product information**

In fundraising, PE investment institutions are prohibited from promoting unspecified objects through public media such as the Internet, instant messaging tools, blogs, e-mail, and other carriers. However, promoting qualified investors through the Internet media and clients that set specific object determination procedures is possible. Technological means can ensure that product information (such as roadshow videos and performance announcements) can be displayed on particular objects by setting permissions. Compliance promotion can also be achieved in the circle of friends and WeChat groups, further enriching promotion channels and forms.

5.5 Issues of Compliance Technology Application and Policy Suggestions

Technology plays two prominent roles in PE compliance management: a connector of the industry and a connector between regulation and the industry. First, by building an information technology platform, the PE fund contracting process is realized online, and transaction data is stored in real-time and immutable, enhancing the industry's intelligence and automation. Second, real-time business data is reported to regulators to improve regulatory efficiency and reduce legal risks.

However, applying compliance technology in PE investment still has problems, such as insufficient digitization, isolated islands of information and data, and data security. Given this, it is necessary to accelerate the digital transformation of PE investment compliance management, improve the degree of industry regulation, solve the data asymmetry problem, and use technology to improve compliance efficiency and reduce the burden of compliance.

5.5.1 *Major Issues*

First, applications of information technology in the industry are insufficient. PE fund management companies rarely use information management systems to carry out fund sales, investment transaction management, share registration, capital clearing, and other operations. GPs have been slow to introduce the fund asset management system compared to LPs. Some smaller PE investment funds cannot bear the costs of self-built information systems and continuous compliance operations. The non-standardization of information is not conducive to the effective regulation of the industry, nor does it conform to the mainstream digitalization trend. According to KPMG's 2019 report "*The digital transformation imperative*",[5] most PE companies are still in the "awareness raising" phase concerning eight key digital innovations, and very few have completed or are implementing technology.

Second, information asymmetry is common. The PE industry has not yet formed effective and credible data and records for many businesses because the information system has limited coverage. Many offline and paper documents are difficult to leave traces effectively, and there is the problem of inaccurate information. The PE industry is characterized by low product standardization, a wide variety of products, and low transparency of industry information. Information sharing and integration among fund management companies, fund sales institutions, investors, and regulators have not been formed. The phenomenon of isolated islands of information and data is common, and information asymmetry among institutions is prominent. It is necessary to enhance the information transparency of specific objects to achieve effective risk management and mutual supervision.

Third, personalized allocation raises costs. Some PE fund management systems fail to meet personalized allocation needs. Although some fund management systems provide customized services, the service cost is too high, raising the cost of operation and compliance.

5.5.2 Policy Recommendations

First, enhance digital awareness and promote the digital development of the industry. According to the "*Trend Analysis of China's Equity Investment Fund LP Market in 2021*" released by Zero2IPO Research, the capital attributes of LPs have changed significantly. State-owned LPs, represented by SOEs/central enterprises and government guidance funds, have accelerated their participation in equity investment, becoming one of the leading forces in the PE investment market. In February 2021, the State-owned Assets Supervision and Administration Commission of the State Council officially issued the "*Notice on Accelerating the Digital Transformation of State-owned Enterprises*," which shows that the government attaches considerable importance to the systematization of asset management. The regulatory environment with higher requirements for efficiency, the expanding fund management scale, and the general environment of digital transformation have all put requirements on PE funds to accelerate the introduction of asset management systems. It is imperative to move towards digitalization, informatization, and standardization.

Second, apply technology upgrades to promote data integration and sharing. Coordinated use of upgraded data collection methods, combined with effective and true

[5] https://home.kpmg/us/en/home/insights/2018/05/the-digital-transformation-imperative.html.

records, solves the problem of inaccurate information and data, realizes traceability, effectively provides evidence in case of disputes, and protects all parties' legitimate rights and interests. Establishing a unified data standardization system and statistical caliber can enhance the fluidity of data among different business departments, realize data sharing among business processes, and form a closed loop of industry capital flow, business flow, and information flow across institutions, clients, and accounts. It enables investors to make decisions based on comprehensive and timely information, allows sales to institutions to judge counterparty risks based on high-quality information, enables managers to make decisions based on multi-dimensional data, and enables regulators to form all-round support for compliance supervision based on information and data from all parties, solving solve the problem of information asymmetry.

Third, promote the application of technology to reduce compliance costs. Learn from advanced international experience to promote supplier pilot, access, and continuous supervision. Encourage technological services that promote and improve the compliance level of the industry, and use technical means to embed compliance and risk control into business processes, so that the compliance process can be automated, traceable, and real-time, significantly reducing the difficulty and compliance cost.

Fourth, promote multi-party cooperation to improve compliance efficiency. The regulatory challenges of PE investment are significant, and compliance supervision involves many regulatory authorities, so it is necessary to constantly strengthen the cooperation of all parties to achieve win–win results. Delineate the regulatory boundaries of different regulatory authorities, promote collaboration in market access, continuous supervision, on-site supervision, and case investigation, encourage sharing of data and information, use technology to enhance compliance supervision efficiency, and then standardize market development.

Fifth, enhance data protection and improve the transparency of specific information. Data acquisition and analysis are indispensable when using compliance technology. To meet the legitimacy of data, PE institutions need to develop standardized data collection and use procedures to ensure information security with strict anti-attack mechanisms and secure data encryption schemes and prevent data tampering, data reselling, data theft, and other improper acts. Meanwhile, a confidentiality agreement shall be signed to ensure that irrelevant personnel will not abuse the data. In addition, the market access conditions and information disclosure processes are clarified to improve PE market transparency, effectively perform the market's self-regulatory function and coordination mechanism, and enhance the transparency of specific necessary information while protecting commercially sensitive information and personal privacy, enabling all parties to manage risks effectively.

References

AMAC. Private equity investment fund industry compliance management manual. Beijing: China Financial and Economic Publishing House; 2021. p. 2021.

Chen YJ. Study on the legal issues of the collection rules of private equity products. Shanghai Finance. 2019;9:51–7. https://doi.org/10.13910/j.cnki.shjr.2019.09.008. (in Chinese).
Clack CD, Bakshi VA, Braine L. Smart contract templates: foundations, design landscape and research directions; 2017. Available at: https://arxiv.org/abs/1608.00771.
Colaert V. RegTech is a response to regulatory expansion in the financial sector. SSRN Working Paper, No.2677116; 2017.
Fu QQ. Application value of compliance technology in data compliance. J Taiyuan Univ (Soc Sci Edition). 2023;4:80–9. https://doi.org/10.13710/j.cnki.cn14-1294/g.2023.04.003. (in Chinese).
Hendrikse R. Regtech 3.0: Easing the cost of compliance. International Banker; 2020.
Hou JN. Private equity funds entered the era of electronic signing the first single signing business completed; 2018. http://www.zqrb.cn/fund/jijindongtai/2018-08-16/A1534351124526.html. (in Chinese)
KPMG. The Pulse of Fintech H1 2020, 2020–9; 2020. https://home.kpmg/xx/en/home/industries/financialservices/pulse-of-fintech.html.
Jin ZF. Thoughts on regulatory technology to solve the compliance dilemma of the financial industry. Financ Technol Era. 2021;9:79–83 (in Chinese).
O'Shields R. Smart contracts: legal agreements for the blockchain, 21 N.C. Banking Inst. 177; 2017. Available at: http://scholarship.law.unc.edu/ncbi/vol21/iss1/11.
Packin NG. Regtech, compliance and technology judgement rule, 93 Chi.-Kent L. Rev. 193; 2018. Available at: https://scholarship.kentlaw.iit.edu/cklawreview/vol93/iss1/7.
Securities Industry Association. The costs of compliance in the U.S. securities industry: survey report; 2006. https://www.sifma.org/wp-content/uploads/2017/06/costofcompliancesurveyreport1.pdf.
Shan CY, Zhao DW. Research on the application of artificial intelligence in compliance technology. Tsinghua Financ Rev. 2019;8:104–6. https://doi.org/10.19409/j.cnki.thf-review.2019.08.027. (in Chinese).
Su HY. Construction of financial data supervision mode under the background of financial technology. Technol Law. 2020;1:68–75. https://doi.org/10.19685/j.cnki.cn11-2922/n.2020.01.009. (in Chinese).
Tao F, Wan XN. Regulatory technology and compliance technology: regulatory efficiency and compliance cost. Financial Regul Res. 2019;7:68–81. https://doi.org/10.13490/j.cnki.frr.2019.07.005. (in Chinese).
Thomson Reuters Regulatory Intelligence. 2023 cost of compliance: regulatory burden poses operational challenges for compliance; 2023. https://legal.thomsonreuters.com/content/dam/ewp-m/documents/legal/en/pdf/reports/cost-of-compliance-report-final-web.pdf.
Tu MH. Private equity fund violations and legal analysis. Legal Expo. 2019;8:67–8 (in Chinese).
Xu X, Liu BL. Application scenarios of regulatory and compliance technologies. Shanghai Insurance. 2019;7:18–21 (in Chinese).
Xueqiu. Survival survey: compliance operating costs of a private equity manager; 2018. https://xueqiu.com/9189223062/117254762. (in Chinese)
Zhou H. Enabling personal information protection with compliance technology. People 's Procuratorate. 2022;16:44 (in Chinese).

Chapter 6
Technology Applications in Private Equity Anti-Money Laundering

The securities industry plays a vital role in the global economy, with participants ranging from professional transnational financial conglomerates to small companies that provide stockbroking or financial advisory services. Securities products are diverse and complex, and many transactions are conducted electronically and across borders. The speed of transactions, global influence, and adaptability of the securities industry provide opportunities for criminals to abuse the financial system for money laundering and terrorist financing. In an era of highly developed technology, how to make full use of new and emerging technologies to enhance the traceability and transparency of financial transactions, and promote the effective implementation of anti-money laundering (AML) and counter-terrorist financing (CFT) measures? It is worthy of in-depth study.

6.1 The Connotation of Money Laundering

Money laundering has become increasingly intertwined with other crimes due to the deepening of economic globalization and integration of the international financial system. Over the past three decades, money laundering has become a major "public hazard" in the international community. It has increasingly become a global problem that needs international cooperation to solve.

In a broad sense, money laundering can be summarized as the disposal of economic benefits from crime. To "wash" the "dirty" money, criminals often disguise the proceeds or sources, such as the funds' true nature, source, location, holder, and beneficiary. The key is to change the form of existence of the original proceeds of crime. To achieve this purpose, money laundering comprises three stages (Association of Certified Anti-Money Laundering Specialist 2017).

Placement. In this stage, money launderers place illegal proceeds into the financial system. Avoidance of the regulatory risk brought about by vast amounts of money

R. Xu and D. Zhao, *Digital Transformation of Private Equity in China*, Contributions to Finance and Accounting, https://doi.org/10.1007/978-981-99-8482-4_6

is usually accomplished by circular investment. The channels include but are not limited to, local or international financial institutions, casinos, stores, and legitimate enterprises.

Layering. It creates multiple financial transactions to dissociate the money from the original source, making it difficult for authorities to detect laundering activity. This stage changes the possession form of illegal funds and creates a complex structure of financial transactions to conceal the origin and ownership of the funds.

Integration. After placing and layering the cash into the financial system, the launderer needs to integrate the scattered funds invested under various channels and make it appear legitimate. This stage usually consists of two sub-stages, "legalization" and "investment." In the "legalization" stage, illegal proceeds are integrated into conventional business activities, such as through loans. In the "investment" stage, the launders invest in normal economic activities (such as purchasing real estate) to make the illegal wealth appear legitimate. At this stage, it is challenging to distinguish between legal and illegal wealth. After the fusion stage, it will be difficult to distinguish between legitimate and illegitimate assets.

The three stages of money laundering require using diversified means, the help of numerous domestic and foreign commercial firms and financial institutions, covering bank savings, securities business, international exchange, real estate transactions, firm cooperation, direct investment, and other channels. The characteristics of such activities determine that modern money laundering requires many specialized techniques. Alternatively, money laundering is characterized by professionalism, technicality, internationalization, and complexity.

6.2 Current Anti-Money Laundering Regulations in the PE Industry

6.2.1 Money Laundering Characteristics of International PE Funds

The Financial Action Task Force on Money Laundering (FATF), an international anti-money laundering authority, notes that corporate vehicles conduct various commercial and entrepreneurial activities and have been misused for illicit purposes, including money laundering and terrorist financing (FATF 2014). PE may also engage in illicit activities.

1. **Contractual PE fund money laundering**

Contractual PE funds are primarily based on a trust agreement that governs the rights and obligations of the principal, trustee, and beneficiaries. Investors generally do not participate in the operation and management of fund assets after delivering funds to the trustee (fund manager). In many cases, criminals use complex structures consisting of corporate entities and trusts set up in different jurisdictions to hide their identities and commit fraud. As the design looks formal and legal, it is easy to attract investment from third parties and transfer and launder criminal funds with seemingly legitimate capital flows.

In 2006, FATF released a case of a trust service provider in the United States, which tricked over 500 clients of $56 million (FATF 2006). It promised to provide asset protection for the clients through trusts and offshore account packages, conceal their assets from the government and creditors, and promise higher investment returns from the trusts. In this case, the service provider used the trusts associated with the offshore bank accounts to transfer the proceeds of the fraud.

2. **Corporate PE fund money laundering**

A corporate PE fund raises funds from specific investors by establishing companies to issue shares, invests the funds following the company's management procedures, and then distributes the benefits from the investment to the shareholders as dividends. The company and the shareholders are the main parties, and the company law and the articles of incorporation govern the rights and obligations of the parties.

In 2010, the FATF released a related case. A lawyer used trusts and company service providers to establish several offshore entities in three countries, including a PE fund company. Equity subscription fees were ultimately transferred to the fund company through several offshore entities to conceal the true source of funds. The investigation revealed that the PE fund was established on behalf of a prominent Minister of Government in an Eastern European country, who used the fund and offshore entities to create several fictitious consultancy agreements entities to conceal millions of dollars in income from power abuse.

3. **Partnership PE fund money laundering**

A limited partnership is the main form of partnership PE fund, including at least one GP and one LP. The GP assumes a certain proportion of the capital contribution, acts as the actual manager of the enterprise, has decision-making power, and bears unlimited joint liabilities for the enterprise's debts. The LP bears limited liability for the enterprise with its capital contributions and does not participate in the management of the enterprise. Hedge funds and VC funds are primarily organized in a limited partnership, with the fund manager as the GP and other qualified investors as LPs. This organizational form is conducive to reducing the conflict of interest between fund managers and investors and achieving self-monitoring of fund managers.

In general, hedge funds are vehicles created to hold and manage investment assets and are structured in various ways that make them potentially unregulated. Hedge funds have a wide variety of sources of funds, including domestic and foreign sources. Some channel funds (such as feeder funds) are set up to invest in other hedge funds, resulting in the opaque identity of hedge fund investors. When a hedge fund uses the trading channels of a securities company, the securities company may not know the identity of the hedge fund investors. International cases have shown that some hedge funds, such as Ponzi fraud, are used to engage in securities fraud.

In 2009, the FATF released a case of two Ponzi schemes in the United States by setting up hedge funds (FATF 2009). Under the first scheme, the fraudsters told investors that their money would be used to purchase equipment that would be leased and resold. Under the second scheme, the fraudsters sold promissory notes purportedly secured by stock in their affiliated legal entities and by precious metals production contracts. Both schemes promised investors high rates of return and guaranteed principal investments. After receiving the funds, the fraudsters used a portion to promote another business and make periodic payments to investors. In contrast, the remaining funds were used primarily for personal expenses.

6.2.2 Current Situation and Problems of Anti-Money Laundering Regulation of PE Funds in China

1. **China's PE fund regulatory system**

(1) PE fund business regulatory system. The laws and regulations of PE funds include the *Securities Law of the People's Republic of China*, the *Company Law of the People's Republic of China*, the *Trust Law of the People's Republic of China*, the *Partnership Law of the People's Republic of China*. Among them, the *Company Law* and *Partnership Law* provide legal protection for the organizational form of PE fund management companies. However, to date, the *Securities Law*, the *Company Law*, the *Trust Law*, and other legal provisions have not stipulated the specific investment funds, the qualifications of managers, the operation methods, the restrictions on investment conditions, and other aspects that have a practical impact on the investment behavior.

On June 30, 2014, the *Interim Measures for the Supervision and Administration of Private Investment Funds* issued by the CSRC made relevant provisions for non-publicly-offered funds, including principles of PE fund business, requirements for registration and filing of PE fund managers, requirements for the filing of PE products, qualified investors and investment operations. It stipulated that the supervisory bodies of non-publicly-offered funds are the CSRC and dispatched institutions. However, the *Interim Measures* do not clarify the nature of PE funds.

(2) Current situation of AML regulation for PE funds. In 2006, *Anti-Money Laundering Law of the People's Republic of China* (*AML Law*) was officially promulgated. It stipulates that financial institutions and specific non-financial institutions should perform their AML obligations, including: taking preventive and monitoring measures, establishing and improving the internal control system of AML, improving customer due diligence, keeping customer identification data and transaction record information, providing large amount transaction and suspicious transaction reports, and implementing special preventive measures against money laundering.

The People's Bank of China has successively promulgated some regulations, including: "Provisions on Anti-Money Laundering of Financial Institutions," "Administrative Measures for Reporting Large Amount and Suspicious Transactions by Financial Institutions," "Administrative Measures for Reporting Suspicious Transactions of Financial Institutions Suspected of Terrorist Financing," "Administrative Measures for Customer Identification and Retention of Customer Identification Data and Transaction Records of Financial Institutions". The regulations define the obligations of fund companies in customer identification, suspicious transaction reporting, and customer identity data and transaction record-keeping. However, the regulations have not yet specifically reflected the regulatory requirements for PE funds.

2. **The money laundering situation in the PE industry**

With the establishment of the National Equities Exchange and Quotations, the Science and Technology Innovation Board (STAR market), and the Beijing Stock Exchange in recent years, the listing channels for investment enterprises have been continuously enriched, the scale of the equity investment market has been expanding, and the number of PE investors has been increasing. In the name of PE investment companies, criminals often commit fraud, illegal fundraising, illegal or disguised absorption of public deposits, and other criminal activities against small and medium-sized investors (especially middle-aged and elderly people) through the Internet, telephone, and other means. In addition, some criminal groups operate in the name of PE investment companies. However, they have not registered with the business administration department or in the name of investment consulting companies as a disguise (Pang and Jin 2012).

3. **Problems of anti-money laundering in the PE industry**

First, the PE fund industry has a weak foundation for AML. The construction of the AML internal control system and AML system in the PE industry starts late compared with banks, insurance, and public funds. Many PE institutions lack complete institutional arrangements such as customer due diligence and identity data preservation. Even though regulatory systems such as the *Anti-Money Laundering Regulations for Financial Institutions* stipulate the requirements for the classification of money laundering risk levels of fund companies' customers and the reporting of suspicious transactions, many PE institutions have not effectively implemented the relevant systems. In summary, the PE fund industry has a relatively weak AML foundation, which criminals will likely exploit.

In addition, practitioners in the PE industry have a relatively weak awareness of AML. PE institutions' managers and business personnel fail to pay enough attention to the AML work. PE institutions and practitioners mainly focus on the profitability of projects, and companies in the PE sector are not yet included in the scope of AML obligations; thus, the practitioners are less willing to cooperate with AML efforts and rarely consider the risk of money laundering. Therefore, the PE industry is more likely to become a tool for criminals to launder money.

(1) Proxy holding is common in the PE industry, and customer' identity identification is rarely implemented. Due to the strong confidentiality of the PE fund

business and the fact that regulators have not included PE funds in daily supervision, PE fund managers have a low incentive to identify the source and true identity of customers' funds.

On the one hand, there is a prevalence of investment behavior using drawer agreements and proxy agreements to purchase shares of PE funds, which makes the true identity of the investors questionable. Cases of holding PE fund shares through proxy agreements can be found on the China Judgment Online website.[1] Some money launderers intentionally conceal the true source of funds when purchasing PE funds. After purchasing with illegal funds, they use PE funds for legitimate investment. Through PE investment, property ownership, use, and benefit are separated. The true beneficial owner can be hidden, facilitating money laundering and allowing property and funds to flow without a trace.

On the other hand, the regulatory requirement of "knowing the source of customers' funds and the purpose of transactions" has not been fully implemented in the actual management process of PE fund institutions. The *Interim Measures for the Supervision and Administration of Private Investment Funds* stipulate that investors should truthfully commit their assets or income and ensure the legitimacy of the source of investment funds. However, the relevant laws and regulations do not stipulate the principle as a practical obligation of PE fund management companies. The problems in practice are as follows. First, most PE institutions do not physically verify the source of funds of individual customers, nor do they require information on the business status of corporate customers or investigate the actual ownership and control structure. In addition, there are no clear regulatory provisions in laws and regulations that require fund managers to hold obligations to verify the identity information of customers and their beneficial owners, understand the sources of customer funds and the purpose of transactions, and conduct continuous due diligence. Second, the collection of customer information in the distribution channel is insufficient. Currently, PE fund companies' sales channels include direct and agency sales. Direct sales channels refer to the direct sales of investment products by PE fund companies. The agency sales channels are generally entrusted to banks, securities companies, insurance companies, and third-party independent fund sales institutions. When identifying customers for the first time, the agent is responsible for registering and verifying the basic information of investors and transmitting the relevant information of customers to the PE fund companies. During the existence of the funds, it is still the distributor's responsibility to identify customers continuously, and the PE fund management companies have little change in customer information. In summary, the integrity and accuracy of the PE companies' data on investors in the distribution channel are insufficient, and continuous identification is difficult. The identification of investors is the foundation of AML work, and incorrect or incomplete information will affect the subsequent AML work, such as classifying customers into money laundering risk levels and analyzing suspicious transactions.

[1] https://wenshu.court.gov.cn/.

(2) Suspicious transaction monitoring is generally not carried out effectively. Investigations show that small and medium-sized PE companies have not built AML monitoring systems due to objective reasons such as insufficient financial support and lack of scale effect. Suspicious transaction monitoring is conducted manually in that small and medium-sized PE companies. Even if some institutions have built AML monitoring systems, the degree of conformity between the system's index construction and the actual business development of PE is not high, and the system construction is far from perfect (Huang 2020). Because PE funds lack sufficient knowledge of some customers' identities and transactions and it is more difficult to obtain relevant information through external channels, coupled with the lack of an AML monitoring system, the detection of suspicious transactions through manual monitoring is a formality.

In addition, few small and medium-sized PE institutions have established departments to conduct list monitoring, and most of them rely on custodians for the relevant monitoring work. Small and medium-sized PE institutions cannot effectively identify persons required by the People's Bank of China to be monitored and customers from high-risk countries or regions of the FATF. Some large PE institutions have conducted list monitoring but rely on their procurement or collection of monitoring lists and lists of persons, while the frequency of list updates is lagging.

(3) PE funds have high professional attributes and confidentiality but low information disclosure requirements. It is difficult for small and medium-sized investors to grasp the actual investment situation of PE funds. In addition, the managers of PE funds tend to keep confidential the investors who participate in the investment.PE investment is to make the industrial investment, which requires investors to have a deep understanding of the industry, to conduct in-depth research on the enterprises they are investing in, and to evaluate the management of the enterprises, which requires a high level of expertise, experience and social resources of the managers.

First, the information transparency is relatively low, and the information disclosure system is imperfect (Duan 2019). Compared with the investors of public funds, PE funds have lower information disclosure requirements and operational transparency, the information disclosure requirements are lower, and the transparency of their operations is relatively low, making their investments more covert. In addition, the *Measures for the Administration of Private Investment Fund Information Disclosure* do not specify information disclosure requirements according to the types of PE funds but rather unify the information disclosure content of PE funds. In practice, as different types of PE funds have very different investment targets, the content of information disclosure may also differ significantly. Compared with private funds invested in the secondary market, PE funds have more targeted investment objectives and fewer channels to obtain information. In addition, some PE fund managers aim to make profits, raise a large number of funds, whitewash investment performance, conceal investment risks, engage in unreasonable related party transactions or transactions with conflict of interest, and charge high management fees (Liu 2018).

Secondly, the current domestic laws do not make mandatory provisions on whether an independent third party should entrust PE investment fund funds. There is a risk of money laundering by illegally misappropriating project funds. In practice, many fund managers have taken the initiative to entrust professional custodians to manage their PE funds to enhance market recognition. Some PE funds have not made fund custodian arrangements and lack a third party for fund supervision. Lack of supervision by a third-party custodian may exacerbate the lack of supervision of PE institutions in terms of fund allocation and investment. In addition, PE fund managers may also misappropriate the funds to obtain illegal interests and repeatedly invest in laundering.

Third, there is no industry-unified valuation system for PE investment projects. The valuation methods are complex and diverse, and there is a money laundering risk of using investment projects to transfer funds. From the perspective of the projects invested by PE funds, it is often difficult for external personnel or third-party professional institutions to understand the companies' internal information and make judgments on the actual financial status, profitability, and market competitiveness of the invested companies. Therefore, PE institutions and invested companies hold the company's core and undisclosed information. The information asymmetry hides money laundering risks. PE institutions and invested companies can obtain illegal benefits or launder money by transferring assets through buying and selling shares at high or low prices.

(4) There is also a money laundering risk in the exit of PE funds. The exit of PE funds is the critical link for investment projects to gain profits and the last link in investment project operation. The main purpose of PE investment is not to control or operate the enterprise but to realize a profit from growing enterprises and reinvested funds to improve the benefit and turnover of the capital. There are three ways to exit a PE fund: share listing, transfer, and liquidation. By taking advantage of the high yield of PE fund exit, criminals transfer assets and hide large amounts of illegal income using false transactions, false contracts, or "buy low, sell high".

6.3 Application of Technology in AML in the PE Industry

In recent years, digital technologies such as big data, biometrics, machine learning, natural language processing, blockchain, and distributed ledger have developed rapidly. The technological innovations have paved new ways for laundering of funds and carrying out illicit activities (Barone and Schneider 2018; Dupuis and Gleason 2020; Tiwari et al. 2020). Meanwhile, it has dramatically promoted financial inclusion, improved the effectiveness and efficiency of AML and CFT measures, and promoted the broader implementation of the global AML and CFT regulatory framework (Zhang et al. 2021; Guo 2021; Xue and Li 2022; Qin et al. 2023).

6.3.1 The Positive Effect of Technology on AML

1. **Improve the efficiency of AML**

With the deep integration of finance and information technology, securities businesses and products show a trend of diversification and personalization. The traditional manual processes obviously cannot be accommodated. The use of new technology not only promotes data standardization but also dramatically simplifies the repetitive manual process of collecting large amounts of unstructured data, which can make information sharing and communication more reliable and convenient.

Meanwhile, automation and other digital programs allow the aggregation and classification of large amounts of data and information from different sources and databases with different structures. Through data aggregation and analysis, AI and big data analysis can be used to conduct AML monitoring and improve AML efficiency (FATF 2020a; Han et al. 2020; Kute et al. 2021; Yuan 2021).

Saaradeey et al. (2019) show that financial institutions rely on fixed monitoring criteria embedded in AML systems for abnormal transaction monitoring, and 90~95% of the irregular transactions screened are false alarms. As this requires manual screening, many resources are not used reasonably. Machine learning technology can dynamically adjust the monitoring rules, increase transaction monitoring pertinence, and reduce false alerts.

2. **Cost Reduction**

Changing market conditions and diverse digital channels have facilitated financial crime. Financial institutions face the challenges of increased costs, complex risks, and growing regulatory pressure on all fronts. AML regulatory authorities in various countries continue to devote significant resources to combating money laundering and terrorist financing crimes, which poses a severe shortage of resources for many emerging markets and developing economies (Coelho et al. 2019).

Financial institutions are being exposed to an increasing level of various types of financial crime, including those involving digital payments, cryptocurrency, third parties and trafficking of proceeds. As the scope of financial crime increases, financial institutions are dealing with a broader set of screening and compliance operations challenges, and bearing higher costs. According to LexisNexis Risk Solutions, the projected total cost of financial crime compliance across financial institutions worldwide is $274.1 billion in 2022, up from $213.9 billion in 2020 (LexisNexis Risk Solutions 2021, 2022). In 2022, the projected total cost of financial crime compliance in North America, LATAM, APAC, Europe, South Africa, and Middle East are $49.9 billion, $6.19 billion, $8.4 billion, $99.8 billion, $3.8 billion, $4.2 billion, respectively. Financial institutions that have invested in technology solutions to support financial crime compliance efforts, have experienced lower costs and fewer compliance operations challenges.

Accelerated digital transformation and tightening regulatory requirements lead financial institutions to terminate financial business with high-risk countries (regions). Using new technologies in AML can significantly reduce AML procedures and human costs, facilitate the inclusion of a broader range of countries and regions in the AML and CFT framework, and mitigate the overall global risk of money laundering and terrorist financing.

3. **Inclusive finance**

Financial institutions must implement risk-based AML and CFT measures to ensure financial inclusion. The intensity of customer due diligence measures should match the level of customer risk rather than an indiscriminate policy for all customers. Using digital ID cards and AML transaction monitoring procedures in customer due diligence and transaction monitoring can reflect customer risk accurately and in real-time at less cost, enabling greater use of simplified due diligence where appropriate. Financial inclusion is also enhanced as new technology minimizes weaknesses associated with manual subjective controls, improves customer experience, saves costs, and provides effective monitoring.

4. **Resource allocation**

Using new technologies for AML and CFT to automate data collection, collation, and analysis can significantly reduce the investment in manual operational labor. It not only facilitates the reallocation of human resources to tasks requiring manual judgment but also improves the accuracy of results. For example, big data analysis in transaction monitoring can save screening analysts time on routine tasks such as data validation and bulk data classification and allow them to focus on more complex analytical tasks.

5. **Dynamic reflection of the risk**

Adequate understanding and assessment of money laundering and terrorist financing risks is an important prerequisite for financial institutions to implement risk control measures effectively. Financial institutions' inadequate risk awareness may lead them to adopt inefficient and burdensome defensive AML and CFT strategies. At the same time, decisions based on insufficient risk assessment, which relies heavily on manual work, will lead to two problems. First, insufficient attention is paid to potential or emerging risks, resulting in the non-detection of money laundering and terrorist financing activities. Second, implementing excessive risk mitigation measures in low-risk situations leads to unnecessary customer acquisition costs and financial exclusion.

New technologies such as machine learning and AI to identify, assess, and manage money laundering and terrorist financing risks can automate risk assessment and reflect the customers' money laundering and terrorist financing risks in real-time. In addition, the accuracy of risk assessment can be further enhanced through the electronic risk assessment process, which facilitates information sharing and increases access to risk assessment data.

6.3.2 Challenges of AML with Fintech

1. **Poor data quality**

Suppose the data relied on by customer due diligence measures and transaction monitoring cannot be guaranteed to be of high quality. In that case, it will not be easy to update and match the information promptly according to the expected standards of financial institutions. Moreover, as the data on the customer identification information and transaction records of financial institutions continue to increase, the poor quality of data and insufficient standardization of data structures will lead to inaccurate data for AML and terrorist financing risk assessment and transaction monitoring analysis. In addition, AML data is created, maintained, and collected from internal and external sources, which may result in inconsistent content for the same information element. For example, a customer's professional identity is recorded as "a" in system A and "b" in system B. When the data is collated or used, we will face the problem of effectively referring to the data and reflecting the real identity and risk status of customers. Poor data quality and inconsistent references from multiple data sources may seriously limit the practical application of some digital technologies in AML and CFT.

2. **Weak calculation and analysis ability**

The data relied on by AML includes customer identification information, transaction records, and external risk information, which are constantly increasing and updated with the business development of financial institutions. New technology used must have sufficiently computing power. In addition, the efficacy and efficiency of system analysis may depend on financial institutions (internal and external) ability to share information since the size, quality, and relevance of data sets significantly affect the accuracy of the analysis (FATF 2020b).

3. **The life cycle of digital technology is limited**

Implementing AML and CFT strategies depends on a control system formed by many control procedures, including sanctions list monitoring, risk-based due diligence, transaction monitoring, risk assessment, and business restrictions. In practice, criminals may use new financial businesses and services for money laundering and terrorist financing activities to avoid regulation. Therefore, AML and CFT strategies must be adjusted in real-time according to changes in money laundering and terrorist financing, and digital technologies face life-cycle constraints. Under such circumstances, the control procedures' static rules and threshold adjustments will make AML and CFT control systems less efficient and effective over time.

4. **Digital technology has inherent defects**

While new technologies have improved data quality, it still requires manual input and review. Manual intervention may lead to a lack of interpretability and transparency of relevant data analysis, thereby reducing the ability of AML and CFT procedures to identify suspicious transactions and other illegal activities and failing to establish their effectiveness as AML and CFT compliance tools. For example, machine learning relies on existing systems and manual updates, may input "bad data," and negatively impact the adopted models. When machine learning is used to identify a suspicious transaction, the errors in the training data will be "trained" into the machine learning system. In addition, while algorithmic decision-making can overcome human biases, the practice has shown that many AI algorithms replicate program developers' conscious or unconscious biases. Its broad applications in the risk control of suspicious transaction subjects may block certain individuals or entities from properly using certain financial products and services.

6.3.3 Application of Digital Technology in AML in PE Investment

1. **Advanced big data analysis**

Advanced big data analysis technology is based on advanced data collection and analysis techniques that can collect information from non-traditional sources (such as open networks, social media, and other sources) and combine them with traditional information to perform comprehensive and systematic analysis. The development and application of data analysis have been greatly promoted by advances in AI and its practical applications in machine learning, natural language processing, and other advanced analysis functions.

Advanced big data analysis technology enables networked monitoring of customer transactions and accurate identification of abnormal transactions. At the same time, it can convert large amounts of structured and unstructured data into information that can be fully utilized and expand the scope of available data by performing contextual analysis with non-transaction data (such as data from public security, market supervision, and management departments, tax departments). Advanced big data analysis technology analyzes suspicious cases by integrating valuable information from different channel sources and telling a coherent story. Therefore, PE institutions can use advanced analysis to more accurately identify suspicious activity, screen customers, and manage risk.

2. **Digital identity and biometric technology**

Digital identity enables PE institutions to conduct identity identification and information update for customers according to compliance requirements and establish or maintain business relations with customers in a non-face-to-face manner, significantly reducing the workload. It also facilitates identity verification for PE institutions in the newly established business relationship and transaction links and improves account access security.

Digital identity allows PE institutions to complete relatively complex customer admission processes at a lower cost. It also simplifies daily operations, can be used repeatedly online, and helps enhance the information interaction between individuals and financial service providers. For example, PE funds can establish channels to deliver financial services using mobile devices and smartphones, provide services for customers by using digital authentication, and enhance the ability of business relationship management.

Biometric technology uses human biometric features that are usually unique, measurable, or automatically identifiable and verifiable, hereditary or invariability, to verify customer identity. In recent years, with the widespread use of intelligent mobiles, more and more financial institutions have been using fingerprint, face, iris, voice, and eye print recognition technologies to assist in customer identification. PE institutions can also use these technologies to monitor and eliminate risks associated with terrorist lists, sanctioned lists, and high-risk lists promptly.

3. **Natural Language Processing**

Natural language processing (NLP) is a branch of AI that uses fuzzy logic to process data and produce usable (but imprecise) output, which simulates human decision-making logic and extracts more helpful information from inaccurate data. NLP can support more accurate, flexible, and timely analysis of customer information, reduce inaccurate or false information, and achieve more efficient matching and searching of data. For example, false alerts can be effectively reduced by screening terrorist-related lists, sanctions lists, and other high-risk lists. At the same time, NLP technology can replace some complex manual operations, such as enhanced due diligence and risk case indexing, that would otherwise be performed manually. Therefore, as natural language processing technology can automate the processing of suspicious case analysis, it can reduce operating costs and improve the consistency of decision-making (FCA 2017).

4. **Application programming interface (API)**

API refers to interfaces between software applications where one application calls upon the functions of another application. It can reduce the "information silos" of fragmented frameworks and increase connectivity between PE firm data. API can improve the degree of automation based on optimizing resources and output accuracy. It can provide aggregated and standardized data feeds to build a complete risk profile for new customers. For example, PE institutions can develop a platform that integrates with various financial service companies using APIs. It can bring a better user experience by providing customers direct access to a range of financial services products through one platform, improving their understanding of their financial situation, and enhancing their knowledge of the various products available in the market.

In addition, within PE firms, APIs also facilitate the exchange of information between business line personnel and AML compliance managers and improve the degree of information sharing.

5. **Distributed ledger technology (DLT)**

DLT can improve the traceability of cross-border and global transactions, making identity verification easier. DLT can better balance information sharing with privacy protection and data security and enhance the efficiency of customer due diligence. For example, with DTL, individuals have their identity information and can proactively verify their identity. They can even automatically take control measures of approval or rejection by establishing smart contracts for verifying data.

In addition, transactions can be managed through a single ledger shared by multiple institutions across jurisdictions or through interoperable ledgers while ensuring data security and meeting regulatory requirements. It will increase the effectiveness of transaction monitoring compared to the existing framework.

Take the application of DLT to monitor high-risk lists as an example. The PE fund industry can establish an AML system integrating blockchain, digital identity, credibility, and other functions. Each PE fund company encrypts the ID numbers and risk labels of high-risk customers identified by the institution and then uploads the information to the blockchain. When other PE firms query the customers, they are matched on the blockchain through a secure computing platform. Due to the use of blockchain encryption algorithms and DLT, risk information can be queried between PE firms without the actual exchange of customer data. It can well balance information sharing with privacy protection and data security and improve client risk management.

6. **Machine learning**

False positive and false negative transactions in transaction monitoring are a challenge that hinders the efficiency improvement and resource allocation of financial institutions in AML. A false-positive transaction is a transaction that has been incorrectly identified as fraudulent by the rules set by financial institutions. It needs to be further screened, analyzed, and eliminated manually. For example, a customer account receives a regular monthly payroll income of 5,000 yuan, and the payment is mainly for daily consumption. According to customer due diligence and regular transaction monitoring, the customer's transaction activities are consistent with normal behavior. However, a sudden surge in the customer's income that exceeds the threshold amount (such as 500,000 yuan from property sales) will indicate abnormal transactions. Since the transaction had a legitimate source and was not suspicious, the abnormal transaction case could be considered a false positive transaction and should be excluded. From an operational point of view, it requires considerable resources to screen and eliminate false positive alerts, significantly increasing the cost of the investigation.

A false-negative transaction, the opposite of a false-positive transaction, is a fraudulent transaction that fails to be labeled as fraudulent and is not monitored by a financial institution. A typical example of a false negative transaction is a student's account used as a money mule account (Esoimeme 2021). Since students have relatively low money laundering risk, the transactions made in their accounts are usually related to daily consumption. Even international students from high-risk countries receive nominal funds from their country of origin for daily consumption and educational expenses. These funds are either spent or withdrawn. Although these transactions come from high-risk countries, there will be no alert in this case due to the low risk associated with the beneficiary and the formal normalcy of the transaction behavior.

Machine learning technology can automatically improve the performance of AML data analysis and control decision-making by constantly updating and iteration. It can also generate realistic behavioral digital profiles for each customer based on transaction data, customer identification information, and data from mobile devices (FCA 2017). Moreover, because machine learning can learn from existing systems and automatically improve and optimize them, it can continuously improve transaction monitoring rules and risk management models, reduce the need to manually set up the rules and models, and reduce the probability of false-positive and false-negative transactions (Jullum et al. 2020; FATF 2021).

In addition, machine learning technology can continuously monitor, analyze and process suspicious transactions and other illegal activities, distinguish them from normal activities in real-time and reduce the workload of AML front-line personnel review. It also allows for a more accurate and complete assessment of customer money laundering and terrorist financing risks, timely identification of emerging threats, and automated countermeasures.

References

Association of Certified Anti-Money Laundering Specialist. ACAMS study guide, 6th Edition; 2017.

Barone R, Schneider FG. Shedding light on money laundering. Is it a damping wave?. Working paper; 2018.

Coelho R, Simoni MD, Prenio J. Suptech applications for anti-money laundering; 2019. https://www.bis.org/fsi/publ/insights18.htm.

Duan HX. Research on risk management methods of private equity fund investment. China Business. 2019;24:50–1. https://doi.org/10.19699/j.cnki.issn2096-0298.2019.24.050. (in Chinese).

Dupuis D, Gleason K. Money laundering with cryptocurrency: open doors and the regulatory dialectic. J Financ Crime. 2020;28(1):60–74.

Esoimeme EE. Identifying and reducing the money laundering risks posed by individuals who have been unknowingly recruited as money mules. J Money Laundering Control. 2021;24(1):201–12.

FATF. Misuse of corporate vehicles including trusts and company services providers; 2006. https://www.fatf-gafi.org/en/publications/Methodsandtrends/Themisuseofcorporatevehiclesincludingtrustandcompanyserviceproviders.html.

FATF. Money laundering and terrorist financing in the securities sector; 2009. https://www.fatf-gafi.org/en/publications/Methodsandtrends/Moneylaunderingandterroristfinancinginthesecuritiessector.html.

FATF. Guidance on transparency and beneficial ownership; 2014. https://www.fatf-gafi.org/media/fatf/styleassets/images/Guidance-beneficial-ownership-transparencyl.pdf.

FATF. Priorities for the financial action task force under the German presidency; 2020a. http://www.fatf-gafi.org/media/fatf/documents/German-Presidency-Priorities.pdf.

FATF. Stocktake on data pooling, collaborative analytics and data protection; 2020b. https://www.fatf-gafi.org/media/fatf/documents/Stocktake-Datapooling-Collaborative-Analytics.pdf.

FATF. Opportunities and challenges of new technologies for AML/CFT; 2021. https://www.fatf-gafi.org/publications/fatfrecommendations/documents/opportunities-challenges-new-technologies-aml-cft.htm.

Financial Conduct Authority. New technologies and anti-money laundering compliance; 2017. https://www.fca.org.uk/publication/research/new-technologies-in-aml-final-report.pdf

Guo ZH. Application and development of compliance technology in the field of anti-money laundering-practice from Hong Kong. Tsinghua Financ Rev. 2021; 12: 96–8. https://doi.org/10.19409/j.cnki.thf-review.2021.12.027. (in Chinese).

Han J, Huang Y, Liu S, Towey K. Artificial intelligence for anti-money laundering: a review and extension. Digital Finance. 2020;2(3–4):211–39 (in Chinese).

Huang LJ. Research on anti-money laundering related issues of fund companies. Account Learn. 2020;15:177–8 (in Chinese).

Jullum M, Løland A, Huseby RB, Ånonsen G, Lorentzen J. Detecting money laundering transactions with machine learning. J Money Laundering Control. 2020;23(1):173–86.

Kute DV, Pradhan B, Shukla N, Alamri A. Deep learning and explainable artificial intelligence techniques applied for detecting money laundering–a critical review. IEEE Access. 2021;9:82300–17.

LexisNexis Risk Solutions. True cost of compliance infographic—2021 overview; 2021. https://risk.lexisnexis.com/insights-resources/research/true-cost-of-financial-crime-compliance-study-for-the-united-states-and-canada.

LexisNexis Risk Solutions. 2022 true cost of financial crime compliance study—global summary; 2022. https://risk.lexisnexis.com/global/en/insights-resources/research/true-cost-of-financial-crime-compliance-study-global-report.

Liu YH. Research on risks and regulatory countermeasures of private equity funds in China—a comparative analysis based on the United States. Res Financ Supervision. 2018; 8, 42–60. https://doi.org/10.13490/j.cnki.frr.2018.08.003. (in Chinese).

Pang ZY, Jin K. Research on anti-money laundering in the field of private equity funds. Financ Theory Pract. 2012;1:63–7 (in Chinese).

Qin YY, Yuan QY, Wei SC, Deng JF, He H. Regulatory technology empowerment research and path exploration for anti-money laundering. Financ Technol Era. 2023;7:85–90 (in Chinese).

Saaradeey S, Ghosh D, Ray R, Ganesan S, Rajagopalan R. Disrupting status quo in AML compliance. ORACLE White Paper; 2019.

Tiwari M, Gepp A, Kumar K. A review of money laundering literature: the state of research in key areas. Pac Account Rev. 2020;32(2):271–303.

Xue HJ, Li TT. The application of science and technology in anti-money laundering in the field of private equity funds. Financ Account. 2022;5:61–72 (in Chinese).

Yuan X. Application of big data in monitoring suspicious funds against money laundering. Financ Technol Era. 2021;12:62–6 (in Chinese).

Zhang ZY, Hu Y, Wang LY, Fang JB. Regulatory technology empowers anti-money laundering supervision. Northern Finance. 2021; 12: 35–9. https://doi.org/10.16459/j.cnki.15-1370/f.2021.12.006. (in Chinese).

Chapter 7
Status and Development Trend of Big Data Technology Application in the Private Equity Industry

In recent years, countries have continued to deepen their big data strategies, including the United States, Europe, Korea, Japan, and Australia (CAICT 2022). In 2022, the U.S. and Europe passed bills to ensure the release of data value under the premise of privacy protection, such as the American Data Privacy and Protection Act, and the European Data Governance Act. Korea and Japan set up specialized agencies to promote digital transformation in various industries, such as Korea's National Data Policy Committee, and Japan's Digital Agency. Australia released National Data Security Action Plan in April 2022. This chapter reviews the development and status of big data technology, and analyzes applications and trends of big data technology in the PE industry.

7.1 The Development and Status of Big Data Technology

Human society is gradually stepping from the information age to the intelligent age, an age of highly abundant data resources. According to Statista, the total amount of global data will reach 2,142 ZB by 2035 (Reinsel et al. 2018), equivalent to 46 times the amount in 2020, with a compound annual growth rate of 29%. The data will come from business activities and individuals and increasingly from data generated by machines after the Internet of Everything.

Advances in cloud computing, machine learning, and other technologies have promoted the development of big data analysis and applications. The value of data lies in discovering the information and associated logic hidden behind the data to predict trends or facilitate decision-making (Wang et al. 2016). It requires sufficient space to store data and professional technical analysis methods to handle the data. The development of cloud computing and machine learning has created the conditions for big data analysis. By 2025, more than 100 zettabytes of data will be stored in the cloud, equivalent to half of the world's data at that time (Arcserve 2020), laying

R. Xu and D. Zhao, *Digital Transformation of Private Equity in China*, Contributions to Finance and Accounting, https://doi.org/10.1007/978-981-99-8482-4_7

the foundation for big data analysis. The development of machine learning, such as pattern recognition and value function fitting, provides technical support for big data analysis. In recent years, machine learning algorithms have been widely used in smart devices such as Apple's intelligent voice assistant and Amazon Echo, reflecting the productivity generated by the collision of machine learning and big data.

After years of high-speed development, China's big data continues to make important breakthroughs, and the market outlook is widely recognized. According to CAICT (2022), China's big data industry scale increased to 1.3 trillion yuan by the end of 2021, with a growth rate of over 30%. The investment and financing amount in China's big data field has shown an upward trend the past few years, and the total investment in big data-related enterprises exceeded 80 billion yuan in 2021, hitting a record high.

Regarding policy, the central and local governments have issued a series of support documents focusing on the big data industry, digital technology, data factor market, and data security (CAICT 2022). At the central level, at the end of 2021, the introduction of the "14th Five-Year Plan for the Development of Big Data Industry" clarified the action plan for developing the big data industry in the next five years. In 2022, the State Council successively passed the "Overall Program for Pilot Comprehensive Reform for Market-based Allocation of Factors", "Opinions on Accelerating the Construction of a Unified National Market", which emphasized on the necessity and urgency of unleashing the value of data factor. At the local level, 31 provinces (autonomous regions and municipalities) have clearly defined the roadmap and timetable for the development of big data technologies, industries and applications through the issuance of thematic plans for big data and plans for the digital economy, highlighting the proactivity of each region in the layout of big data.

7.1.1 Key Features of Big Data

IBM proposed that big data has the "5V" characteristics, including velocity, volume, value, variety, and veracity. The initial discussions about big data focused on the "3V" characteristics ("velocity, volume, and variety") of big data. As the debate progressed, its attributes of low-value density and veracity to be tested were increasingly recognized by data scientists.

Volume is a fundamental characteristic of big data, referring to a large amount of big data. Only when the amount of data is large enough can it be recognized as big data. For example, the skin cancer detection system developed by Stanford University uses nearly 130,000 images of lesions (Susskind 2020), more than a human doctor could see in a lifetime. With this large number of lesion images, the monitoring system can help doctors diagnose diseases without the so-called "intuition" of a general practitioner. The first version of Google's Go system, AlphaGo, is based on the data of 30 million games played by top human chess players. The vast amount of learning experience unmatched by any human player is an important reason for AlphaGo defeating the world champion of chess.

Velocity refers to the speed of data generation and transmission. Streams of data from smart devices, smartphones, and social media are continuously created and sent to the end destinations. The data needs to be analyzed and processed by data analytics organizations in near real-time to help companies or individuals make the best decisions at the right time. For example, Tesla continuously collects a vast volume of driving data from non-autonomous vehicles, approximately 1 million miles of driving data per hour (Susskind 2020). Tesla uses the data to polish its autonomous driving system, Autopilot. In the medical field, wearable devices are gaining popularity. According to International Data Corporation (IDC), in the third quarter of 2021, 138.4 million wearable devices were shipped worldwide, up 9.9% year-over-year. These devices collect user health data in real-time and can be provided not only to medical institutions to help doctors serve their patients but also to insurance companies and other organizations, leading to related product development and reasonable pricing.

Variety refers to the diversity of data types. Big data comes from diverse sources and may vary in value. The collected data can be unstructured, semi-structured, or structured. Unstructured data lacks a fixed structure and can appear in different formats, such as video, images, and text. It does not fit into mainstream relational databases, cannot be analyzed using traditional data models, and is usually stored as a whole in a binary data format. Semi-structured data has not been organized into specialized repositories but has relevant information. It is easier to process than unstructured data, and tags can split semantic elements or hierarchize fields. Structured data is data that has been organized into a formatted repository. It is easy to retrieve and allows for efficient data processing and analysis.

Value refers to the value that big data can provide. However, because of the large scale of data, the value density is relatively low. In data applications, extracting from complex and large amounts of data is necessary to find valuable information. Different organizations may use similar big data tools to collect and analyze data, but the data value relates directly to what the organizations can do with the data. The value of big data is widely recognized. A typical case is Google's influenza forecasting, Google Flu Trends. In 2009, Google engineers built the H1N1 flu trend forecast model based on online search terms. The model successfully predicted the timing and intensity of the H1N1 outbreak two weeks earlier than the United States Centers for Disease Control and Prevention prediction.

Veracity refers to the quality and accuracy of data. It is challenging to ensure that all collected data are complete and accurate because of the diverse sources and large scale of big data. Some data may be missing, inaccurate, or unable to provide accurate and valuable insights. In subsequent big data applications, removing the false and retaining the true is necessary.

7.1.2 Classification of Big Data

The United Nations Global Working Group on Big Data for Official Statistics Task Team on Cross-Cutting Issues (UNGWG) classifies big data into three categories according to the data source (UNGWG 2013).

1. **Big data generated by social networks (human-sourced information)**

This information refers to big data generated by human experiences, previously recorded in books and works of art and later in photographs, audio, and video. Human-sourced information is now almost entirely digitized and stored everywhere, from personal computers to social networks. It includes social networks such as Facebook and Twitter, blogs and Instagram, video data from platforms such as YouTube, Internet search data, SMS and other mobile phone data, user-generated maps, emails, and other data. The data are loosely structured and often ungoverned.

Social network data can be crawled online through the toolkits of R, Python, Java, and other program toolkits. For example, the Quantmod toolkit for data analysis software R can crawl data from Yahoo, FRED, Google, and other websites. The R toolkit Rblpapi and Python toolkit BLPAPI can crawl data from Bloomberg. The data crawling toolkits for Twitter include R toolkittwitteR and Python toolkit twitter. The corresponding R and Python data crawling toolkits for LinkedIn are Rlinkedin and python-linkedin, respectively.

Data crawled from social networks can be analyzed and processed to guide business decisions. For example, big data from social networks can reflect the real-time sentiment of the public and influence the stock market in the short term, helping to predict short-term stock market fluctuations. RavenPack is a big data analysis company that helps clients (mainly financial institutions) optimize their investment strategies. Analyzing news and social media data from more than 22,000 data sources can help clients optimize their investment strategies and use data to drive asset management. RavenPack researchers build a news sentiment index that uses smoothed sentiment of various durations from 1 week to 90 days (3 months) to analyze the impact of short- and long-term sentiment and overlays the signals from the sentiment index on traditional quantitative investment strategies (QIS). It has been applied to Asia Pacific equity portfolios. The traditional multi-factor framework for the Asian markets includes momentum, market capitalization, volatility, growth, value, and quality factors. Analysis using MSCI's GEM3 model (new Barra Global Equity Model) factor exposure framework reveals that the sentiment index has little correlation with other factors, indicating that it can add value to a portfolio. The multi-factor model with the sentiment index overlay significantly improved over the previous model. The red line in Fig. 7.1 below shows the portfolio's performance with the sentiment factor overlay. In contrast, the blue line indicates the portfolio's performance without the sentiment factor overlay. When the asset under management is \$1 billion, the information ratio improves by 64% from 0.45 to 0.74, and the annualized return improves by 35% from 167 basis points to 225 basis points (RavenPack 2021).

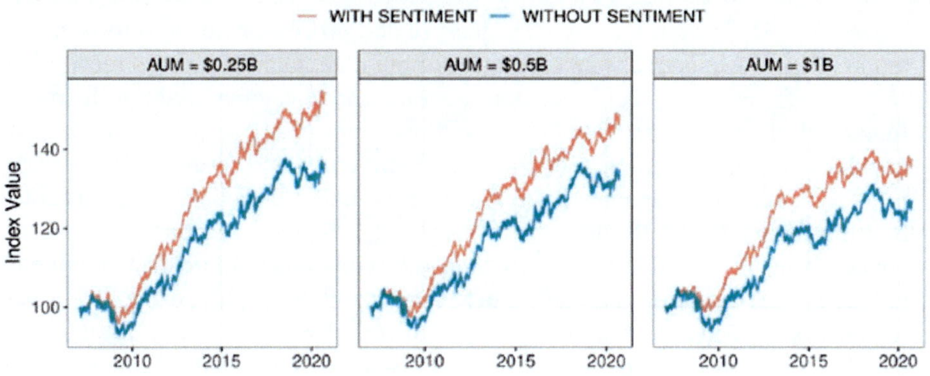

Fig. 7.1 Cumulative performance of the APAC multi-factor indices for a monthly rebalancing frequency and different levels of AUM *Source* RavenPack (2021)

2. Big data generated in traditional business systems (process-mediated data)

It covers data from traditional business processes that public agencies ("administrative data") and enterprises generate. The processes record and monitor business events of interest, such as registering a customer, manufacturing a product, and taking an order. The process-mediated data collected is highly structured and stored in relational database systems, including transactions, reference tables, relationships, and the metadata that sets its context. Traditional business data is the vast majority of what IT manages and processes in operational and business intelligence systems. Data generated by public institutions is usually stored for decades. Currently, many international institutions, including the International Monetary Fund (IMF), the World Bank, the Organization for Economic Cooperation (OECD), and the Bank for International Settlements (BIS), provide the public and institutions with a large amount of data resources at the international level for free. Government statistics departments and relevant agencies also have economic and financial market statistics, usually updated less frequently.

In contrast, data generated by enterprises are updated frequently, even in real-time, including bank records, stock trading information, business transactions, credit card transactions, and e-commerce data. These data can be used for high-frequency trading in the financial markets and for analyzing and predicting stock price fluctuations, which are of high value to investors and generally not free of charge. According to Eagle Alpha, the five highest-priced data categories are credit data, consumer transaction data, geographic location data, application use and network traffic data, and B2B data sets (Eagle Alpha 2020).

Considering the value of business transaction data, many big data companies have emerged to track business transaction data. Consumer transaction data is a popular type of business big data and attracts wide attention. Many big data companies track and collect such data. The Yodlee department of Investment collects credit card and debit card transaction data and sells them to hedge funds and research companies such as Earnest Research, 1010data, and Second Measure after anonymous processing. The research companies analyze and process the data to form research reports. Eagle Alpha tracks 28 categories of big data, including cargo receipts from ships at different ports, consumer transactions, and consumer credit, to help hedge funds and PE companies make investment decisions (Eagle Alpha 2021). BuildFax tracks more than 84 billion data points of commercial and residential structures to provide insurance companies, investment firms, and other clients with insights on housing renovation, solar devices, roof age, and maintenance history.[1] PriceStats collects price information from more than 1,200 retailers in more than 50 countries, publishes daily inflation series for more than 20 countries, purchasing power parity indices for 10 economies and shortage data for 11 countries, as well as inflation data for food and beverage, furniture and household equipment, health and beauty, energy and transportation, entertainment and electronic products industries in the United States.[2]

3. **Big data generated by the internet of things (machine-generated data)**

With the advent of the Internet of Everything, the number of sensors and machines used to monitor and record all events and conditions in the physical world has grown significantly. The output of these sensors is machine-generated data, ranging from simple sensor records to complex computer logs, and it is well structured. As sensors proliferate and data volumes grow, it is becoming an increasingly important component of many enterprises' information stored and processed. Its well-structured nature is suitable for computer processing, but its size and speed are beyond traditional approaches. Hence, it requires the application of big data analysis techniques.

Machine-generated data can be divided into two categories based on the source: sensor big data and computer system big data. The former includes big data generated from fixed sensors such as weather/pollution sensors, smart homes, traffic sensors/webcams, security/surveillance videos/images, and scientific sensors, and mobile sensors such as mobile phones, cars, satellite images. The latter includes all kinds of logs and web logs.

Fixed sensors are often installed in shopping malls, retail stores, transportation hubs, and other locations to track customer flow. For example, Teledyne FLIR has installed more than 2,600,000 sensors in the United States that provide accurate counts of people entering and exiting a given space, help improve retail store operations, and provide the public sector with information about people at transportation hubs to enhance operational efficiency.[3] Sensormatic has developed a shopping tracking solution (ShopperTrak), from headcount devices at store entrances to location-based technology that monitors shopper movement. Sensormatic comprehensively analyzes shoppers' mobile footprints and customer behavior in stores and shopping centers.[4]

[1] See the official website at https://www.buildfax.com/.

[2] https://www.pricestats.com/inflation-series.

[3] See official website at https://www.flir.com/.

[4] See official website at https://www.sensormatic.com.

Among mobile sensors, satellite image data and geographic location data generated by mobile phone positioning are the most popular alternative types of data. One of the reasons for the popularity of satellite image data is the dramatic decrease in the cost of launching satellites. Twenty years ago, launching a traditional geospatial imaging satellite cost tens of millions of dollars and years of preparation. Today, commercial launch advances have dramatically reduced space launch costs. National Aeronaut and Space Administration (NASA)'s cost of launching 27500 kg into low earth orbit is about 1.5 billion or 54,500 dollars per kg. In contrast, SpaceX's Falcon 9's cost of launching 22,800 kg is $62 million, or 2,720 dollars per kg (Jones 2018) Planet can place shoebox-sized nanosatellites in low Earth orbit. At present, there are more than 180 satellites in orbit. The company has introduced the Planetscope Monitoring system,[5] which enables global monitoring with high-resolution, continuous, and real-time monitoring daily. Satellite image data is used not only in the scientific field but also in the commercial sector. Orbital Insights uses satellite image analysis technology to track and measure global oil reserves. Oil is generally stored in storage tanks, and the tank's floating roof changes with the oil level. The oil storage in the tank can be calculated based on the floating roof changes. Using high-resolution satellite images provided by DigitalGlobe and Airbus, Orbital Insights tracks the projection shape changes of more than 20,000 oil storage tanks worldwide to estimate global oil reserves. The results highly match those of the U.S. Energy Information Administration.

Geographic location data generated from mobile phone positioning has similar application scenarios as big data generated from fixed sensors installed in shopping malls and retail stores, which can be used to determine the customer flow of specific stores. Avan Research Through Technology[6] is a big data company that determines the customer flow information of physical stores by tracking the location of smartphones. By monitoring more than 1000 mobile apps that users agree to share location information, the company has access to data of more than 300 billion locations per month, which is valuable to financial institutions and commercial real estate companies that invest in listed/unlisted companies such as retail businesses, hotels, restaurants, and theaters. On December 2, 2016, Avan Research Through Technology used the collected flow information to predict a seven percentage point increase in Lululemon sales. The estimate was larger than the general market expectation but was verified when Lululemon announced its sales data on December 7. It also successfully predicted a rise in Lululemon's stock price.

[5] See official websitehttps://www.planet.com/products/monitoring/.

[6] See the official website at https://advanresearch.com/.

7.1.3 The Main Applications of Big Data Technology in Business

With its massive data size and real-time data updates, big data can provide users in the business sector with an information advantage and explore new signals that bring excess returns.

Big data is vital in business decision-making and improves operational efficiency in many business fields (Rabbi 2018; Koman et al. 2022). Big data analysis plays an increasingly important role in business decisions for enterprises. Through big data analysis, companies can gain more insight into consumer needs and promote sales growth with precision marketing. The International Institute for Analytics (IDA) estimates that by the end of 2020, companies using big data will have gained 430 billion dollars in productivity gains compared to their competitors who have not adopted big data analysis tools.

In the credit field, big data can be used as a supplement to traditional credit data. Using alternative data and new analytical techniques, it can better depict the credit status of enterprises and individuals, alleviate the problem of information asymmetry, increase the availability of credit, improve the ability of financial institutions in risk identification and risk pricing, and reduce the probability of systemic financial risks. Alternative data used in the field of credit investigation can reduce the information monopoly of banks and promote effective credit allocation (Giannetti et al. 2017), reduce the information asymmetry between banks and borrowers, and weaken the impact of adverse selection (Pagano and Jappelli 1993). At the same time, sharing big data credit information can reduce the moral hazard problem in the credit market, increase the borrowers' cost of default, and motivate borrowers to maintain their credit (Padillar and Pagano 2000). By sharing big data credit information, the quality of banks' credit can be improved, and the borrowers' default risk can be measured more accurately. Besides, information sharing will reduce the overall risk of banks and the probability of systemic bank failure (Houston et al. 2010).

In retail field, big data can give users a comprehensive customer portrait. Algorithms analyze user data, such as basic information, social attributes, consumption behavior, browsing records, social media traces, and living habits. Valuable information is then explored and used to form a customer portrait, including user interests, consumption preferences, and consumption ability, risk preferences. The customer portrait helps sales staff to deeply explore customer needs and improve the value of single customers.

Big data can also be used in various fields, including healthcare, energy, logistics and transportation, and manufacturing. For example, the medical field can use big data from medical devices to identify disease risk factors or help doctors diagnose patients' diseases. The energy industry can use big data to track the power grid, implement risk management or conduct real-time market data analysis. The logistics and transportation industry can use big data to build a national logistics network, monitor each node's capacity and transportation demand, allocate resources rationally, and ration goods and capacity in real time to improve the transportation efficiency of the logistics network. The manufacturing industry can use big data technology to solve the overproduction problem that has plagued the manufacturing industry for centuries. Collecting and analyzing retail big data and mobile Internet data can improve the accuracy of demand projections, reduce inventory, and avoid overproduction or oversupply.

In PE investment, social media, community, and inventory big data play an increasingly essential role. It helps PE funds identify investment opportunities and screen investment projects (Petersone et al. 2022).

7.2 Application of Big Data Technology in the PE Industry

Digital transformation is a trend in PE investment. Technologies such as big data, cloud computing, AI, blockchain, and more emerging technologies are being applied to the financial industry and investment process (Guan 2017; Hu 2022; Shu 2022). At the initial stage of the investment process, big data analysis and AI significantly reduces information asymmetry and provides higher prediction accuracy than human analysts, enabling better screening of investment projects. In the due diligence stage, big data can help PE companies track changes in target companies' personnel and income. In the management stage, big data helps PE companies better to understand the correlation between portfolios from more dimensions and optimize investment transaction decisions.

7.2.1 Application of Big Data Technology in the Project Searching and Screening Stages

In the project collection and screening stage, PE companies can utilize social media big data and big data from business activities to improve screening efficiency. If the target company is a startup or even not yet established, business data of seed companies and startups are scarce. The focus of PE investments at this stage is to identify startup teams with a high probability of success. Therefore, social media data is an important source of big data, mainly used to identify potential entrepreneurs and startup teams. Even before the establishment of a startup, PE companies set up models to identify and screen potential entrepreneurs who have the propensity to quit and start their businesses by analyzing the social media activities of senior technicians and product managers of large technology companies and establishing contacts with them before they start their companies. After the establishment of the enterprise, team-related data remains an essential factor in evaluating the company. Many factors, including board members and other venture investors, are important input variables in the big data model. For target companies in the growth and maturity stage, big data generated from business processes can help PE companies better determine the value of the target company. As a company grows, transaction history, consumer data, customer growth, and other stylized variables become essential input for scoring and forecasting models.

In the project screening phase, big data technology can screen and identify promising entrepreneurs based on quantifiable factors, which helps reduce unconscious bias in investment decisions. Investment decisions based on intuition, pattern recognition, and personal social networks are likely to have unconscious biases that lead to a lack of investment diversity. By not bringing biased factors into the model, data-driven project screening can remain neutral to factors such as gender and ethnicity, increase the diversity of portfolio companies, and ultimately bring higher diversification returns.

In addition, big data from online investments such as crowdfunding can help PE companies track investment trends and identify potential entrepreneurs (Zhu and Zhou 2016). Analyzing data from crowdfunding sites and investment networks can track new deals, identify innovative products and services being launched or attracting broad interest, and gain insights into the team structure, expertise, funding status, and entrepreneurial history. This information helps identify high-potential entrepreneurs and startups and reduces the possibility of investment failure.

Big data technology has been widely used in project search and screening. For example, Connetic,[7] a venture capital firm from the Midwest of the United States, can decide whether to conduct a manual investigation in only eight minutes through its automated pre-screening platform, Wendal. It reduces the screening cost of PE investments, improves screening efficiency, and effectively reduces bias in PE investments. Among the companies invested by Connetic, 51% are headed by women or ethnic minorities, well above the industry average of 6–8% in the United States. Hatcher+, a venture capital firm incubator from Singapore,[8] extensively uses big data technology in the project's preliminary selection and evaluation stages. In the initial selection stage, the company created an evaluation system called Hatcher + Quality Score, which pre-screens all projects and uses a 1% screening rate to select winners from many investment projects to enter the next stage. In the investment evaluation stage, the firm created a scoring system called the Hatcher + Opportunity Score based on more than 450,000 venture investments over the past 20 years and scored the investability of candidate projects. Social Capital, a venture capital firm, established an automated system to help companies invest without meeting target startups. The system scores the target company based on the data uploaded. Companies with high scores can get investment support. Automated decision-making without meeting prevents prejudice. By mid-2018, the company had evaluated more than 5,000 startups and invested in 60 of them, with a portfolio company that is quite diverse in terms of geography, investor gender, and ethnicity. Most invested companies are outside the Bay Area and New York (two dominant venture capital business regions), and many are located overseas. About 80% of the founders of invested

[7] See the official website at https://connetic.ventures/.

[8] See the official website at https://hq.hatcher.com/.

companies are non-white, and 30% are female, well above the industry averages of 14 and 6–8%.

7.2.2 Application of Big Data Technology in Project Evaluation

The application of big data technology in the project evaluation depends on the growth stage of the target company. For startups, there is scarce operational history data, and PE investment decisions rely on the target company's business plan and other relevant information the startup team provides. A relatively subjective judgment is ultimately made based on an understanding of the target company's status in the market and a thorough analysis of the startup team. Currently, the assessment judgment of startups is usually based on qualitative data, and quantitative assessment models based on big data are not yet common. For target companies in the growth or maturity stage, tangible data such as historical operating, financial, and customer information play a vital role in project evaluation. PE companies can use big data technology to integrate internal business data with external market and consumer information data. They can also use big data sources such as business IT systems and website data services to leverage equity investment activities. Business systems, often in the form of customer relationship management (CRM) systems, are the core of IT systems for PE investment and can be used to record meetings with target companies and track detailed communication details. Network data includes data provided by third-party market analysis platforms such as Statista, Mattermark, App Annie, Flurry, and enterprise transaction monitoring companies. These external data are combined with internal market information data to predict market trends and new investment opportunities, assess business conditions and ultimately evaluate target companies.

A typical case of using big data technology to empower PE investment evaluation is 645 Ventures, a New York-based early-stage venture capital company. The company has developed a comprehensive operations support platform called 645 Voyager to help in due diligence on its target companies. Due diligence on any potential target is automatically recorded in the system, and all information about potential investment targets, such as changes in personnel and income, is automatically updated.

7.2.3 Application of Big Data Technology in Post-Investment Management

With the application of big data technology, PE companies have a closer relationship with portfolio companies. PE companies can use big data technology to track front-line data that reflects the actual status of the business and use data analysis to identify and address potential issues in advance. The access to front-line business data also facilitates data sharing across portfolio companies. For example, an analysis of the effectiveness of a company's marketing strategy can be a valuable reference to other portfolio companies that have the same target fields.

Applying big data technology can help companies strengthen growth impetus and discover new opportunities. SignalFire is a PE firm that uses big data technology to serve portfolio companies with a focus on startups. Its founder team is mainly composed of engineers and data analysts. Since its establishment in 2015 in San Francisco, assets under management have exceeded 1 billion dollars. The application of big data in PE began in the recruitment process through a "beacon talent" platform. The platform helps invested enterprises to track the world's top engineers, data scientists, product managers, designers, and industry leaders in real-time. For the market analysis, SignalFire tracks more than 2 million data sources and 50 trillion data points, providing investment firms with unique insights into market intelligence.[9] Leveraging the big data and big data analysis mined, SignalFire helps firms with product pricing and cohort analysis. For example, big data can estimate the impact of discounts on revenue growth and profitability and analyze the advantages and disadvantages of new products compared to competing products.

7.2.4 *Key Elements of Big Data Technology Applied to PE Investment*

High-quality data sets are the first key element. The data-driven strategy requires large-scale and high-quality data. Many companies acquire big data from social media and business processes by cooperating with third parties. Some also hire data collection professionals or outsource data collection to third parties. They integrate the external data with internal data from the invested enterprises. The collected data organized in this customized form will ultimately become proprietary data of PE companies.

Models are the second key element. The validity of models must be assessed before they can be used for investment decisions. High-quality large data sets can present valuable conclusions or findings only through information mining. Machine learning techniques such as logistic regression and deep learning models are commonly used to analyze big data sets in the PE industry. Many companies have developed scoring functions to evaluate investment targets. Some companies have also developed predictive models that predict variables such as the room for growth, valuation changes, and the likelihood of attracting additional investment and use the key signals output from these models to screen and evaluate target enterprises in a pre-investment stage. Models vary according to the target enterprises' investment strategies, industry, and growth stage. However, without exception, these models are

[9] See the official website at https://signalfire.com/.

improved and updated repeatedly with training data and test results. Some companies adopt a strategy-driven approach to compile and build data and algorithms. In contrast, others focus on data- and model-driven approaches, using data and models to determine investment strategies.

7.3 Trends of Big Data Technology in the PE Industry

7.3.1 Importance of Big Data Will Gradually Exceed Personal Social Networks

Traditionally, the PE investment has relied heavily on personal social networks. The search and investment of a PE project highly depend on the fund managers' proprietary social network. If a PE firm lacks sufficient capital to purchase a target company, it must make joint deals with peers. The success of joint deals also depends on the social network. A larger, more solid social network generates a higher likelihood of finding partner firms. In the screening phase, PE investment decisions rely heavily on traditional data sources such as news or financial statements, historical patterns, and investment "intuition" to make judgments about the value of a target company.

With the development of big data technology, investors pay more attention to a broader range of information. Data and models replace personal social connections turning PE investments from an art to a science. In the age of big data, almost anything can be important information for PE investors, from credit card spending records to GPS cell phone locations, social media to surveillance footage, and satellite imagery to online job postings. Using big data, PE companies seek out the companies most in need of capital, build models that can accurately predict the potential of a particular product or startup, and track changes in a company's popularity and profitability. It is increasingly important in decision-making and implementation in various stages, such as investment target search, screening, investment monitoring, and post-investment management.

Applications of big data in the PE industry have accelerated due to influx of capital, an increase in the number of startups, and competition among PE companies. Nowadays, the PE industry is attracting more and more capital, and the competition to find the right investment target has intensified. Many firms have begun to search and screen target companies using big data technology. According to an Ernst & Young survey, 94% of companies will adopt more predictive analysis techniques in the PE investment process in the next two years. When big data applications prove beneficial to value creation in PE investment, the competitive advantage from new technology applications will attract other companies to follow suit, driving the popularity of big data technology in the PE industry. However, big data technology is only a tool in the PE investment process. Most PE companies adopting a data-driven strategy still combine big data technology with traditional deal evaluation, and big data technology will not replace the investment process.

7.3.2 *Teams of Data Scientists Will Become an Integral Part of Changing the Governance Structure of PE Companies*

Big data is increasing in size and quality, and machine learning models are improving. Hence, data and algorithms will have a more significant share of the competitive advantage of PE companies, and even pure data-driven investment platforms may emerge. This change will affect the talent needs of PE companies and even change the organizational structure. PE companies need the right talent and resources to effectively integrate data-driven investment processes, which requires them to change recruitment strategies to include more people with computer technology backgrounds. Today, data scientists and engineers have become essential to venture capital firms such as SignalFire. With the popularity of big data in the PE industry, PE companies will emphasize building teams of data scientists and engineers. Even PE companies that get big data technology support from third-party companies need people who understand computer science to facilitate communication and cooperation. As the changes occur, the traditional partnership model may be challenged, and the organizational structure of PE companies may be closer to that of technology companies.

References

Arcserve. The 2020 data attack surface report; 2020. See https://1c7fab3im83f5gqiow2qqs2k-wpengine.netdna-ssl.com/wp-content/uploads/2020/12/ArcserveDataReport2020.pdf.

China Academy of Information and Communications Technology. January 2023. White Paper on Big Data; 2022. http://www.caict.ac.cn/english/research/whitepapers/202303/t20230316_416841.html.

Eagle Alpha. The data on data; 2020. https://www.eaglealpha.com/2020/05/27/the-data-on-data/.

Eagle Alpha. Alternative data report 2021: year in review; 2021. https://www.eaglealpha.com/2021/11/18/eagle-alphas-1st-annual-alternative-data-report-2021/.

Giannetti M, Liberti JM, Sturgess J. Information sharing and rating manipulation. Review of financial studies, forthcoming, Swedish house of finance research paper no. 15–11; 2017.

Guan XL. The road of financial technology development in private equity industry under the new situation. Tsinghua Financ Rev. 2017;12:90–1. https://doi.org/10.19409/j.cnki.thf-review.2017.12.027. (in Chinese).

Houston JF, Lin C, Lin P, Ma Y. Creditor rights, information sharing, and bank risk taking. J Financ Econ. 2010;96:485–512.

Hu M. Application and enlightenment of fintech in the private equity investment industry in the United Kingdom and the United States. Finance. 2022;03:89–94 (in Chinese).

Jones, H. The recent large reduction in space launch cost, 48th international conference on environmental systems; 2018.

Koman G, Tumová D, Jankal R, Mičiak M. Business-making supported via the application of big data to achieve economic sustainability. Entrepreneurship Sustain Issues. 2022;9(4):336–58.

Padillar AJ, Pagano M. Sharing default information as a borrower discipline device. Eur Econ Rev. 2000;44:1951–80.

Pagano M, Jappelli T. Information sharing in credit markets. J Finance. 1993;46(5):1693–718.

Petersone S, Tan A, Allmendinger R, Roy S, Hales J. A data-driven framework for identifying investment opportunities in private equity. arXiv e-prints; 2022. https://doi.org/10.48550/arXiv.2204.01852

Rabbi F. Application of big data in promoting sustainable solutions for business-a review. Glob J Appl Sci Technol. 2018;3(11):1–6.

RavenPack. News sentiment as a factor for enhancing quantitative investment strategies for Asia Pacific stocks; 2021. https://www.ravenpack.com/research/news-sentiment-factor-enhancing-quantitative-investment-strategies-asia-pacific-stocks/.

Reinsel D, Gantz J, Rydning J. Digital world—from the edge to the core; 2018. https://www.seagate.com/files/www-content/our-story/trends/files/idc-seagate-dataage-whitepaper.pdf.

Shu L. The application and impact of big data technology in the private equity investment industry. Financ Account. 2022;4:32–8 (in Chinese).

Susskind D. A world without work: technology, automation, and how we should respond, chapter 11 Big Tech. London: Penguin; 2020.

United Nations Global Working Group on big data for Official Statistics Task Team on Cross-Cutting Issues. The 2013 UNECE classification of big data; 2013.

Wang H, Xu Z, Fujita H, Liu S. Towards felicitous decision making: an overview on challenges and trends of Big Data. Inf Sci. 2016;367:747–65.

Zhu H, Zhou ZZ. Analysis and outlook of applications of blockchain technology to equity crowdfunding in China. Financ Innov. 2016;2(1):1–11 (in Chinese).

Chapter 8
Status and Development Trend of Artificial Intelligence Application in the Private Equity Industry

The capital management demand in China is expanding, and the preference for equity assets has increased. Meanwhile, the PE market has increasingly relied on digital technology. Although traditional financial institutions have advantages in capital management business by utilizing abundant capital, resources, number of branches, and experience, fintech companies have gradually penetrated the capital management market. In the future, with fully realized digital transformation, China's investment management institutions will be able to provide more inclusive, efficient, and convenient investment management services.

8.1 The Development of AI Technology

AI is a branch of computer science. It is a technology that simulates, extends, and expands intelligent human behaviors (such as learning, reasoning, thinking, and planning), enabling computers to act on higher-level intelligence principles. Artificial intelligence (AI) is the core technology of the technological revolution and industrial transformation (Zhang et al. 2017). Since its birth, AI has been maturing in theory and technology and expanding in application areas. During the covid-19 pandemic, the new generation of emerging technologies represented by AI has accelerated the evolution of traditional industries and brought substantial economic benefits.

Countries worldwide have recognized the importance of AI in promoting economic transformation and industrial upgrading. Xi Jinping, General Secretary of the Communist Party of China Central Committee, stressed that accelerating the development of new-generation AI is a strategic issue, key for China to seize the opportunities in the new round of technological revolution and industrial transformation.[1]

[1] Refer to https://chinaplus.cri.cn/chinaplus/news/china/9/20181031/203609.html. According to Du et al. (2023), AI chip is critical for the development of AI industry, while China's AI chip

R. Xu and D. Zhao, *Digital Transformation of Private Equity in China*, Contributions to Finance and Accounting, https://doi.org/10.1007/978-981-99-8482-4_8

Two critical documents issued by the State Council have elevated the development of AI technology to a national strategic level. In July 2017, the State Council issued the Development Plan for New Generation of Artificial Intelligence, which elevated the development of AI to a national strategic level and vigorously promoted the development of AI in various fields. In the same year, the People's Bank of China issued the Thirteenth Five-Year Plan for The Development of Information Technology in China's Financial Industry. The Plan states: "Strengthen the research and application of financial technology and regulatory technology, steadily promote the research of system architecture and cloud computing technology application, deeply carry out the innovation of big data technology application, standardize and popularize the Internet financial-related technology applications, and actively promote research on blockchain, AI and other new technology applications".

To promote the industry's management norms and technical standardization, in 2020, the National Standardization Administration Committee, the Central Internet Information Office and five other departments jointly issued the *Guidelines for the Construction of the National New Generation of Artificial Intelligence Standard System*, which provides a detailed description of the development of the AI standard system. In addition, local governments have introduced many development strategies and supportive policies, mainly in the areas of top-level design, technology R&D, talent cultivation, industrial layout (Guo et al. 2023). The deep integration with the real economy releases a new impetus for the development of the industry.

In January 2022, China issued its "14th Five-Year Plan for the Development of the Digital Economy", which listed AI as one of the key sectors to enhance innovative capacities.

China's market demand for AI is huge. According to the Shenzhen Artificial Intelligence Industry Association, by the end of 2021, the scale of China's AI core industry will reach 341.6 billion yuan, an increase of 5% over 2020 (Shenzhen Artificial Intelligence Industry Association 2022). Meanwhile, the registration of new AI-related enterprises has risen year by year (Fig. 8.1). Data released by Qichacha Finance shows more than 1.09 million existing AI-related enterprises in China, of which 420,800 were added in 2022, with a year-on-year growth of 18.5% (Qichacha Finance 2023).

Finance is one of the most important areas of AI technology application. AI has brought good opportunities for transforming financial business models in recent years. AI has deeply integrated with financial business through multi-modal perception, deep learning, cross-border integration, and group intelligence opening. As a result, it promotes the digitalization and intelligent transformation of business scenarios, the financial supply-side structural reform, and the optimal allocation of

---

technology is still in the primary stage, breakthrough of AI chip technology bottleneck requires advancement in core technology, industrial chain, and commercial application. In addition, related entities in China were slow to develop AI ethics frameworks (Lee 2018; Hickert and Ding 2018) before 2019, while there was a surge in attempts to define ethical principles since 2019 (Roberts et al. 2021). For example, China's Ministry of Science and Technology established the National New Generation Artificial Intelligence Governance Expert Committee in March 2019, and the committee released eight principles for the governance of AI in June 2019.

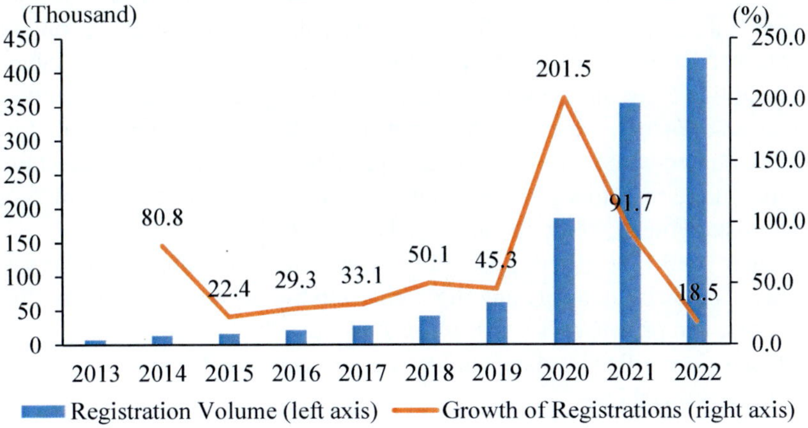

Fig. 8.1 Registrations and growth rate of AI-related companies in China. Qichacha Finance (2023) *Source*

financial resources. It also develops innovative service models, reshapes the financial development model, and speeds up the transition from traditional finance to intelligent finance.

Compared with Internet finance, intelligent finance further promotes the reallocation of production factors, reduces costs, reduces information asymmetry, changes the original production relationship, enhances the effect of economies of scale, changes the traditional financial logic, and becomes the driving force for the intelligent development of the financial industry. First, intelligent finance helps financial institutions improve efficiency and reduce costs. Intelligent customer service has dramatically alleviated the pressure of manual services, significantly reducing time-consuming business processes. Second, intelligent finance improves the flexibility, adaptability, and inclusiveness of financial products and services. The flexibility is enhanced by fully integrating customer information and providing personalized and customized financial services and products (Zhang et al. 2017). Adaptability is reflected as intelligent finance adapting to various scenarios' financial needs. Inclusiveness is improved as intelligent finance innovates a range of products and services that traditional finance cannot cover. Third, intelligent finance improves risk prevention and control capabilities. For example, an abnormal transaction identification model can be built with big data and machine learning technology and accurately identify abnormal transaction behaviors.

AI technology provides possibilities for improving asset allocation, an evolution, and an upgrade of existing fintech applications (Astebro 2021). The application of AI in finance mainly includes five key technologies: machine learning, biometrics, natural language processing, voice technology, and knowledge mapping. First, machine learning conducts feature learning by transmitting data between hierarchical structures, performs well for various financial data, and improves financial risk assessment and early warning. Second, biometrics is applied to business processes such as identity verification and online double recording to automate customer interactions and significantly impact the core value chain, including risk control and customer service. Third, natural language processing is valuable in information mining from unstructured data. Natural language processing is often used in automation-related scenarios such as text compliance checking and data retrieval. It is also combined with voice technology to enable intent recognition and multi-round dialogue, further creating intelligent customer interaction modes and reducing operational costs. Fourth, voice technology is mainly used in customer service robots, compliance, and other scenarios. Fifth, knowledge mapping technology has been applied to credit risk control and other fields, but the application depth is still limited. Both public and private sector institutions may use these technologies for regulatory compliance, surveillance, data quality assessment, and fraud detection (Financial Stability Board 2017).

8.2 Policy Environment of AI and PE Industry

Policies inevitably influence the development of China's PE investment industry. In recent years, China has continued to launch favorable policies, prompting emerging technologies such as AI to various financial industry fields. The covid-19 pandemic accelerated China's digitalization process, promoting the new infrastructure (including AI), and the digital transformation toward intelligent financial services. China has intensively introduced laws, regulations, and policies about AI, showing its determination to elevate AI development to a national strategic height.

In 2017, the People's Bank of China established the Fintech Committee to conduct in-depth studies of the development process of fintech at home and abroad, as well as its impact on economic and social development. At the same time, it is necessary to actively explore and build a fintech regulatory mechanism applicable to China, and strengthen synergistic cooperation at home and abroad, especially in intelligent finance.

On December 14, 2018, the Ministry of Industry and Information Technology (MIIT) issued the "Three-Year Action Plan for Promoting the Development of a New Generation of Artificial Intelligence Industry (2018–2020)",[2] which specifies the goals for the development of the AI industry. The Plan puts forward specific goals for developing the AI industry in four aspects: large-scale development of essential AI products, significant enhancement of basic core capabilities, deepening development of intelligent manufacturing, and establishing an intelligent industrial support system.

In June 2019, China launched the Science and Technology Innovation Board ("STAR Market"), which allows technology-focused fintech companies to be listed. The board offers multiple benefits. It provides a better exit channel for PE and VC funds, enables the valuating of local fintech companies in Chinese market, and

[2] Three-Year Action Plan for Promoting the Development of a New Generation of AI Industries (2018–2020), Ministry of Industry and Information Technology Official Website, 2017.

facilitates brand building and timely information transfer between companies and the market.

In August 2020, the "Guidelines for the Construction of a National New Generation Artificial Intelligence Standards System" were formulated by five central government departments, including the Standardisation Administration of China (SAC), the Cyberspace Administration of China (CAC), the National Development and Reform Commission (NDRC), the Ministry of Science and Technology (MOST), and the Ministry of Industry and Information Technology (MIIT). It outlines a two-stage (by 2021 and 2023) strategy to be achieved by the national AI standards system. The purpose is to promote the continuous self-optimization of AI technology in the open-source and open industrial ecosystem and to form a new pattern in which standards lead to the comprehensive and standardized development of the AI industry.

To prevent security risks and promote the healthy development of in-depth synthetic services, the CAC has tightened regulations associated with deep synthesis technologies (DST) and generative AI services, including ChatGPT.[3] In December 2022, the CAC issued regulations prohibiting the creation of AI-generated media without clear labels, such as watermarks, and the regulations took effect on January 10, 2023. Under the regulations, new deep synthesis products are subject to a security assessment from the government.

Nearly 30 countries and regions worldwide have released AI-related strategic plans and policy deployments, including the United States, China, the European Union, Japan, South Korea, India, Denmark, and Russia.[4] About 80% of countries intensively released relevant policies and official plans after 2016. For example, the United States National Science and Technology Committee released the National AI Research and Development Strategic Plan in 2016. It updated it in 2019, and the United Kingdom House of Commons released Robotics and Artificial Intelligence in 2016. China National Development and Reform Commission released the Three-Year Action Implementation Plan for "Internet+" Artificial Intelligence in 2016. The United States, in particular, has been committed to maintaining its global technological hegemony, positioning AI at the core of its strategic blueprint, and has been actively promoting AI research. Its policy has gradually evolved from guidance and support to seizing the strategic "commanding heights". In 2019, the United States successively promulgated three guidelines, including "Maintaining United States Leadership in Artificial Intelligence" (Executive Order 13,859 of the President, February 11, 2019), "National for Artificial Intelligence Research and Development Strategic Plan", "The American AI Century: A Blueprint for Action". The European Union focuses on industries, manufacturing, medical care, energy, and other fields, emphasizes creativity, and promotes AI to empower manufacturing and intelligent upgrading in related areas. The European Union issued the Declaration on Cooperation on Artificial Intelligence in 2018.

[3] In September 2023, Tencent debuts its large language artificial intelligence model "Hunyuan", which is similar in power and capabilities to GPT-3 and available for enterprise use in China.

[4] A brief description of public strategies for supporting AI in Germany and Hessen could be found in Bredt (2019).

In recent years, regulations of the PE fund industry have been generally tightened, while supportive policies have also been promulgated. The CSRC issued "*Provisions on Strengthening the Supervision of Private Investment Funds*" on December 30, 2020. Its purpose is to strengthen the supervision of PE funds further, strictly control the incremental risks, steadily resolve the existing risks, crack down on all kinds of illegal behaviors, foster the development of the industry, and protect the legitimate rights and interests of investors and relevant participants. The six main aspects are to regulate the name and business scope of PE fund managers, optimize the supervision of PE fund managers, refine the requirements for non-public offerings and qualified investors, clarify the criteria for PE fund investments, strengthen the regulatory requirements for PE fund managers and practitioners, and clarify legal responsibilities and transitional arrangements.

8.3 The Current Market Situation of the PE Industry

8.3.1 The Demand for Equity Assets Has Surged

The total wealth of China's households has glowed rapidly in the past two decades and has vigorously promoted the rapid development of the large asset management industry, which has entered a period of explosive growth. According to the National Institution for Finance & Development (NIFD) statistics, by the end of 2019, China's total social assets were 1655.6 trillion yuan, and the social net assets were 675.5 trillion yuan (Li and Zhang 2021). The wealth stock of China's household sector reached 512.6 trillion yuan, and the wealth per capita reached 366 thousand yuan. In the past decade, the year-on-year growth rate of China's social wealth in most years exceeded the GDP growth rate. In the past two decades, the compound annual growth rate of China's social net wealth has reached 16.2%, exceeding the compound annual growth rate of nominal GDP (12.8%). The proportion of non-financial assets to total assets has risen in recent years. The proportion of housing assets to net assets exceeding 40% since 2018 and accounted for 93% of non-financial assets in 2019. The ratio of stocks to financial assets reached 52% in 2019, while that of currency and deposits declined and accounted for 36.44% (Fig. 8.2).

According to *China's National Balance Sheet 2020*, the proportion of risk-free deposits has decreased with the gradual development and maturity of China's asset management industry. That of stocks and equity and securities investment funds rise faster than households' wealth. The investment preference of high-net-worth groups has been gradually changing. They used to focus on bank deposits, fixed-income products, and real estate trusts but are switching to stocks and equity, private equity products, and financial derivatives.

The development of AI overlaid with big data technology is setting off a new round of industrial revolution. Since 2016, China has vigorously promoted intelligent wealth management, and the industry has developed rapidly in the past few

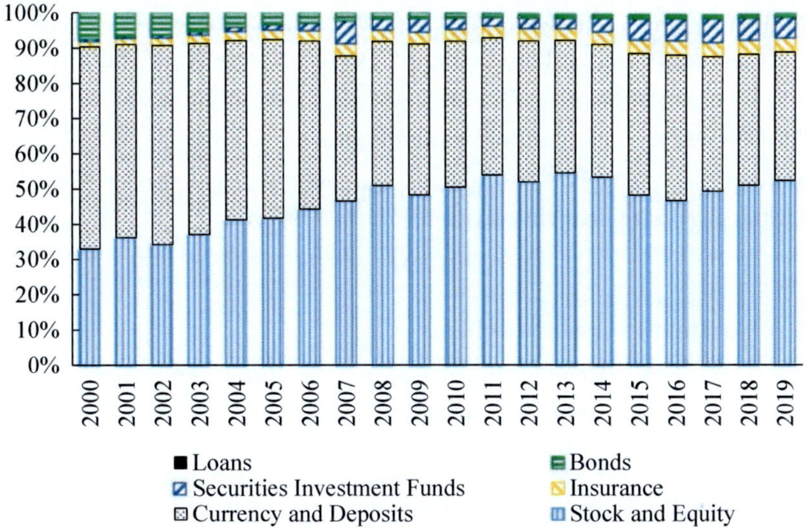

Fig. 8.2 Composition of net financial assets of Chinese households (2000–2019). Li and Zhang (2021) *Source*

years. With the continuous development of regulation, technology and information system, the intelligent wealth management platform will continue to be upgraded. Today's online financial customers will be potential customers of intelligent financial platforms in the future (Zhao and Li 2021).

8.3.2 The Pain Points of the Traditional PE Industry

The PE funds cooperate with many brokerage firms, and the product accounts are highly fragmented. This practice generates some pain points. First, it causes difficulties in operation at the transaction level. Second, the funds must deal with different custodians' system differences. Third, providing timely services to clients is difficult due to the scattered products. Fourth, third-party investment management institutions have insufficient risk control capability. Fifth, raising funds is often difficult due to the private placement attributes of PE funds.

1. **Difficulty in operating the trading system**

With a growing number of cooperative institutions, PE funds are increasingly difficult to operate at the transaction level. Generally, the investment management organization that sells the fund products on commission operates the account transactions. Even some investment management institutions require private placement of different products due to various sales departments. If split into three products, then three accounts must be managed simultaneously for trading, which is challenging to coordinate even within an investment management institution, not to mention multiple investment management institutions. Different institutions may use different trading systems and terminals and are bound to face a massive workload in the case of a large volume of products.

2. **Insufficient accuracy of financial advice**

Traditional financial services rely on the knowledge and experience of professional staff when providing financial advice to clients. However, financial advisors' varying knowledge and experience make it difficult to ensure a unified quality of service and accurate advice.

3. **Lack of timely services to clients**

To expand the scale, PE fund companies usually seek distribution from several investment management institutions, whose distribution capacity varies. As the number of investment management institutions grows, the workload of fund managers increases dramatically. However, PE companies have to save personnel expenses by reducing costs, which makes it challenging to cover timely services.

4. **Inadequate risk control capability of third-party investment management institutions**

China's investment management market has formed a competitive pattern of three groups: third-party investment management institutions, mainstream financial institutions, and emerging digital investment management institutions. Among them, the third-party investment management institutions started earlier and have established a full range of channels in the market, accumulated many customers, and had a high market share. However, such institutions are relatively weak in active asset management and have inadequate risk control capabilities.

5. **Difficulties in raising funds**

Due to the restriction of a private placement, attracting customers through a public channel and reaching the target group is usually challenging. It is often easy to ignore the differential needs of customers.

8.4 Application Scenarios of AI Technology in the PE Industry

Nowadays, the financial industry is already in deep integration of information technology and business services. With the continuous iteration and update of financial technology, the PE industry has also started the digital transformation, entirely using big data, cloud computing, AI, blockchain, and other financial technologies. Various business models, operation methods, products, and services have been transformed and reshaped, enhancing service efficiency. The fund company has also used cloud computing, AI, blockchain, and other financial technologies to improve service efficiency, reduce costs, improve customer experience, enhance the competitiveness of products and services, and support its transformation and development.

PE practitioners are actively exploring the application of new digital technologies, empowering the PE industry with more inclusive, efficient, and convenient investment management services. PE institutions are fully aware of the value of emerging digital technologies and have been applying the technologies to facilitate digital transformation. Every stage of the "fundraising, investment, management, and exit" process of the PE industry is closely linked to the innovative application of digital technology (see Table 8.1). Among them, the application of AI technology is the most common one.

1. **The fundraising stage—smart customer acquisition**

Clients have different risk-bearing capacities, investment willingness, and different demands for products and services. PE companies can collect customer needs, investment, and consumption data through various channels such as mobile applications, social media software, and online questionnaires. Then the companies use AI and big data technologies to accurately portray user-profiles and make marketing plans for products and services accordingly, conduct precise marketing and personalized recommendations, and monitor customer data in real-time. Continuous optimization of marketing strategies and establishing a large user database help attract and retain customers. The main application scenario of AI in this field is personalized recommendations.

2. **The investment stage—intelligent investment research and robo-advisor**

(1) **Intelligent Investment Research**

Intelligent investment research means using AI technologies for financial data research involving big data, machine learning, natural language processing, and knowledge mapping. For traditional industry research in the PE industry, practitioners conduct information retrieval, collection, classification, research, and analysis manually. It shows low efficiency in data processing, and the quality of research highly

Table 8.1 Emerging digital technologies in the asset management industry

Stage	Business segments	AI	Big data	Blockchain
Fundraising	Precise customer acquisition	√	√	√
	Intelligent marketing	√	√	
	Intelligent customer service	√		
Investment	Intelligent investment research	√	√	
	Robo-advisor	√	√	
	Intelligent anti-fraud	√	√	√
Management	Intelligent risk control	√	√	√
	Intelligent operations	√		
Exit	Intelligent clearing			√
	Data control	√	√	√

Source Ba et al. (2020)

depends on the professionalism of the practitioners. In contrast, the in-depth use of AI technology can simplify the process of data collection and digitization, save time and costs, and improve research intelligence. For example, natural language processing technology can process and extract unstructured data from news and information, policy releases, and social media, expanding data breadth. Data mining can be used to analyze the potential relationships hidden in the data and build a knowledge graph, which significantly improves research efficiency.

For data collation and analysis, the knowledge management platform collects and integrates data[5] in a unified framework for management. Based on a complete financial industry thesaurus and business model, it extracts various types of information through machine vision and natural language processing technology. The next step is automatically labeling and classifying the documents according to report type, industry, publishing institution, author, rating, and other dimensions.

For report writing, the benefits of using AI technology include the following. Firstly, it can collect all kinds of unstructured texts[6] and automatically transform them into structured data using machine vision technology. In such a way, it solves the pain point that a large amount of valuable information in unstructured data is challenging to use effectively. Secondly, robotic process automation (RPA) technology can be used to simulate the operation process of employees. The extracted data can be traced back to the designated system platforms and applications 24 h daily. In such a way, it solves the pain point of low efficiency and high risk in the data transfer process. Thirdly, natural language processing, machine learning, and visualization technology can automatically learn data from massive financial industry charts and realize the best data visualization. In data acquisition, it can quickly and accurately acquire existing data, automatically calculate, integrate and analyze data according to the customer's search intent, and display the meaning to customers through the best visualization path. In such a way, it solves customers' pain points in the data search process.

(2) **Robo-Advisor**

Robo-advisor refers to PE companies using AI technology to provide investors with personalized asset allocation solutions. It facilities the PE companies to understand investors' information (such as financial needs, risk preferences, and financial situation) and intelligently adjust holdings according to market dynamics to meet investors' diversified and personalized investment needs (Wang 2021). Robo-advisor is mainly a traditional investment advisor service that realizes automation in the asset allocation process and generally has functions such as investor risk assessment and portfolio analysis. On the other hand, the robo-advisor optimizes the allocation and personalization of customer assets based on the customer's targets and market dynamics. On the one hand, based on the modern asset portfolio theory, robo-advisor

[5] For example, internal and external market information, research activities, research reports, stock rating changes, earnings forecast changes, simulation portfolio changes, enterprise intrinsic value, research minutes.

[6] For example, announcements, research reports, contracts, financial reports, legal documents, bills, documents, operation reports.

can automatically analyze the risk, return and correlation of various assets and form the optimal portfolio strategy. On the other hand, robo-advisors use AI technologies to generate optimized investment strategies through algorithmic models and achieve the best risk-adjusted return through continuous learning and improvement of the models.

Robo-advisor has three key capabilities. First, it accurately identifies customers' real investment objectives and constraints. Second, it fully uses market information to diversify investments and strengthen portfolio model development capabilities. Third, it provides high efficiency of risk control by monitoring market dynamics in real-time and automatically, instantly identifying portfolio risks, providing early warning, and timely adjusting asset portfolios.

Robo-advisor has five advantages. First, it extends the coverage of investment advisor services. Second, the cost is low, and the operation is simple and convenient. Robo-advisors mainly rely on AI-related infrastructure and technology to automate formulating investment strategies, network marketing means, and expand scale effect. The management fees are generally between 0.25 and 0.5%. Third, the wide range of investment targets is conducive to forming optimal asset allocation. Fourth, the service process is simple, transparent, efficient, and precisely matches the customers' asset management objectives. Fifth, it avoids the influence of psychological factors of customers and managers in the investment process, which makes investment decisions more professional and objective.

3. **The management stage—intelligent operation and intelligent risk control**

(1) **Intelligent operation**

To share data and information across departments, PE companies must establish an enterprise-level big data platform and break through the barriers between departments by clarifying data management responsibilities, improving data governance mechanisms, and promoting data management standards. At present, the applications of AI technology help realize multi-dimensional data connectivity, break the data barriers, dissolve the information silos, build intra-enterprise and inter-enterprise business collaboration, and release the core value of big data as a fundamental strategic resource. The mainstream applications of intelligent operation are daily processes and investment project management. Most PE companies have used EHR online human resource management platforms to provide online personnel management solutions, compensation and benefits solutions, and process and performance management solutions. Daily process management uses big data technology to expand the dimensions of employee performance evaluation and analyze the portrait of employees with good and bad performance, which highly improves the efficiency of daily management. In addition, some companies set labels for sample contracts by developing and designing contract document management systems. With machine learning and natural language processing technology, they automatically mine the rules between contracts and labels and put the rules into new contracts to realize automation of contract label setting, judge the classification attributes of labels, effectively carry out classification management, and improve the efficiency and refinement of operational management. For fund project management, the construction and updating of an enterprise data platform can dynamically display the situation of project establishment and approval, issuance, due diligence management, and other matters during the project's life cycle. Some PE companies have started to use blockchain technology to empower project management to ensure the security and integrity of project material management.

(2) **Intelligent risk control**

The low-risk control capability of the traditional PE industry is a pain point of the industry. The risk control system has gradually matured through years of exploration. However, the conventional risk control model has presented many problems, restricting improving the industry's risk control level. The industry's risk control model aims to measure counterparties through subjective and objective evaluations. In subjective evaluation, the traditional model often judges by an inherent impression of counterparties and the accumulated experience of cooperation but lacks an overall grasp of the complex environment, leading to loopholes in risk control. The objective evaluation focuses on the counterparty's lending history, collateral assets, and credit rating. However, the informatization[7] of risk control decisions is insufficient and lacks standardized data support.

Intelligent risk control is a means for PE companies and third-party investment institutions to collect and integrate risk control data with AI technology and use machine learning technology to learn risk patterns to set up corresponding risk management firewalls and warnings. PE institutions and third-party investment institutions have actively layout infrastructure and tried to implement intelligent risk control technology. A public opinion monitoring system collects data from the Internet, third parties, social media, and other channels and processes. It analyzes the data with AI technology to realize timely alerts and early risk warnings. Timely, accurate, and intelligent public opinion monitoring improves the company's ability to control risks and provides strong support for the management decisions of business departments.

4. **The exit stage—intelligent data management**

Intelligent data management is not only the development of software and management strategies but an integrated data management strategy by integrating software and hardware to enable more efficient storage, utilization, and data protection. The exit of a PE investment is the last and core stage of the PE investment cycle. The exit paths of equity investments show diverse characteristics due to the diversity of invested companies and the external environment. Intelligent data management converts the designated data into the optimal exit solution and maximizes benefits and controls costs, using data warehousing, data visualization, and analysis technologies combined with big data, data mining, machine learning, and other cutting-edge technologies.

[7] There is a lack of the macroeconomic situation, information in the industry, real-time public opinion and other multi-dimensional information.

Through the process, AI can also reshape corporate information disclosure. The increasing AI readership motivates firms to prepare filings that are more friendly to machine parsing and processing (the so-called "feedback effect" as compared with the use of AI by investors), implying the growing roles of AI in the financial markets and their potential impact on corporate decisions (Cao et al. 2020).

8.5 Application Cases of AI Technology in the PE Industry

As the capital market matures, PE fund companies are also developing rapidly. Most PE fund companies have smaller asset management scales, weaker revenue capacity, and less digitalized business operations than public fund companies, banks, and insurance companies. In the digital transformation process, PE companies also face the high cost of self-developed and self-built systems. They often cooperate with third-party institutions and cloud-based platform services to achieve the digitalization of business operations. A typical third-party fintech service provider in the industry is JingData's "Investment Management System". It provides practitioners with many solutions, including marketing and promotion, business process, risk management, data analysis, investment research, and regulatory reporting with the help of "PaaS (Platform as a Service) + hybrid cloud technology". It boosts the digital transformation of the asset management industry.

Case 1: JingData's "Investment Management System"

JingData,[8] as a financial technology service provider, has developed its own "Investment Management System" platform to support the digital transformation of China's investment management institutions. The platform applies "PaaS + hybrid cloud technology" architecture to provide system support for investment management institutions in the "fundraising, investment, management, and exit" process, helping institutions realize middle and back office integration and reduce system development costs and improve investment efficiency.

For investment management institutions, JingData's "Investment Management System" is a one-stop solution with six core functions. First, the lifecycle management of investment projects covers project entry, due diligence, and exit and uses data intelligence to improve efficiency. Second, fund data management assists investors in the relationship, portfolio, and transaction management to improve fund operation efficiency. Third, it offers transaction-based multi-account management, automatic revenue distribution, and intelligent settlement. Fourth, compliance management consists of a mainstream compliance library, built-in mainstream risk management models, real-time risk warning, and promotes risk control capabilities. Fifth, built-in standard investment analysis model and visual presentation support investment decisions and analysis, including a diagram of dynamic asset structure, asset relationship analysis, and underlying asset analysis. Sixth, it provides comprehensive digital office

[8] https://www.jingdata.com/.

services, including process approval, document storage, schedule management, and work progress monitoring.

For investment managers, the system is a one-stop work platform with the following functions. First, it intelligently finds and recommends investment targets, associates data from different sources and tracks in real time, and compares investment targets with competitors in the same industry. Second, it helps to speed up the project process by realizing online tools, structured presentation of TS/SPA terms, real-time review of reports and meetings by IC portal, and intelligent reminder function of delivery. Third, during the post-investment management stage, it can import the company's operational data in batches, uses an external portal to facilitate data collection, and monitor risks in real-time to-do. Fourth, it reduces office work with the functions of automatic circulation of internal and external approval nodes, team schedule visualization, progress tracking and reviews at any time, and document data sharing.

Case 2: China Galaxy Securities—Technology Empowers PE Investment and Research Capabilities

Improving investment returns and working efficiency are the two constant themes of the PE industry, which also reflect the core competitiveness of PE, and ultimately determine whether PE institutions can survive in the fierce market competition. To bring the PE industry back to its essence, China Galaxy Securities is committed to building an intelligent service platform, creating a comprehensive and ecological service for PE companies. Since trading involves network connection, system response speed, and buying and selling decisions, Galaxy Securities meets the diversified needs of PE institutions for trading strategies, platforms, and trading speed through a diversified intervention portfolio. In a typical transaction, there is room for technology upgrades and efficiency improvement in all aspects, from data acquisition, data processing, and strategy formation to transaction execution. In the trade execution stage, Galaxy Securities provides comprehensive, specialized, and customized one-stop services that can significantly improve execution effectiveness and reduce the risk of manual operations.

In addition, Galaxy Securities provides integrated operation services, including PE creation, legal support, compliance services, operation services, product services, and financial and tax services for PE institutions through collaboration with third-party institutions, increasing efficiency for PE institutions in all aspects.

8.6 Prospects for AI Technology Application in the PE Industry

8.6.1 Technology Empowers the PE Industry

Along with the in-depth application of technology in the PE industry, various emerging digital technology tools have gradually penetrated specific modules of the industry. Technology has become a key driving force for PE institutions to cultivate core competitiveness in the digital economy. The fundamental goal of the digital transformation of PE firms is to improve managers' ability and the stable and sustainable operation of PE institutions. On the one hand, fund managers' service capability improvement through digital transformation is the basis of their market positions. On the other hand, PE institutions manage risks to earn profits, and only through continuous innovation to adapt to the changes in the external environment can they achieve sound and sustainable development.

In digital transformation, PE firms need to reach a consensus from a strategic perspective, change their perceptions in concept and seek ecological development. First, a strategy must be designed and planned systematically to form a consensus internally and form the company's digital transformation culture. Second, the company should take the initiative to change the traditional perception and improve the active management ability. Overturn of the conventional concept boosts understanding of the changes brought by digitalization and its far-reaching impact on the future. Third, the development concept of financial integration and service symbiosis should be established. The business ecosystem demands diversity, and PE institutions should participate in win–win cooperation with industry peers and service customers in a connected and open way. The PE industry serves China's real economy and national wealth management and promotes the healthy development of industry and finance ecology.

8.6.2 The PE Industry Needs to Utilize AI Technology Further

The continuous development of digital technologies and the scorching competitive market environment has pushed the PE industry to improve and optimize its service system, actively applied AI technologies to solve industry pain points, and brought customers better products and service experience (Xu and Zhao 2020). In the future, China's intelligent PE industry needs to make better use of AI technologies, such as machine learning, computer vision, natural language processing, and knowledge mapping, to penetrate deeply into the whole process of "fundraising, investment, management, and exit" (Zhao and Huang 2022). And it also promotes the continuous updating, improvement, and optimization of business links, such as intelligent customer acquisition, robo-advisor, intelligent investment research, intelligent risk control, intelligent operation, and intelligent data management.

8.6.3 Investor Education Needs to Be Elevated to a Strategic Level

Customers' demand for intelligent financial services has gradually increased, and the maturity of customers has further improved. Chinese financial customers are increasingly cautious in choosing products and services. For customers, professional financial knowledge is the base of reasonable financial decision-making. For investment service providers, more vital professional ability and management and operation capabilities can provide better customer investment service. With the rapid development of the PE industry, traditional financial advisors lag and cannot provide customized services. The demand for professional financial advisors has surged, as has the demand for intelligent professional financial advisors.

In such circumstances, PE institutions have elevated investor education to a strategic level. Customers have not yet formed systematic knowledge about intelligent services and have insufficient trust in the institutions. Some clients do not even understand the benefits of intelligent and online financial management due to a lack of experience. At the same time, due to the "digital divide", some senior customers with high wealth prefer traditional services and lack trust in intelligent financial services. Better investor education will release the demand of these customers.

8.6.4 Regulatory Technology Continues to Promote the Development of the PE Industry

Regulatory technology ushers in breakthrough development, and regulation of the PE industry is further strengthened. In the digital era, the PE industry has undergone significant changes, and regulatory technology has become critical for the sustainable development of the financial sector. New technologies represented by big data, blockchain, and AI bring great benefits, but also make regulators face more significant challenges. There is a need for regulation concerning algorithms and organizations (Haenlein and Kaplan 2019; Wang and Ma 2022).

The lagging regulatory technology has negative impacts on the finance market. First, it cannot effectively regulate China's financial management market. The uncoordinated and inconsistent regulatory mechanism makes it difficult to provide the market with rational guidance, warning, and restraint. Second, backward financial supervision cannot support the call to carry out compliance and legal innovation, so the market's multi-level and diversified investment and finance needs can hardly be met. The Guiding Opinions on Regulating the Asset Management Business of Financial Institutions released in 2018 included robo-advisors in the scope of regulation for the first time. With the implementation of the rules and regulatory technology, effective regulation will bring development opportunities and a healthier environment for innovation in the robo-advisor market.

References

Astebro TB. An inside peek at AI use in private equity. J Financ Data Sci. 2021;3(3):97–107. https://doi.org/10.3905/jfds.2021.1.067.

Ba SS, Qiong Y, Zhou G et al. China Asset Management Industry Development Report; 2020.

Bredt S. Artificial intelligence (AI) in the financial sector—potential and public strategies. Front Artif Intell. 2019;2:16.

Cao S, Jiang W, Yang BZ, Zhang AL. How to talk when a machine is listening?: Corporate disclosure in the age of AI. NBER Working Paper 27950; 2022.

Dawei Z, Qiyan H. Application and development of artificial intelligence technology in private equity investment industry. Western Finance. 2022;9:19–23. https://doi.org/10.16395/j.cnki.61-1462/f.2022.09.015. (in Chinese).

Du CL, Wang TZ, Wang CW. The development status, challenges and countermeasures of artificial intelligence chip technology in China under the digital economy. Sci Technol Manage Res. 2023;12:1–10 (in Chinese).

Financial Stability Board. Artificial intelligence and machine learning in financial services market developments and financial stability implications; 2017. https://www.fsb.org/2017/11/artificial-intelligence-and-machine-learning-in-financial-service/.

Guo XY, Liu WB, Qian Y. Status of artificial intelligence industry and technology development in China. Qual Certification. 2023;4:46–8. https://doi.org/10.16691/j.cnki.10-1214/t.2023.04.00. (in Chinese).

Haenlein M, Kaplan A. A brief history of artificial intelligence: on the past, present, and future of artificial intelligence. Calif Manage Rev. 2019;61(4):5–14.

Hickert C, Ding J. Read what top Chinese ofcials are hearing about AI competition and policy. New America; 2018. https://www.newamerica.org/cybersecurity-initiative/digichina/blog/read-what-top-chinese-officials-are-hearing-about-ai-competition-and-policy/.

Lee KF. AI superpowers: China, silicon valley, and the new world order. Boston: Houghton Mifin Harcourt; 2018.

Li Y, Zhang XJ. China's national balance sheet 2020. Beijing: China Social Sciences Press; 2021.

Qichacha Finance. ChatGPT triggers AI boom! Annual registration growth rate of domestic AI-related enterprises has been positive for 9 consecutive years [EB/OL]; 2023. 07 Feb 2023. https://baijiahao.baidu.com/s?id=1757139730742010625&wfr=spider&for=pc. (in Chinese).

Roberts H, Cowls J, Morley J, Taddeo M, Wang V, Floridi L. The Chinese approach to artificial intelligence: an analysis of policy, ethics, and regulation. AI & Soc. 2021;36:59–77.

Shenzhen Artificial Intelligence Industry Association. The white book on the development of artificial intelligence in 2022; 2022. http://www.saiia.org.cn/index.php/hangyebaipishu/. (in Chinese).

Wang QX. Research on the investor protection system of smart investment under the new "Securities Law." J Fujian Univ Financ Manage. 2021;4:27–34 (in Chinese).

Wang SH, Ma RG. The construction of the black box supervision system of the intelligent investment advisory algorithm in the context of financial data security. Soc Sci. 2022;2:86–95 (in Chinese).

Xu RH, Zhao DW. Develop artificial intelligence technology to crack the pain points of the securities industry. Tsinghua Financ Rev. 2020;8:89–92. https://doi.org/10.19409/j.cnki.thf-review.2020.08.026. (in Chinese).

Zhang S, Yao LN, Sun AX et al. Deep learning based recommender system: a survey and new perspectives. ACM Comput Surv. 2017; 52(1). https://doi.org/10.1145/3285029
Zhao DW, Li JQ. Intelligent finance era. Beijing: People's Daily Press; 2021. (in Chinese).
Zheng XL, Zhu MY, Li QB, Chen CC, Tan YC. FinBrain: when finance meets AI 2.0. Front Inform Technol Electron Eng. 2019; 20(7): 914–24.

Chapter 9
Status and Development Trend of Blockchain Application in the Private Equity Industry

As an essential part of the digital economy revolution, blockchain is rapidly developing and penetrating various fields of China's economy as a new generation of information infrastructure. Its supporting role in China's economic and social development has emerged. Blockchain technology has immutability, data storage in a distributed structure, data anonymity, value transfer, automatic network consensus, and programmable contracts. The research on these features' impact on the PE investment industry is insufficient. This chapter analyzes the current development status and applications of the domestic and international blockchain industry, and the application and prospect of blockchain technology in PE industry. It proposes future regulatory focuses for applying blockchain technology in PE investment.

9.1 Development Status and Applications of the Blockchain Industry

9.1.1 Global Perspective: The Blockchain Industry Grows in Leaps and Bounds, and Emerging Fields Gain Momentum

1. **Blockchain becomes a multi-national strategy, and cryptocurrency policy is bifurcated**

An increasing number of countries have elevated the blockchain industry to the level of national strategy and introduced various measures to encourage blockchain technology innovation and industrial development.

In October 2020, the United States government announced the National Strategy for Critical and Emerging Technologies, which considers blockchain a regulated technology to protect national infrastructure security. Most state governments in the

R. Xu and D. Zhao, *Digital Transformation of Private Equity in China*, Contributions to Finance and Accounting, https://doi.org/10.1007/978-981-99-8482-4_9

United States have clarified their regulatory stance on blockchain technology, and many state governments have enacted or promulgated laws related to the blockchain. In addition, countries including Germany, Australia, and Singapore have also clarified their policies on the development of blockchain. On September 18, 2019, the German federal government adopted and released the "German Blockchain Strategy", which believes that blockchain technology will be an integral part of the Internet in the future and can effectively promote the development of Germany's digital economy. In February 2020, the Australian government released a 52-page blockchain industry roadmap, highlighting the potential of blockchain technology and suggesting ways to design industry-specific regulatory frameworks. Singapore has also invested heavily in technology innovation, with the government allocating $12 million in December 2020 to promote innovation and the adoption of blockchain for commercial use. Singapore is seen as a strong forerunner since it already has regulations in place, including its Payment Services Act and its Digital Token Payment Act, and is in the process of issuing regulations related to stablecoin issuances (KPMG 2023).

While blockchain technology is being researched and developed, countries are also strengthening the supervision of the virtual money market. China has long banned domestic trading of virtual currencies, and has successively issued policies to crack down on virtual currency trading and "mining" activities. Despite many cryptocurrency investors and blockchain companies in the United States, there is no clear regulatory framework for virtual currency. While the United States Securities and Exchange Commission (SEC) generally treats cryptocurrencies as a security, the Commodity Futures Trading Commission (CFTC) refers to bitcoin as a commodity, the Ministry of Finance refers to it as a currency, and the Internal Revenue Service (IRS) classifies cryptocurrencies as property for federal income tax purposes. Cryptocurrency transactions in the United States fall under the regulation of the Bank Secrecy Act and must be registered with the Financial Crimes Enforcement Network (FinCEN).

Meanwhile, countries including the European Union, Canada, Japan and Australia have clarified cryptocurrencies' asset classes and adopted an aggressive policy. Cryptocurrencies are legal in most parts of the European Union, with governance and taxation varying by individual member countries. Canada classifies crypto investment companies as a money services business, and cryptocurrencies are taxed similarly to other commodities. Cryptocurrency trading platforms and dealers can operate upon registration, and Canada became the first country to approve a bitcoin exchange-traded fund (ETF) in February 2012. According to the Payment Services Act, Japan recognizes cryptocurrencies as legal property and treats the transactions income generated as "miscellaneous income" and taxes investors accordingly. Australia classifies cryptocurrencies as legal property, subject to capital gains tax, and exchanges can operate freely. In the United Kingdom, cryptocurrencies are considered property. Cryptocurrency exchanges must register with the Financial Conduct Authority (FCA) and are prohibited from offering crypto derivatives. Investors are required to pay capital gains tax on profits from crypto transactions. On September 7, 2021, Saldova's Bitcoin Act came into effect, making it the first country to adopt bitcoin as a legal tender.

2. **Blockchain spending grows in scale, and the banking sector takes the lead**

Blockchain and other distributed ledger technologies show great potential to improve the efficiency of business operations and create new ways of delivering value. Various industries and companies are implementing these technologies and integrating them into infrastructure and industry planning. According to Statista, global spending on blockchain solutions is expected to reach almost $19 billion by 2024.[1]

According to the Global Blockchain Survey 2021: The New Age of Digital Assets released by Deloitte, which surveyed a sample of 1,280 executives and practitioners in 10 regions around the world, the vast majority of participants (80%) said that the solutions provided by the blockchain, digital assets or cryptocurrencies would bring new revenue streams to their industries.

According to the China Academy of Information and Communications Technology (CAICT), the number of new blockchain enterprises worldwide has declined, and the industrial pattern has taken shape. Driven by the traction of new technologies such as NFT, Web3.0, and meta-universe, the number of new blockchain enterprises worldwide in 2021 saw a rapid growth momentum. As of September 2022, there are 6,914 blockchain-related enterprises in the world. The number of blockchain enterprises in China and the U.S. still leads the world, with a combined share of 52% (CAICT 2023).

In addition, by industry, the banking industry is in a leading position in blockchain adoption, followed by telecommunications, media and entertainment, manufacturing, healthcare and life sciences, retail, and consumer goods. Blockchain adoption of retail and consumer goods is expected to grow fastest by 2024.

3. **Major economies are exploring central bank digital currencies**

Central Bank Digital Currency (CBDC) is a digital currency backed and issued by central banks. As cryptocurrencies become increasingly popular, central banks worldwide are more willing to issue CBDCs. The Atlantic Council's GeoEconomics Center launched the Central Bank Digital Currency (CBDC) Tracker to provide the latest information for global CBDC research. Figure 9.1 shows the number of countries with CBDCs in exploration phases. By the first half of 2023, 109 countries actively explored or engaged in CBDCs across various phases. Among these countries, 45 were involved in research, 32 were engaged in development, and 21 were in the pilot stage.

Several countries have now fully launched CBDCs. On March 31, 2021, the Eastern Caribbean Central Bank (ECCB) launched its central bank digital currency, DCash, thereby becoming the first monetary union central bank to issue a CBDC. In the Caribbean, digital cash systems are being implemented in countries including the Bahamas, Saint Kitts and Nevis, Antigua and Barbuda, Saint Lucia, and Grenada.

Nigeria launched e-Naira on October 25, 2021, becoming the first country outside the Caribbean to issue a CBDC. In addition, among the world's four major central banks (Federal Reserve of the United States, European Central Bank, Bank of Japan,

[1] https://www.statista.com/statistics/800426/worldwide-blockchain-solutions-spending/.

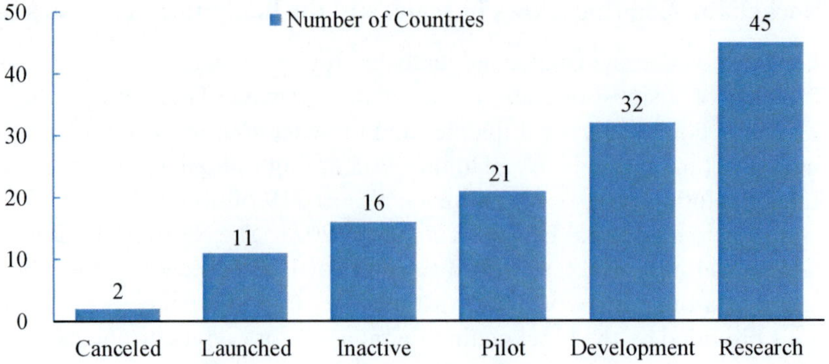

Fig. 9.1 Number of countries with central bank digital currencies (CBDCs) in exploration phases (by Phase Status). *Sources* Finbold.com, Statista.com, Atlanticcouncil.org

and Bank of England), the Federal Reserve is the only central bank that has not committed to a digital currency testing program.

Fourteen countries, including China (digital currency named e-CNY) and South Korea (Digital Won), are currently in the pilot phase of CBDCs and are preparing for a possible full launch.

9.1.2 Domestic Perspective: The Blockchain Industry is Steadily Advancing, and the e-CNY Achieves Promising Results

1. **Policy for the development of blockchain technology, rectification of virtual currency trading, and "mining" activities**

The blockchain technology has entered the Chinese government's official publicly released documents since 2016. In October 2016, the Ministry of Industry and Information Technology (MIIT) released the "White Paper on China's Blockchain Technology and Application Development (2016)" (MIIT 2016). In December 2016, the blockchain technology was listed as a strategic frontier technology in the State Council's "13th Five-Year Plan" national informationization plan, which is necessary for achieving the preemption of the new generation of information technology.

In China, The development of blockchain technology has become a national-level strategy in 2019. During the 18th collective study of the Political Bureau of the Nineteenth CPC Central Committee, General Secretary Xi Jinping stressed that "blockchain should be taken as an important breakthrough in independent innovation of core technologies", "clarify the main direction, increase investment, focus on conquering some key core technologies, and accelerate the development of blockchain technology and industrial innovation".[2] Since then, the central and local governments have been putting forward various supportive and regulatory policies to accelerate the development of blockchain technology.

In March 2021, blockchain was included in the Outline of the 14th Five-Year Plan (2021–2025) for National Economic and Social Development and Vision 2035 of the People's Republic of China, which proposed to build a digital China and promote the development of digital industries. Emerging digital sectors, including artificial intelligence, big data, blockchain, cloud computing, and cybersecurity, will be grown stronger, and the quality of such industries as communications equipment, core electronic components, and critical software will be improved. At the local government level, as of September 2022, 29 provinces and municipalities have included the development of blockchain technology in their 14th Five-Year Plans, and 319 blockchain industrial policies have been issued, covering a wide range of industries or fields such as government data sharing, finance, supply chain and logistics, healthcare, and agriculture (CAICT 2023).

In June 2021, the Ministry of Industry and Information Technology (MIIT) and the Office of the Central Cyberspace Affairs Commission (Cyberspace Administration of China, CAC) jointly issued the "*Guidance on Accelerating the Application and Industrial Development of Blockchain Technology*", focusing on supply chain management, product traceability, data sharing and other areas of the real economy. Promote the integration of blockchain applications to support the digital transformation of industries and high-quality industrial development. Promote the application of blockchain technology in public services such as government services, evidence collection, and smart cities, and support the transparency, equality, and accuracy of public services.

In January 2022, blockchain is listed as one of the key sectors to enhance innovative capabilities in "14th Five-Year Plan for the Development of the Digital Economy." In the same month, the CAC and 15 other departments (including the MIIT, the PBC) jointly announced a list of national blockchain innovation and application pilots (CAC 2022). The initiative covers 15 pilot zones and 164 entities in various industries, and aims for the large-scale implementation of blockchain technology across businesses and government organizations in China. The notice states that the pilot should explore the full role of the blockchain in promoting data sharing, optimizing business processes, reducing operating costs, improving collaboration efficiency, and building a credible system. In the same year, related government departments accelerated the construction of blockchain in transportation and justice. For example, in May 2022, the Ministry of Transport issued *Guidelines for the Construction of an Electronic Platform for Imported Dry Bulk Cargoes Import and Export Business Based on Blockchain*, emphasizing the applications of the blockchain technology in the transportation industry; the Supreme People's Court issued the *Opinions of the Supreme People's Court on Strengthening the Judicial Application of Blockchain*, proposing to give full play to the role of blockchain in promoting judicial credibility, serving social governance, preventing and solving.

[2] https://www.gov.cn/xinwen/2019-10/25/content_5444957.htm.

While supporting the innovation of blockchain technology in industrial applications, China has also maintained a suppressive stance on cryptocurrencies since 2021. It is mainly due to the potentially illegal activities and market disruption related to virtual currencies.

In September 2021, the People's Bank of China issued the Notice on Further Preventing and Disposing of the Risk of Speculation in Virtual Currency Transactions. It further specifies the attributes of virtual currencies and virtual currency-related activities, proposes a working mechanism to deal with the risk of speculation in virtual currency transactions, and strengthens the regulation. On September 22, 2020, President Xi Jinping announced at the UN General Assembly (UNGA) that China would aim to reach peak CO_2 emissions before 2030 and achieve carbon neutrality by 2060. Virtual currency mining, as a project with high energy and power consumption, must be strictly controlled in the target context.

In early March 2021, the Inner Mongolia Development and Reform Commission issued a draft for comment, proposing clean up and shut down virtual currency mining projects. Subsequently, Xinjiang, Qinghai, Sichuan, Yunnan, and other provinces have carried out similar activities. On September 24, the National Development and Reform Commission and 11 other departments jointly issued a Notice on Rectification of Virtual Currency Mining Activities. The action was followed by Jiangsu, Zhejiang, Fujian, Jiangxi, and Hainan provinces.

2. **The number of blockchain-registered enterprises continues to rise, and the industry is about to enter a "steady recovery period"**

Since 2021, the number of blockchain-registered enterprises has continued to rise. According to the website "Blockchain Home" of the National Computer Network Emergency Response Technical Team/Coordination Center of China (CNCERT/CC),[3] by the end of December 2021, more than 93,600 blockchain-related enterprises have been registered in China. Regarding regional distribution, the density of blockchain-related enterprises is high in coastal areas and Sichuan, Chongqing, Jiangxi, and Hainan provinces. The coastal province Guangdong accounts for about 37.23% of total blockchain-registered enterprises, the highest density in the country. In terms of business forms, blockchain applications and solutions account for 36.4% and 29.8%, and blockchain infrastructure (12.24%), industry services (11.90%) and underlying platform (9.56%) together constitute a complete business pattern.

Gartner, a leading consulting firm, published a report named *Hype Cycle for ICT in China, 2021* to evaluate the emerging technologies in China. According to the report, China's blockchain technology is about to complete the process of transition from the "sliding into the trough" stage to the "climbing the slope" stage, and the next step is "entering the plateau", which is expected to be mature and effective in a broader range (Gartner Research 2021). According to the White Paper on Blockchain 2022 published by the CAICT, China's blockchain industry has formed a relatively perfect industrial chain, consisting of over 1,400 blockchain enterprises. According to Statista, the market size of blockchain applications in China increased from 0.33

[3] https://www.cert.org.cn/publish/english/index.html.

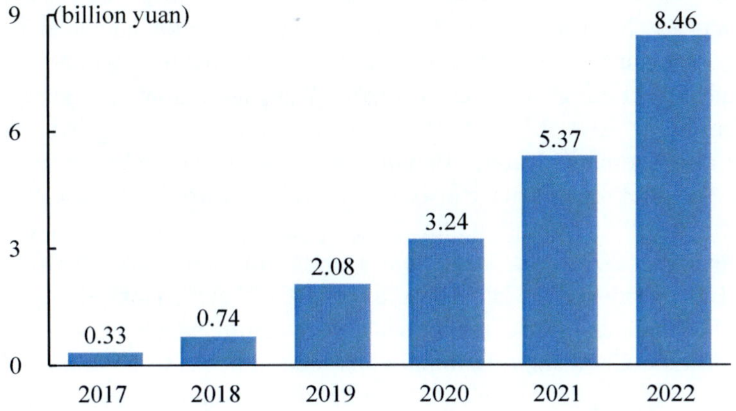

Fig. 9.2 Blockchain market size in China 2016–2022 (in billion yuan). *Source* Statista

billion yuan to 8.46 billion yuan in 2022[4] (Fig. 9.2), and was projected to surpass 27 billion yuan by 2025 and nearly 69 billion yuan by 2030.

Asset management and public services are essential scenarios for blockchain applications. In addition, blockchain has equally important applications in some emerging scenarios. For data sharing and privacy computing, the use of massive data in the era of the digital economy requires the blockchain to be combined with various data security technologies (Zhao et al. 2021). In addition, emerging fields such as non-fungible token (NFT) and meta-universe are also in a vigorous development stage, with technology giants and other startups exploring relevant application scenarios.

3. **E-CNY needs to overcome three challenges**

The e-CNY is a digital form of legal tender issued by the People's Bank of China (PBC), which aims to meet the public's cash demand in the digital economy. It is supported by a reliable, stable, fast, efficient, continuously innovative, and open competitive financial infrastructure in the retail payment sector. It is expected to promote the development of China's digital economy, enhance the development of inclusive finance, and improve the operation of the monetary and payment system. It will support the development of China's digital economy, strengthen financial inclusion and improve the efficiency of the monetary and payment system.

In 2014, the PBC set up a legal digital currency research group to conduct special research on the framework, key technologies, issuance and circulation environment, and relevant international experience. In 2017, the PBC established the Digital Currency Institute to study digital currency issuance and the commercial operation framework. In late 2017, with the approval of the State Council, the PBC began to organize commercial institutions to jointly carry out research and development experiment of legal digital currency (e-CNY). The research and development test has completed the top-level design, function development, and system debugging.

[4] https://www.statista.com/statistics/1285636/china-blockchain-market-size/.

In October 2020, based on the "4 + 1" closed pilot launched in Shenzhen, Suzhou, Xiongan New Area, Chengdu, and the 2022 Winter Olympics, six pilot sites were added, including Shanghai, Hainan, Changsha, Xi'an, Qingdao, and Dalian, thus forming a "10 + 1" pilot layout. At the same time, six provinces, including Guangzhou, Zhejiang, Tianjin, Fujian, Jinan, and Hubei, which were initially not listed as the pilot regions, have also been considered striving for e-CNY pilot in the 14th Five-Year Plan or other policy documents.

In November 2021, Mu Changchun, Director of the Institute of Digital Currency of the PBC, introduced the latest progress of e-CNY at the Hong Kong Fintech Week 2021. Mu Changchun also mentioned three significant challenges to the official launch of the e-CNY. First, terminal construction needs to be improved. Although the current e-CNY pilot project has been operating smoothly, the construction of the system usage environment is still on the way. Second, the security and risk management mechanism needs to be improved. The system must be safe and stable during the whole life cycle of the e-CNY. Therefore, the security management of the operating system must be ensured, including encryption algorithms, financial information security, data security, and business continuity. Third, the regulatory framework should be further clarified. The newly released *Law of the People's Republic of China (Draft for Comments)* has included physical forms of cash and e-CNY. Based on updating the original laws and regulations, e-CNY must be supplemented by different regulatory measures and management methods.

The e-CNY has so far been used mainly for domestic payments. The pilot of digital RMB has been accelerating. By the end of 2022, the pilot program had been expanded to 26 pilot areas in 17 provinces (cities and districts), including: Beijing, Tianjin, Hebei Province, Dalian, Shanghai, Jiangsu Province, Zhejiang (Hangzhou, Ningbo, Wenzhou, Huzhou, Shaoxing, Jinhua), Fujian (Fuzhou, Xiamen), Shandong (Jinan, Qingdao), Changsha, Guangdong Province, Guangxi (Nanning, Fangchenggang), Hainan Province, Chongqing, Sichuan Province, Yunnan (Kunming, Xishuangbanna), Xi'an. There are 10 digital RMB operating financial institutions, namely Industrial and Commercial Bank of China, Agricultural Bank of China, Bank of China, Construction Bank, Bank of Communications, Postal Savings Bank, China Merchants Bank, Industrial Bank, Alipay, and WeChat Pay. A number of application modes have taken shape in wholesale and retail, catering, tourism and payment of administrative fees, which cover both online and offline scenarios.

In July 2023, former central bank governor Yi Gang revealed the progress of e-CNY at an event organized by the Monetary Authority of Singapore (MAS). As of June 2023, the cumulative transaction volume of e-CNY reached 1.80 trillion yuan, and the e-CNY in circulation had reached 16.50 billion yuan, taking account of only 0.16% of the cash in circulation in China.[5] The total number of e-CNY transactions

[5] The PBC has included e-CNY in the statistics of currency in circulation (M0). The official website of the PBC showed that since December 2022, "currency in circulation (M0)" includes e-CNY in circulation.

reached 950 million,[6] and 120 million wallets were opened. The figures cement China's position as a leader among countries developing a CBDC (Reuters 2023; MyPayPass 2023).

9.2 Blockchain Application in the PE Industry and the Prospects

Blockchain is a technical solution for maintaining a distributed database through a decentralized approach. It is a sequence of correlated data blocks generated using cryptographic methods, each containing information about network-wide transactions over time, for verifying the validity of the information and generating the next block of data. These data blocks are connected like a chain and share information. Generally speaking, blockchain can be regarded as a distributed network bookkeeping technology. Its technical features, such as sharing, encryption, and immutability, enable it to provide encrypted and open bookkeeping services and allow participants to obtain accurate account records of their money, property, or other assets.

9.2.1 Advantages of Applying Blockchain to PE Investments

First, the decentralized structure, information immutability, distributed bookkeeping and storage, and blockchain's programming flexibility help solve the problems of efficiency bottlenecks, transaction delays, fraud, and operational risks prevalent in the financial services sector. As summarized by Ali et al. (2020), blockchain brings financial sector benefits, including increased transparency of transactions, improved traceability and reduced risk of fraud, and beneficial impact on pricing and costs in the market.

Second, under the existing technical conditions, blockchain can effectively solve the technical problems in PE investment, such as low frequency, miscellaneous documents, data loss, complex processes, and third-party custody risks, and can significantly improve the efficiency of transactions and reduce irregularities such as black box operations.

Third, the PE over-the-counter market is more compatible with the scenarios of blockchain-distributed bookkeeping and other functions, and is also more suitable for the application of blockchain technology. The over-the-counter market comprises real-name transactions, non-guaranteed settlement and clearing, relatively discrete transactions, low real-time requirements, and low liquidity. It is relatively easy to

[6] As of August 31, 2022, the cumulative number of e-CNY transactions in the pilot areas is 360 million and the cumulative transactions amount 100.04 billion yuan, meaning that the transaction volume increased by nearly 1700% in 10 months.

correct transaction errors and has a higher tolerance for global risks. Compared to a more centralized clearing procedure, the decentralized clearing process can also solve bankruptcy and liability issues (Csóka and Herings 2018). Therefore, it is more likely to make substantial breakthroughs if blockchain is applied in over-the-counter markets such as regional equity trading markets, inter-institutional markets, and brokerage counter markets. It will be conducive to optimizing the construction of PE investment platforms, which is significant in improving the equity market in the multi-level capital market and the domestic direct financing system.

Fourth, blockchain technology can improve the valuation of intangible assets in PE investment. The evaluation of intangible assets is a complex problem, especially with the rise of new high-tech enterprises with a high proportion of intangible assets. The application of blockchain technology can make the price of equity assets more transparent, reduce information asymmetry and thus make the equity value closer to the intrinsic values, making the valuation of intangible assets more accurate. Besides, a substantial amount of valuable data is generated on the Internet by every individual, and blockchain technology is a potentially viable solution to data islands and a tool for establishing data ownership, while ensuring genuine and reliable information and minimizing the costs of data acquisition by credit agencies (Ali et al. 2020). In addition, an essential benefit of blockchain adoption is identified by Chod et al. (2020), that is, blockchain technology helps firms to secure favorable financing terms at lower signaling costs.

Fifth, blockchain technology helps improve equity exit regulation. The inaccuracy and lack of timeliness of equity information reduce the effectiveness of the law. Specifically, PE regulation delay may be related to untimely updates of equity information in the centralized system, and the long-standing communication issues between regulatory authorities. Equity information inconsistencies may further increase the difficulty of regulation. Blockchain technology can ensure the uniqueness and validity of equity information because registration and transaction of equity information is recorded in the equity trading platform and is immutable. Besides, since the data is open and transparent on the blockchain, the relevant parties will be urged to update the data promptly, thus solving the problem of poor timeliness.

9.2.2 Technical Analysis of Blockchain Application for PE Investment Platform

For data storage, blockchain can establish a decentralized data flow platform, which can track the whole process of data transactions, ensure the immutability of transaction data and the reliability of data sources, and effectively avoid large-scale data loss or leakage caused by attacks on centralized institutions or mishandling of permissions. For data management, blockchain data is accompanied by time tags, verified and recorded by a consensus mechanism, and cannot be tampered with or forged

(Wang et al. 2021). It can realize equity asset confirmation, authorization, and real-time monitoring. It can also prevent error information from being generated in transactions. For the transaction process, the decentralized structure of blockchain can spontaneously generate credit. It uses blockchain-automated smart contracts[7] and accessible programming to realize automatic clearing and settlement, which can avoid the complicated clearing process and high clearing costs of traditional centralized clearing systems and realize convenient equity asset transactions. At the same time, the instantaneous arrival and settlement of blockchain-based transactions also make equity asset transactions more efficient, economical, and safer.

The blockchain-based PE platform generally consists of two layers. The bottom layer is a blockchain P2P-style network for creating each user's account, recording transactions, and interconnecting accounts to form a decentralized distributed ledger. The upper layer mainly stores users' data, and uses the data to realize various platform functions, including equity registration, purchase, and transfer. On the platform, each user has a private key after opening an account, and no one can obtain the account's data without authorization. If a user needs to buy, sell or transfer equity assets, the platform will call the underlying blockchain and write the assets' basic information to the counterparty's blockchain account by executing a smart contract, realizing instant settlement, and quickly recording the changes. During the transaction process, information acquisition and registration of equity changes, provision and acceptance of transaction-related services, issuance of commission orders, settlement, and delivery are all carried out on the blockchain-based platform. Each transaction record is clearly and accurately recorded on the blockchain, which all blockchain nodes can query. Each node in the same blockchain network has a replicated copy of the blockchain, and the damage to any node does not affect other nodes and the entire network, ensuring the platform's security.

9.2.3 Application Scenarios of Blockchain in PE Investment

1. **Transaction Records**

In November 2015, Nasdaq officially launched Nasdaq Linq, an equity management system for private companies based on blockchain technology. As an essential part of Nasdaq's PE market, Linq's primary function is not to trade, but to design a way to keep many equity paper credentials and worksheets in the financing process for investors. Blockchain will provide a more accurate solution for PE back-office operations on the platform. All parties established a strong trust relationship and are confident in protecting their interests.

[7] A smart contract is a set of conventions defined in digital form, including agreements on which contract participants can enforce these conventions. Smart contracts can be automatically executed in blockchain according to a default contractual agreement without trusting a third party (Egelund-Müller et al. 2017; Sun et al. 2018; Paulavičius et al. 2019).

Linq's demonstration effect has led some institutions in the industry to design blockchain depository structures. According to media disclosures, global capital management giant Northern Trust has carefully operated a PE blockchain technology platform. The platform stores information such as equity issuance, fee calculation, income distribution, and contribution requests involved in financing, investment, and exit, which can be accessed anytime.

2. **Due Diligence**

Blockchain technology can make due diligence more effective.

Investors do due diligence because of information asymmetry. The startup company may not disclose detailed information during the initial communication with investors. Generally, investors do due diligence after the related parties agree on some intentional terms, such as investment amount, shares, and priority rights.

It is a challenge to understand more about the actual internal situation through due diligence and then make judgments and decisions on whether to invest and how to invest. And blockchain will provide the solution. The entrepreneurial team can encrypt and store the due diligence information on the blockchain and decrypt and release the appropriate information to investors when required.

(1) **Blockchain technology helps investors understand the entrepreneurial team**

Uploaded information on the blockchain is immutable and can be synchronized to credit investigation and judicial authorities, which largely guarantees the credibility of the data. On the blockchain, through effective authorization and permission control, the resume of the entrepreneurial team can be verified, especially the learning and working experience of the team members and proof of no crime of the core team members. The education and working experience of the entrepreneurial team can be verified to consider whether their ability matches entrepreneurship. The past cooperation records of the entrepreneurial team can be viewed and used as a reference for risks of future disputes or disagreements. At the same time, due to the traceability of blockchain information, investors will leave traces on the blockchain. In addition, cryptographic designs such as zero-knowledge proof can be carried out if needed to verify the identity experience without directly providing explicit information, which guarantees the security of the personal data of the entrepreneurial team.

(2) **Blockchain technology helps investors conduct financial due diligence**

Blockchain technology will effectively assist investors in conducting due diligence on the financial situation of the entrepreneurial team. It can store not only the financial data but also the financial process of the entrepreneurial team.

On the one hand, the blockchain collects the company's financial statements for all years to compare the historical performance of the company and understand its growth. On the other hand, the blockchain can be docked to the electronic visa agency to provide solutions for financial processes. The application process and results will be stored in the blockchain to offer credible materials for investors to understand the company's financial operations.

(3) **Blockchain technology helps investors conduct legal due diligence**

Blockchain effectively assists investors in conducting legal due diligence. The legal due diligence involves many contracts, agreements, and documents. The information is important and sensitive, and highly confidential. Like the entrepreneurial team information query, confidential company information security can be guaranteed on the blockchain through effective authorization, authority control, and cryptographic design such as zero-knowledge proof.

3. **Index Compilation**

In recent years, the PE index has become a hot research topic for major PE institutions, custodian banks, and research institutions. Relevant indices are compiled by integrating different industries, countries, client types, global capital flows, and other factors to obtain operable information from the data. In practice, clients can use the index to compare the performance of submarkets or various investment opportunities to optimize or adjust asset allocation. State Street Bank and Cambridge Associates compiled some of the well-known PE indices.

However, compiling the index requires a large amount of customer data. Effectively using customer data without revealing their identity and assets becomes a major concern. Blockchain provides a solution. The blockchain model changes the traditional "labor-intensive" process of manually generating price indices from the customer's transaction data after obtaining their permission. Customer data will be protected through the encryption settings of the blockchain. Using smart contracts, customers can authorize the institution's data access through signatures. After authorization, various data types will be used to support index compilation through smart contracts. It is even possible to customize the design so that the institution does not see the data content, and every data retrieval will be recorded in the blockchain.

9.2.4 Examples of Blockchain Applications in the PE Industry

There have been many successful cases of blockchain technology applied to PE investments. The most representative is the PE trading platform Linq, officially launched by NASDAQ Exchange in October 2015 and jointly developed with the blockchain technology company Chain. It is an equity trading and financial service platform based on Bitcoin's blockchain technology. It can solve the problems of data errors or human tampering and improve the efficiency of trading. In addition, blockchain equity trading platform projects such as Overstock, Equibit, Bitshares, and Hyperledger Fabric have been put into market use or are in trial operation (see Table 9.1). Many foreign stock exchanges or financial institutions also invest in research and development and trials of blockchain equity trading platforms.

In China, trials and applications of blockchain in PE investment are emerging. TERS is a well-known blockchain equity registration system, announced in June

Table 9.1 Some foreign blockchain equity trading platform projects

Financial institution or company	Projects	Development
Overstock	TΦ	In August 2015, the United States company Overstock announced the launch of an equity trading platform TΦ, which is believed to be the world's first blockchain-based equity trading platform. It provides services for share trading and clearing of non-listed "unicorn" companies
Nasdaq	Linq	In October 2015, the Nasdaq exchange officially launched Linq, a PE trading platform based on Bitcoin blockchain technology. It is jointly developed by Nasdaq and blockchain technology company Chain, and completed its first transaction in December 2015
EDC	Equibit	In November 2016, EDC, a Canadian blockchain technology company, announced the establishment of its equity trading platform Equibit. The crowdfunding is completed in 2017
NorthernTrust	Hyperledger Fabric	In February 2017, NorthernTrust, a top North American private bank, released its Linux-based blockchain PE trading platform developed jointly with IBM, claiming to be the world's first fully functional blockchain equity trading platform
Bitshares	Bitshares	Bitshares, established in 2013, is a decentralized trading platform that can trade various forms of digital assets. It launched its equity trading business in 2016. By the end of 2017, three projects with a market capitalization of 100 million dollars (peerplay, yoyow, obits) had been traded on the platform

2016 by Taiyi Cloud Technology, the first blockchain company listed on the National Equities Exchange and Quotations, and the Northern Industrial Equity Exchange. The launch of TERS makes the Northern Industrial Equity Exchange the first equity exchange in China to try to use blockchain technology. In January 2018, ShareX, launched by potential stock blockchain startups, was entrusted with the equity transfer plan of well-known companies such as Ant Financial Services. In addition, blockchain startups such as YI,[8] Bubi Tech[9], and SharesLink have also made progress in developing blockchain equity crowdfunding and trading platforms.

[8] https://www.xiaoyi.com/.

[9] https://www.bubi.cn/.

9.2.5 *Prospects of Blockchain Technology Applications in the PE Industry*

Blockchain technology can improve the transaction efficiency of PE investment. Blockchain technology ensures immutability so that the transaction and registered information cannot be easily modified, and credibility is enhanced accordingly. Each transaction is recorded on the blockchain at a fast speed, which ensures efficiency and accuracy. In addition, blockchain technology simplifies the transaction process, enhances information and communication efficiency, automatically generates smart contracts, and releases the asset by delivering tokens and generating the asset's code.

Blockchain technology can improve the credibility of private equity registration. China's business registration legally provides for formal review only. The registration of information is a corporate action that shareholders themselves cannot perform, which may cause agency risks. Knowledge of equity registration on blockchain enhances the credibility of the information due to its transparency and immutability. By using blockchain, equity holders can check the company's equity registration and rely on the blockchain to ensure the data's trustworthiness, reducing agency risks. In addition, blockchain technology also enhances the authenticity of equity registration. The registration information for shareholding is scattered. The shareholders' register is an internal document, and retrieving such data requires a high cost. The use of blockchain technology for shareholding registration enhances the authenticity and accuracy of the shareholding registration information, since the stakeholders ensure the accurate and effective transmission of information for their interests.

Blockchain technology empowers supervision and enhances regulatory efficiency. Blockchain technology integrates equity information and covers all the transaction information. Such complete data is convenient for regulators to conduct complete big data analyses. The authenticity of information on blockchain help reduces the use of regulatory resources and costs. The information on the blockchain is real-time, and every transaction will be fed back to the blockchain in time, enhancing the timeliness of supervision and avoiding the regulatory lag caused by the slow update of equity information.

9.3 Future Regulatory Focuses on Blockchain Application in PE Investment

Given the significant advantages and bright prospect of blockchain application in PE investment, it is foreseeable that the construction of blockchain PE investment platform will enter a rapid development stage and the market will continue to expand. However, significant risks are also brought by blockchain technology, including legal risks, security risks, and operational challenges (Ali et al. 2020; Wang 2022; Cao 2023; Deng 2023). In this regard, how to better monitor the application of blockchain technology in PE investment has become a common concern of the industry and academia.

9.3.1 Emphasis on Security Maintenance of Platform Operation

Every network platform provider must ensure the security and reliability of its platform, but the situation of PE platforms is more complex. If a blockchain PE platform generates unexpected systemic errors or crashes due to hardware defects (such as insufficient computing power) or software vulnerabilities, all platform users would face operational difficulties, and there is no individual solution. Because the hardware involved is distributed and independent in the network, integrity, availability, continuity, security, and accuracy are closely related to the centralized platform system. Once the platform system collapses, all equity transactions or transactions related to financial assets on the platform will not be carried out normally, and the complexity of the economic disputes caused is positively associated with the scale of the platform and the amount involved, which may have a considerable impact on the real economy. In addition, system docking and compatibility issues in competition and mergers between platforms, and network accidents, such as viruses or hacker intrusion, can also trigger similar risks. For example, in June 2016, the DAO, a famous blockchain Ethereum project in the United States, was attacked by hackers, and users lost more than 50 million dollars. Many disputes arising from the accident have not been fully resolved.

Given the importance of node users and the whole market, it is necessary to formulate relevant regulations to address the security issues of PE platforms. When the platform system crashes or is attacked, actions may include suspension of transactions, rollback or cancellation of transactions for different situations, and mediating the interests and risk relationship between platform providers, network service providers, and users. In addition, attention should also be paid to issues such as competition or mergers between platforms and access of platform participants, which also affect the security of platform operations. Giving full play to the predictability of laws and regulations can ensure the platform's adaptability to unexpected security issues, and avoid or reduce the overall risk.

9.3.2 Address Potential Risks of Smart Contracts

Smart contracts demand different regulatory treatments from traditional contracts (Cong and He 2019). A vital aspect of the blockchain PE platform operation is allocating and acquiring assets through smart contracts. Its implementation is entirely determined by the internal rules of the blockchain, namely, code and algorithms, and enforced, significantly improving the efficiency and security of equity transactions. When there is a default or other suspension events, a smart contract may suspend the implementation of the contract content automatically and then automatically calculate the repayment amount and execute it according to the code conditions, such as the contract default terms, or implement measures such as transferring the relevant collateral to the auction.

However, smart contracts still have defects. Smart contracts are flexible in content programming but inflexible in execution after programming. Once a smart contract is written and implemented, it will be executed strictly according to the code. It will not be able to react and adapt to changes in circumstances, force majeure situations, or other changes in the transaction process. Even if an unexpected problem occurs after the agreement is signed, the program in the smart contract will continue to be strictly executed until the end of the operation or error. The lack of flexibility will easily lead to transaction risks, causing unnecessary losses, and even the risk of bankruptcy. Exemption and the corresponding technical means of smart contracts in risk management, authorization, and due diligence are still blank, affecting the wide use of smart contracts. In addition, there are still potential vulnerabilities in smart contracts, which hackers may use to disrupt regular transactions. The DAO incident is a typical case.

Moreover, in addition to the programming defect, the unclear legal status of smart contracts is also an obstacle to implementing the dynamic adjustments, especially regarding the highly subjective unfairness or integrity issues. It requires contract law or relevant laws and regulations to clarify the legal nature and effect of smart contracts and then set up abstract rules that can be adapted to certain situations. Suppose notary offices, judicial authentication centers or regulatory agencies become blockchain nodes. In that case, they can directly deal with the disputes among stakeholders and risks brought about by the strict implementation of smart contracts.

9.3.3 Set up "Supervision Account" to Control Illegal Financial Activities

PE platforms may be used to commit financial crimes, such as money laundering, illegal fundraising, terrorist financing, or other illegal securities activities, such as insider trading and market manipulation. Blockchain technology can potentially improve governance regulation, especially regarding security and accessibility (Warkentin and Orgeron 2020; Lu 2018). Therefore, regulators must track and review specific transaction data and information through blockchain-based PE platforms.

Regulators can set up "supervisory accounts" on blockchain-based platforms and use privileged functions of the account to check all blocks in the blockchain, obtain the required transaction data, and screen the data according to timestamps to track and audit suspicious transactions more effectively. The privileged functions may include synchronizing various types of information in the blockchain in real-time, freezing or unfreezing assets in specific accounts, conducting penetrating reviews of specific accounts, suspending or resuming trading, and mandatory transferring or rolling back particular transactions. The privileged operation instructions can be sent by the "supervisory account" to specific smart contracts employing a message signed by the private key, triggering the corresponding privileged operation actions. The blockchain-based platform can appropriately increase the design of privileged operation requirements to support the "supervisory accounts" and properly incorporate centralized mechanisms to facilitate more active and traceable audit arrangements, streamline the regulatory process, and reduce regulatory costs.

9.3.4 Legislation and Policy Recommendations for the Regulation of Blockchain-based PE Investment Platforms

Blockchain's applications in the PE industry require thoughtful modifications of existing legal and regulatory frameworks combined with new legal solutions (Yeoh 2017; Yu et al. 2022). On the one hand, tight regulation at early stages could be counterproductive. Going by this, it is further claimed that regulators should not intervene yet but rather find ways to accommodate new approaches within existing frameworks than risk the stifling the innovation with overly prescriptive rules (The Economist 2015). Others believe that excessive reliance on the automation of laws, contracts, and information flows could lead to the tyranny of codes (Lee et al. 2015). It poses the adaptability challenge for legal frameworks.

1. **Modify or formulate existing relevant laws and regulations**

The primary task of blockchain financial regulation is to amend or formulate relevant legal rules and supplement the provisions related to the financial application of blockchain so that the laws and regulations can guide and regulate the application and development of blockchain in the financial industry. For example, the contract law should be modified to clarify the legal attributes of smart contracts, including the nature, constituent elements, and the rights and obligations of participating subjects. The property law should be amended to clarify the confirmation of data and information ownership, the establishment, change, or extinction of usufruct rights, and security interests of virtual property. The company law should be revised to confirm the registration of shareholding changes on the blockchain-based platform, record the election of the shareholders' meeting and board of directors, and record the effectiveness of the decisions of the shareholders' meeting and the board of directors. Financial laws such as securities, commercial banking, and bill law should be amended accordingly. At the same time, special regulatory rules should be formulated to address the operational risks of blockchain-based PE investment platforms, potential risks of smart contracts, and "supervisory accounts" to regulate and standardize the operation of blockchain-based PE investment platforms in a more targeted and efficient manner.

2. **Formulate and implement unified standards for blockchain applications in PE investment**

Research shows that the common foundation of cross-regional blockchain financial regulation lies in developing and implementing uniform standards for blockchain finance. Basic protocols such as TCP/IP on the Internet stipulate the basic format and corresponding rules for information transmission and management on the Internet. Only by unifying various standards can blockchain financial regulation cover the whole industry and be effective. The R3 blockchain consortium, formed in 2015 by top banks such as Citibank, Bank of America, and HSBC, is working to develop a unified standard for blockchain banking applications. In May 2016, the Chain Open Standard 1, an open-source blockchain financial application protocol, was announced jointly by a blockchain technology provider, Chain, and well-known financial institutions, including Citigroup, Fidelity, and NASDAQ.

China has also explored this field. Led by the ChinaLedger, 11 commodity, equity, and financial asset exchanges began to create an open-source blockchain protocol in May 2016, and develop cross-industry standards to ensure regulatory compliance. It is suggested that China's financial regulators can take the lead in studying and developing unified standards and rules for blockchain PE applications and in cooperation with various industry associations, regional equity markets, Internet trading platforms, and other units. It can be used to develop rules for enhancing platform security, preventing potential risks of smart contracts, and establishing "regulatory accounts". It will enable effective regulation of blockchain PE investment platforms and PE markets.

3. **Adopt the "regulatory sandbox" approach to supervise innovation projects in blockchain-based platforms**

A regulatory sandbox is an innovative financial regulatory mechanism in which financial regulatory authorities test innovative financial projects within a certain period and scope to verify the operation of their innovative financial products and services. During the test, the regulatory authorities lower the target projects' entry threshold and appropriately relax the regulatory restrictions. For projects that pass the test, the regulatory authorities can permit the relevant authorized institutions to promote the project. For projects that fail to pass the test due to adverse impacts during the trial, the regulator can request to stop the project within a certain period. Through the regulatory sandbox, regulators can effectively prevent and control the spread of financial risks while promoting fintech innovation.

The supervision of blockchain-based PE investment platforms can also adopt the regulatory sandbox approach. Blockchain-based PE platform projects that apply for sandbox testing may operate in a designated PE market "special zone". The market performance will be carefully observed during the test, and risks will be strictly controlled. For blockchain-based PE platforms that operate well in the trial, regulators could publicize the test results and legal status, allowing them to serve the market. The regulators can use the regulatory sandbox to facilitate the development and innovation of blockchain-based PE platforms and accumulate experience for formulating relevant policies and measures by participating in the regulatory sandbox to fully understand the financial nature, risks, and operational practices of innovative projects. At the same time, during the pilot stage of innovative financial products or projects, regulators can use the buffer period during the test to build a regulatory framework based on feedback information to introduce relevant regulatory policies or regulations promptly after the innovative products or projects are launched.

References

Ali O, Ally M, Dwivedi Y. The state of play of blockchain technology in the financial services sector: a systematic literature review. Int J Inf Manage. 2020;54: 102199. https://doi.org/10.1016/j.ijinfomgt.2020.102199.

Cao X. Legal risks and regulatory path of blockchain finance. Investment Cooperation. 2023;2:13–5 (in Chinese).

China Academy of Information and Communications Technology. (2023). White Paper on Blockchain (2022); 2023. http://www.caict.ac.cn/english/research/whitepapers/202303/t20230316_416842.html.

Chod J, Trichakis N, Tsoukalas G, Aspegren H, Weber M. On the financing benefits of supply chain transparency and blockchain adoption. Manage Sci. 2020. https://doi.org/10.1287/mnsc.2019.3434.

Cong LW, He Z. Blockchain disruption and smart contracts. Rev Financ Stud. 2019;32(5):1754–97.

Csóka P, Herings PJJ. Decentralized clearing in financial networks. Manage Sci. 2018;64(10):4681–99. https://doi.org/10.1287/mnsc.2017.2847.

Cyberspace Administration of China. Sixteen departments including the CAC jointly announced a list of national blockchain innovation and application pilots; 2022. http://www.cac.gov.cn/2022-01/29/c_1645059212139691.htm.

Deng L. Crime risk in blockchain finance and its prevention and control. J Jiangxi Police College. 2023;2:22–9 (in Chinese).

Egelund-Müller B, Elsman M, Henglein F, Ross O. Automated execution of financial contracts on blockchains. Bus Inf Syst Eng. 2017;59(6):457–67.

Gartner Research. Hype cycle for ICT in China; 2021. https://www.gartner.com/en/documents/4003537

KPMG. The pulse of Fintech H1 2023, 2023–7. https://assets.kpmg.com/content/dam/kpmg/xx/pdf/2023/07/global-pulse-of-fintech-h123-report-web.pdf.

Lee JA, Long A, Steiner S, Handler SG, Wood Z. Blockchain technology and legal implications of 'crypto 2.0'. Bloomberg BNA Banking Report. 2015.

Lu Y. Blockchain and the related issues: a review of current research topics. J Manage Anal. 2018;5(4):231–55. https://doi.org/10.1080/23270012.2018.1516523.

Ministry of Industry and Information Technology. White paper on the development and application of blockchain technology in China (2016). Beijing: Ministry of Industry and Information Technology of the PRC; 2016. (in Chinese)

MyPayPass. Yi Gang: Digital RMB transaction volume reached 1.80 trillion, an increase of nearly 1,700% in 10 months. 1 Aug 2023; 2023. Access at https://www.mpaypass.com.cn/news/202308/01174506.html.

Paulavičius R, Grigaitis S, Igumenov A, Filatovas E. A decade of blockchain: review of the current status, challenges, and future directions. Informatica. 2019;30(4):729–48.

Reuters. China's digital yuan transactions seeing strong momentum, Says Cbank Gov Yi. July 19; 2023. Access at https://money.usnews.com/investing/news/articles/2023-07-19/chinas-digital-yuan-transactions-seeing-strong-momentum-says-cbank-gov-yi.

Sun Y, Fan L, Hong X. Technology development and application of blockchain: current status and challenges. Strategic Study Chin Acad Eng. 2018;20(2):27–32.

The Economist. The promise of the blockchain: the trust machine: the technology behind bitcoin could transform how the economy works. The Economist. 2015.

Wang X, Mei J, Zhang Z, Xie X. Research on the mechanism of blockchain technology to equity management innovation. Converter. 2021;2021(7):441–8.

Wang Y. Financial regulatory risk governance and mechanism construction under blockchain technology. Heilongjiang Finance. 2022;4:77–80 (in Chinese).

Warkentin M, Orgeron C. Using the security triad to assess blockchain technology in public sector applications. Int J Inf Manage. 2020;52: 102090. https://doi.org/10.1016/j.ijinfomgt.2020.102090.

Yeoh P. Regulatory issues in blockchain technology. J Financ Regul Compliance. 2017;25(2):196–208.

Yu P, Gong R, Sampat M. Blockchain technology in China's digital economy: balancing regulation and innovation. In: Regulatory aspects of artificial intelligence on blockchain. IGI Global; 2022. pp. 132–157. https://www.igi-global.com/chapter/blockchain-technology-in-chinas-digital-economy/287688.

Zhao XF, Zhang SH, Lu T, Dai BR, Li C. Blockchain service system design for private equity. Comput Appl Softw. 2021;10:33–8 (in Chinese).

Chapter 10
International Practice of Technology Applications in the Private Equity Industry

Accelerated digitalization has transformed financial institutions and markets (FSB 2019, 2022),[1] and different countries adopted various regulatory approaches to supervise fintech development, which in turn affects the development of the fintech industry (World Economic Forum 2017; JD Finance 2017). The application of technology in the PE industry has become diversified and popularized (Guan 2017; Hu 2022). This chapter explores the practice of technology application in the PE industry by reviewing the practice of representative companies in the United States, the United Kingdom, Japan and Singapore, which has certain reference significance for developing China's PE industry.

Generally, traditional financial institutions embrace technology advancement to improve services, explore business model innovation, and strengthen risk management. They either partner with technology companies, spin off their fintech, or both. Fintech companies have broadly engaged in business lines, such as payments, wealth management, lending, digital banking, insurance, and credit scoring. In China, the fintech market is dominated by internet giants[2] such as Baidu, Ant Financial, Tencent (known as "BAT"), and JD Finance, which use their large customer bases and datasets to build an integrated ecosystem of financial services, including payments, financing, wealth management, insurance, etc. (Mahoney 2019; Xu and Xu 2020).

[1] The FSB has been investigating how innovation is transforming financial institutions and markets. Although markets have developed differently across jurisdictions, there are commonalities that warrant international discussion (FSB 2019). Impacts of innovation on jurisdictions depend on the state of development of the financial services industry and the regulatory environment. In addition, FSB (2022) find that the COVID-19 pandemic has accelerated the trend toward digitalisation of retail financial services.

[2] China's regulatory authorities have implemented new requirements to enhance the regulation of large non-financial companies that have significant interest in financial services (Carstens et al. 2021).

R. Xu and D. Zhao, *Digital Transformation of Private Equity in China*, Contributions to Finance and Accounting, https://doi.org/10.1007/978-981-99-8482-4_10

10.1 The United States Uses Digital Systems to Manage Funds and Create Artificial Intelligence Services

The United States PE industry has a history of nearly 100 years, accounts for more than 50% of the global PE market scale, and has become a leader in the market. Private funds, crypto assets, fintech, data analytics, initial public offerings, and Special Purpose Acquisition Companies are five of the key capital market trends identified by the Chair of SEC Gary Gensler (2021). In the digital era, technology is gradually integrated into the PE industry in the United States. Big data analysis is used to guide investment decisions, and emerging technologies are used to develop digital platforms, launch intelligent investment products, construct digital systems to encrypt capital management, and strengthen the dynamic monitoring of risk. Technology empowers the PE industry, creating more diverse operational channels and broader investment space.

10.1.1 JPMorgan Chase[3] Develops Multiple Technology Tools to Empower Investment Services

1. **Use big data to analyze customer habits and provide a reference for decision making**

JPMorgan Chase established the JPMorgan Chase Institute, aiming to combine the power of big data analysis with information from 30 million customers to build a more granular snapshot of the economy and help policymakers make more informed decisions. It uses big data technology to access the daily transaction habits of tens of millions of customers, measure individual responses to weekly and monthly income fluctuations, and conduct data mining to portray consumer business profiles. The big data collected by JPMorgan Chase Institute is updated quarterly to provide a continuous source of rich data for deeper analysis across 15 key industries. In addition, it also analyzes residents' shopping preferences based on massive transaction data, uses fluctuations in residents' income and expenditure to analyze possible investment directions, and provides ideas for developing investment advisory products that can inform PE investments. Big data analysis is also applied to investment guidance for small businesses. It analyzes small businesses' job and financial status by analyzing payroll data and provides recommendations for investors. JPMorgan Chase leverages its vast consumer and corporate accounts network to build big data and analyze the United States investment market environment, providing strong support for its innovative investment advisory products and guiding PE investments.

[3] https://www.jpmorganchase.com/.

2. **Develop a blockchain platform to process private transactions**

JPMorgan Chase established the Blockchain Center of Excellence to develop blockchain technology and launch a licensed blockchain platform, Quorum, designed to meet the needs of financial institutions and corporations to process private transactions (Choo 2021). In February 2019, JPMorgan Chase launched a cryptocurrency[4] JPM Coin, to address the expensive and inefficient settlement process in financial markets with volatile cryptocurrency prices. JPM Coin is pegged to the U.S. dollar and can be exchanged for $1 from JPMorgan Chase's bank account and used to track cash for compliance and instant settlement of payment transactions between customers. When connected to the public blockchain network through a hybrid platform, JPMorgan Coin can interoperate between JPMorgan Chase's private ledger and a secure, scalable public blockchain. By doing so through the hybrid network, JPMorgan Chase benefits from the liquidity and market access of the public blockchain, while ensuring privacy and security through the permission chain.

3. **Adopt artificial intelligence technology to adjust investment portfolios**

JPMorgan Chase launched its robo-advisor product "You Invest" in July 2019, renamed "Self-Directed Investing" after two years of operation, to recommend and automatically adjust investment portfolios. It adopts a "zero commission + account opening bonus" model to attract new customers, gradually establish a stronger bond with them, and increase user stickiness. Self-Directed Investing not only builds portfolios to match individual consumers' risk preferences, financial goals, and time horizon, but also automatically adjusts to optimal portfolios by monitoring changes in market conditions, product values and other relevant factors in real time, thus helping customers improve investment returns. The application of artificial intelligence technology has enabled JPMorgan Chase to absorb a large amount of capital quickly, generated massive revenue for the company, and contributed to the flourishing of the United States PE market.

10.1.2 Morgan Stanley[5] Develops Proprietary Platform to Provide Services

1. **Use big data technology to monitor risks in real-time**

Morgan Stanley places great emphasis on data-driven and digital transformation and considers data to be the most critical asset[6] that can be used to enhance the firm's

---

[4] In September 2022, the U.S. releases the First-Ever Comprehensive Framework for the Responsible Development of Digital Assets, which guides responsible innovation, ensuring U.S. leadership in the global digital asset ecosystem.

[5] https://www.morganstanley.com/.

[6] As a new type of production factor, data is the basis of digitization and intelligence, and has been profoundly changing the modes of production, lifestyle and social governance (CAICT 2022).

services and increase revenue. To this end, Morgan Stanley has built its own user information database containing massive customer and business data and processed, high-value business data (wire data). Wire data provides the most comprehensive and intuitive view of business operations and is highly valuable. Data transmitted over massive networks is reconstructed into structured data in real-time, faults can be easily located, and troubleshooting is carried out accordingly, which meets the business needs without affecting the production system. Compared to Internet big data, this data source is more timely, comprehensive, and insightful and can show the status of the application stack and the entire delivery chain. Morgan Stanley has been using "Hadoop" technology since 2010 to build an infrastructure that meets its rapidly growing big data needs. Hadoop technology can efficiently process structured and unstructured data, analyze data in real-time, help companies identify problems quickly, and follow up on investment projects. Hadoop technology provides Morgan Stanley with a scalable, flexible, and powerful portfolio analysis solution. The agile ecosystem built by Morgan Stanley with Hadoop and other open-source architectures has a long life cycle and is highly innovative. The company constantly improves its data collection, filtering, and analysis tools to make better decisions.

2. **Use artificial intelligence to provide investment advisory services**

Morgan Stanley believes that artificial intelligence-driven services have changed how people search for financial services, making it critical for financial advisors to serve consumers anytime and anywhere. The company's Next Best Action (NBA) core platform and Goals Planning System (GPS) is the foundation for a robust fintech ecosystem that provides online trading, investment advice, big data analysis, and a range of other services to the wealth management departments. The main functions of NBA platform are to provide investment advice, issue operational alerts and help investment advisors handle daily trivial matters. The GPA system is used to identify and quantify clients' long-term investment objectives and to keep tracking on a cyclical basis. According to client needs, the NBA platform and GPS integrate complementary software to maximize user experience and wealth management efficiency. On the advisor side, intelligent investment advisors process clients' personal preferences and market changes through sophisticated algorithms and provide customized investment recommendations to wealth advisors. On the client side, the company has started to provide individual and exclusive investment advisory services to investors since December 2017 through the self-developed digital investment platform "Access Investing". Clients with more than $5,000 in investments regularly received investment advice, portfolio performance, market updates, and Morgan Stanley's internal research reports with investment guidance. Morgan Stanley continues to upgrade its smart technology systems to better serve clients and improve business efficiency through artificial intelligence and machine learning, enabling financial advisors to easily provide accurate answers to complex consumer questions and extend business coverage.

Countries and enterprises work together to construct a data factor market, and release the value of the data.

10.1.3 Citigroup[7] Promotes Company Growth Through Multiple Partnerships

1. **Use big data technology to improve service efficiency**

Citigroup has recently adopted a big data-driven strategy to promote business growth, improving service efficiency and quality. To meet customers' demands for speed and convenience, Citigroup launched new e-commerce and digital wallet solutions. Citi Pay SM, a tokenized omni-channel digital wallet, promotes tokenization of digital payment, certifies multiple issuance platforms, and leverages massive amounts of customer wallet data to build analytics models. It significantly improves response rates, efficiency, balance, and spending retention rate, thereby reducing the cost of acquiring data and delivering services. Citi also uses new models to deconstruct data as granularly as possible and synthesize structured and unstructured data sources to discover where most effective areas of big data, and leverages technology capabilities to address individual business cases. Big data analysis is then applied to customer retention and the acquisition and analysis of transaction records to detect anomalies. The practice helps Citigroup algorithmically analyze target market data, identify or predict problems promptly, and correct customer transaction anomalies in advance. Citigroup has built its big data integration platform architecture that cleans up duplicate data and reduces data migration costs, enables data to be retrieved promptly, and ensures that data accurately matches commonly used enterprise reference models.

Regarding delivering payments, Citigroup's Treasury and Trade Solutions (TTS) provides integrated cash management and trade finance services to multinational corporations, financial institutions, and public sector organizations worldwide. With the industry's most comprehensive digital platforms, tools, and analytics TTS leads the way in providing innovative and tailored solutions to its clients. Its products include payments, receivables, liquidity management and investment services, working capital solutions, commercial card programs, and trade finance. Based on the belief that customer experience drives sustainable differentiation, TTS has been committed to achieving business transformation by developing capabilities, customer advocacy, network management, and service delivery to provide a seamless end-to-end customer experience and achieve convenience, cost savings and risk reduction. Leveraging big data technology, Citigroup also uses a variety of technology strategies to help clients optimize working capital globally. Optical character recognition continues to drive back-office innovation to improve efficiency and enhance the customer experience.

2. **Introduce artificial intelligence to optimize business processes**

In December 2018, Citigroup invested in Privitar, a UK-based data privacy company, and introduced artificial intelligence technology to help clients make fast, data-driven decisions. It ensures data security and privacy through more intelligent machine learning and cloud computing use. Citi enhanced its capabilities to focus

[7] https://www.citigroup.com/citi/.

entirely on providing solutions, not products, to its institutional clients. TTS offers the industry's most versatile and powerful digital platforms, tools, and analytics. Citigroup also cooperates with fintech company HighRadius to create and launch "Citi Smart Match," which uses artificial intelligence and machine learning technology to significantly improve the efficiency and automation of the cash application process, matching outstanding invoices with payments received by corporate customers. Citi has partnered with Ernst & Young and Seth Software to develop an advanced risk-scoring engine using artificial intelligence. The program can simplify the time-consuming and highly manual processes of reviewing large volumes of global trade transactions while ensuring compliance. The project helps Citigroup optimize processes from the back office to the front office by expanding the use of digitalization, automation, and advanced analytics. The real-time solution can more effectively detect transactions with potential compliance issues in advance,[8] manage and compare a large number of data points in transactions, provide more information and data to help decision-makers review global trade transactions, transform the traditional manual process into an artificial intelligence process, streamline the processes and improve service efficiency. Additionally, Citigroup's payment outlier detection solution, available in 90 countries or regions, uses advanced analytics, artificial intelligence, and machine learning to identify unusual payments proactively and allows customers to review, approve or reject such unusual payments through Citi's institutional e-banking platform. Making full use of artificial intelligence and machine learning technology, Citi has strengthened the control and monitoring of payments and met customers' expectations for speed in processing payments.

3. **Invest in blockchain to develop business**

Citigroup has partnered with Nasdaq to launch a pioneering blockchain and global banking integration, using distributed ledger to record and transmit payment instructions to achieve direct payment processing and automatic reconciliation. Real-time visibility of payment transactions on the blockchain ledger improves operational efficiency and simplifies reconciliation. Effective integration of blockchain technology and global financial systems can achieve greater operational transparency and ease of reconciliation. The partnership also combines blockchain technology with Citi's global network using API technology. Citigroup provides payment processing services for "Allianz Global Corporate & Specialty SE" and successfully pilots blockchain technology for a global proprietary insurance program that facilitates cash transfer between countries. By partnering with leading digital ecosystems, Citigroup has embedded its services into the platforms customers use daily, thus improving customer participation. Citigroup and Chicago Mercantile Exchange Group jointly announced the launch of a blockchain platform that helps both groups reduce logistical-related costs and shorten financing time, freeing up billions of dollars in collateralized funds. Using this system to improve efficiency, Citigroup can achieve

[8] The volume of regulatory change was expected to increase, and this was seen as a compliance challenge for both corporate boards and compliance officers. Respondents of a survey by Thomson Reuters Regulatory Intelligence (2023) said that the overall cost of compliance staff was expected to increase.

real-time monitoring of collateral and instant confirmation of clearing house transactions. By investing in blockchain technology, Citigroup can reduce labor costs and increase efficiency. In January 2019, Citigroup invested in Symbiont, a blockchain technology platform, to promote the development of data management, mortgage loans, private equity, and syndicated lending. The use of blockchain technology helps Citigroup achieve its customer-centric mission and facilitates active collaboration with customers, providing synergies, cost savings, rationalization, and mergers and acquisitions for Citi's growth.

10.2 The United Kingdom Establishes Big Data Centers and Cloud Platforms to Explore Development Paths

The United Kingdom is a global leader in the development and regulation of PE funds and hedge funds, and other PE fields. It has comprehensive regulatory and policy support systems, high-tech investments, and applications, which have important implications for China's fast-growing PE industry. For fintech, the UK government was early to recognize the importance of fintech and has strongly supported the development of the sector. In 2014, HM Treasury proposed to build the UK into a world fintech center. In the 2017–2018 Business Plan published by the Financial Conduct Authority (FCA), FinTech and RegTech are prioritized for development (FCA 2017). The United Kingdom is working to create the right regulatory environment to support a sustainable crypto and digital assets ecosystem, represented by the "regulatory sandbox" tools for fostering fintech (Ernst and Young 2016; KPMG 2023). In 2023, the UK passed the Financial Services and Markets Act 2023, which includes measures to enhance the UK's leadership and competitiveness in the financial services and fintech spaces. In particular, the Act enables changes meant to make the UK an attractive place to IPO, sets the foundation for regulating crypto assets to promote adoption, and establishes sandboxes to facilitate testing new technologies in the sector. The Bank of England is committed to embracing fintech to deliver its mission by upgrading its payments infrastructure to enhance security and support innovation and its regulatory rules and regulations to mitigate potential risks (Bank of England 2019; Gispert and Chatain 2023). The United Kingdom's PE firms establish data centers and cloud platforms to meet the needs of investment business expansion and clients' investment. In addition, some companies set up internal R&D centers to attract professional talents, develop artificial intelligence technology, and empower the company's highly efficient operation.

10.2.1 *Actis Capital[9] Exerts Efforts to Improve Customer Satisfaction*

1. **Establish data centers and expand the market**

Actis Capital attaches great importance to sustainable infrastructure. It has partnered with technology companies to build data centers in Asia and Africa, leveraging the growing demand for digital infrastructure to enhance its Internet Data Center (IDC) capabilities. Through its data centers, Actis Capital offers world-class, operator-neutral data center programs to international users. The data centers provide exclusive consulting services covering technical and design requirements, efficiency improvements, cost reductions, and operational monitoring. By continually introducing innovative ways to engage users, the data center tailors messaging applications for Asian customers to ensure the company can maintain a leading position in the competition. The data center monitors data in real-time and anticipates the explosive growth of IT, domestic and international consumption, e-commerce, and digital banking. The company has a growing need for data storage. Data localization is more convenient than cloud storage and can reduce data transfer latency issues, so the data center is gradually shifting from cloud storage to data localization. A decentralized content hosting strategy facilitates timely data extraction, analysis of customer consumption information, and more efficient investment advice to customers. The company also actively explores the integration of artificial intelligence and data centers. The proliferation of artificial intelligence-based applications has become one of the growth drivers of data centers. Data centers have also become physical assets to accommodate the "brains" of artificial intelligence.

2. **Establish a cloud platform to increase customer stickiness**

Actis Capital has partnered with Indian companies to build a cloud platform in India and launch innovative products through the cloud platform. The products include targeted customer participation activities, consumer analysis, in-store consumer financing of partner brands, and online customized products for customers. The innovative products connect customers and products in real-time, generate over $1 billion in consumer credit annually, and contribute to customer loyalty. The cloud platform enables customers to receive the company's services more conveniently, avoid the confusion of information inconsistency caused by multiple terminals, and reduce reconciliation costs and the risk of information mismatching. The cloud platform helps companies analyze customers' consumption preferences in detail by integrating and summarizing their past consumption information, thus simplifying the service process, accurately providing customers with investment and consumption solutions, and enhancing customer stickiness.

3. **Introduce artificial intelligence to improve customer experience**

---

[9] https://www.act.is.

Actis Capital believes that emerging markets have successfully leapfrogged the mobile phone and banking industry and that artificial intelligence will likely have a similar growth trend. The data of digital transactions via smartphones is a key driving factor of artificial intelligence development. The company promotes financial inclusion by introducing artificial intelligence algorithms, which can capture value from vast undeveloped data accessed via smartphones. Artificial intelligence breaks through regional restrictions to regularly provide tailored and secure investment solutions for customers worldwide. Customers also enjoy various value-added services, including instant installment payments, access to different rewards, loyalty programs, and instant discounts. Artificial intelligence enables fast and insightful service and decision-making and provides clients value-added services and multiple options to improve their investment experience.

10.2.2 Apax Partners[10] *Explores New Ideas by Leveraging Digital Transformation*

1. **Create a Digital Service Platform**

Apax Partners emphasizes digital transformation, building digital services platforms in partnership with high-tech companies to create a digital edge. It sees accelerating demand for digital products and platforms across all industries, making it the next step to becoming a global leader in technology services. It plans to provide cutting-edge technology solutions to its clients, contributes to developing critical skills, and builds strong customer loyalty for the next generation of technology creators. It supports customers' success by building superior PE and capital solutions digital platforms.

Apax Partners establishes joint ventures to accelerate the development of investment products and technologies, leveraging advanced digital and cloud technologies to expand in key markets. In such a way, it supports investments of Apax and the customers, promotes the rapid expansion of products and capabilities, and provides a new level of end-to-end, cloud-based investment solutions. In particular, in insurance investments, Apax Partners helps its customers shape and deliver leading digital technology, using new technologies to develop and expand its property and casualty technology solutions. The solutions support a full range of functions from underwriting, policy administration, and agency support to rating, billing, and claims, encompass all aspects of insurance investment, and enable customers to make insurance investments more secure and convenient.

Apax Partners also has agreements with global information technology companies to provide Internet technology services and software products for customers in the investment industry. The services and products include consulting, business optimization, and extensive expertise in mobility, data analytics, big data, testing, and

[10] https://www.apax.com/.

application development. The software products business consists of a suite of core software products in the banking, financial services, and vertical insurance fields. In addition, Apax Partners cooperates with leading Italian Internet technology service and solution providers to offer innovative solutions for designing and implementing digital transformation, improving customer experience and customer satisfaction. The solutions include digital customer engagement, next-generation Internet technology infrastructure, cloud financial services solutions, cybersecurity, Internet of Things, and big data.

2. **Use artificial intelligence to provide services**

Apax Partners has partnered with UK-based artificial intelligence company Faculty to develop an AI-as-a-Service model using artificial intelligence technology. The AI-as-a-Service model can be applied across Apax's businesses, from optimizing its marketing expenditure to more accurate projections of customer investment needs and predicting client investment risks and stresses. Apax Partners believes that too many organizations fail to realize the value of artificial intelligence due to a lack of tools to integrate it into business. In the era of intelligent technology, Apax Partners needs high-performance technology to release the power of data and maximize the impacts, which helps clients make better, more effective, and robust investment decisions and improve return on investment. By introducing artificial intelligence through cooperation, Apax Partners guides customer investments, provides advice, and offers powerful, fair, and interpretable artificial intelligence tools and advanced data privacy, enabling them to realize the tremendous value of artificial intelligence.

10.2.3 Man Group[11] Builds a Professional Team and Enhances Services with Technology

1. **Create a big data platform to serve customers**

Man Group recognizes that responsible investment is the foundation of fiduciary responsibility to customers and beneficiaries, thus creating a group-wide big data platform to support investment decisions and risk management. By developing big data technology, building an internal data repository, and introducing data analytics tools, Man Group can ensure that its investment and sales teams have the necessary data and reporting capabilities to enhance and support customer relationships. Man Group integrates multiple data sets into a coherent whole. It develops a powerful analytics engine, Remote observation System Automation (ROSA), to aggregate analytics in an internally developed system. The system can combine internally generated data with datasets from various third-party data providers and query them through intuitive custom query tools. To improve the speed and stability of the big data analysis engine, Man Group created a separate centralized data repository, Cortex,

[11] https://www.man.com/.

which is the source of all data for customer reports and internal assessment of fund performance. Man Group created an in-house proprietary big data platform that can integrate and analyze data, improve the ability to add frameworks for additional data sets, manage benchmark links to funds, and meet its intuitive and efficient reporting goals. On this basis, Man Group also provides clients with rich investment deposit and risk analysis so that customers can better understand their investment status and accept the investment guidance proposed by the Man Group.

2. **Introduce a cloud platform to develop a trading platform technology**

The trading platform technology is responsible for cutting-edge technology solutions for Man Group's asset management and trading business, including a wide range of functions such as portfolio management, order management, sales and marketing, trade execution, accounting, operations, compliance, regulatory reporting, and risk. The group builds dedicated teams and a trading platform through in-house and third-party, local, and cloud-based solutions. In addition, the trading platform technology is committed to improving customer experience and maintaining customer stickiness through continuous platform improvements, architecture tools, and models, business analytics, project management, design, development, data management, and visualization. The group has also partnered with professional technology companies to provide cloud-hosted sales and marketing content management solutions and use powerful cloud platform tools to update data dynamically. By building an internal hybrid cloud through Digital Recycle, the group reduces start-up costs, monitors investment and risk data in real-time, and provides more professional services for customers.

3. **Establish Oxford-Man Institute for Quantitative Finance to study artificial intelligence techniques**

The group established the Oxford-Man Institute for Quantitative Finance (Oxford-Man Institute) in 2007. By collaborating with the University of Oxford in artificial intelligence technology, the group hired outstanding quantitative talents to lead the research work, promote communication within and between the group and academia, help improve the group's approach and guide practical investment activities. Artificial intelligence, particularly machine learning technology, plays a helpful role in the group's investment management, helping the group to research and develop faster system investment strategies and algorithms for trade execution and intelligent order routing. Through the learning and development of artificial intelligence technology, the group continues to improve its investment management strategies and guide the investment direction, becoming a pioneer in the PE industry in using technology for market trend tracking and trade path optimization.

10.3 Japan's PE Industry Innovation Through Artificial Intelligence

Japan is a leader in Asia's PE markets. Technology leads the innovative development of the Japanese PE industry, and provides high-quality services to companies. This subsection discusses the application of technology in the Japanese PE industry, taking Ant Capital Partners and Nomura Group as examples. One approach is to set up specialized agencies. Ant Capital Partners set up a special support office for "Artificial Intelligence (AI)/Digital Transformation (DX)". A second approach is to use AI technology to promote machine learning fully. Nomura Group actively develops new asset management methods using cutting-edge technologies such as machine learning. A third approach is introducing quantum cryptography and quantum computer technology to address potential risks. Nomura Group verified the application of quantum cryptography technology in the financial field.

10.3.1 Ant Capital Partners[12] Establishes "AI/DX" Support Office

Ant Capital Partners is one of the fastest-growing PE firms in Japan, and is the top PE firm in the small-cap M&A sector in Japan. Its three merger and acquisition funds established since 2001 have attracted total committed capital of $331 million, three secondary market investment funds launched since 2003 have attracted total committed capital of $284 million, and three venture capital funds launched since 2004 have attracted total committed capital of $216 million. Ant Capital Partners, which typically acts as a lead investor in venture capital investments, is a leader in secondary market PE investments in Japan and East Asia.

Technology plays a pivotal role in Ant Capital's PE investments. The AI/DX support office is dedicated to facilitating the digital transformation of PE investments by replacing systems, introducing business intelligence tools, and helping portfolio companies improve business growth potential through AI-based data analysis and Internet of Things strategies.

The AI/DX support office comprises experts in fields including artificial intelligence, data science, cybersecurity, and system construction and provides the best strategic planning and advice according to the environment. In addition, Ant Capital guides on general Internet technology issues and tailors services to its invested companies. For example, a restaurant with multiple branches may be worried about assigning employees according to their hospitality skills, work shifts, and other factors. The AI/DX support office can set up a unique system for the restaurant to quantify the skills of each employee and the impacts on sales to help the invested company make appropriate staff assignment and replenishment decisions.

---

[12] https://www.antcapital.jp/.

10.3.2 Nomura Group[13] Improves Service Quality Through Artificial Intelligence

The Nomura Group is a global financial services organization that provides investment advisory services to domestic retail investors and securities brokerage services, securities underwriting services, investment banking advisory services, asset financing, merchant banking, asset management, and financial management services to global clients. Nomura Capital Partners was established in 2018 as the PE arm of the Nomura Group. It manages the group's main investment businesses and provides equity solutions for corporate restructuring, revitalization, business succession, and management buyouts using its capital.

1. **Improve efficiency through artificial intelligence**

(1) **Integrate artificial intelligence and social media to develop new indices**

Nomura Securities, a Nomura Group company, has developed two indicators, "SNS x AI Business Confidence Index" and "SNS × AI Industrial Production Index" as part of the Ministry of Economy, Trade and Industry's Internet of Things business initiative (New Index Development Business Using Big Data).[14] Specifically, the SNS x AI Business Confidence Index leverages AI to gather tweets related to business sentiment from an online sample, automatically assigning a score to the sentiments based on how negative or positive they are. The SNS × AI Industrial Production Index also uses AI to mine information regarding work or the economy, and predict the Industrial Production Index using machine learning. The indices are published weekly.

The two indices have the following characteristics. First, they are highly instantaneous. The weekly frequency facilitates more rapid investment decisions. Second, collecting and analyzing data through artificial intelligence is cheaper than questionnaires. Third, it has a large sample size. Existing economic indicators, such as the Economy Watchers Index for Current Conditions, are based on questionnaire surveys, and the sample size is generally limited to a few thousand. In the "SNS × AI Business Confidence Index", artificial intelligence can extract about 15,000 tweets from social media. The large sample size is conducive to improving prediction accuracy and providing more diversified opinions.

(2) **Develop new asset management methods using cutting-edge technologies**

Nomura Group continues to develop new asset management models based on its unique perspective and approach to providing clients with more investment opportunities.

Nomura Asset Management is researching and developing new asset management technologies using advanced techniques, including machine learning. Some of the research results have been presented at Association for the Advancement of Artificial Intelligence (AAAI) and the International Joint Conference on Artificial Intelligence

---

[13] https://www.nomuraholdings.com/jp/innovation/.

[14] https://www.nomuraholdings.com/innovation/.

(IJCAI), the world's top conferences in artificial intelligence. For example, new portfolio optimization recommendations based on extreme risk scenarios, a versatile stock price forecasting method that can be applied to various market analyses.

2. **Refer to quantum cryptography and quantum computer technology**

The Nomura Group is actively introducing quantum cryptography and quantum computer technology to the financial sector. On the one hand, with the increasing threat of cyber attacks in recent years, the digital transformation of financial institutions has been accelerating, and the system cooperation between companies has been strengthened. Since the environment surrounding the system has also changed significantly, there is an urgent need to enhance security measures further.

On the other hand, cryptography, which secures data communications inside and outside systems, has long been considered free from the risk of being deciphered by third parties because it requires highly complex calculations and long computation times. However, with the rapid development of quantum computer technology capable of breaking passwords quickly, the potential threat is increasing, and new security measures are urgently needed to address future threats.

In December 2020, Nomura Holdings, Nomura Securities, the Japan Institute of Information and Communication Technology (NICT), Toshiba, and NEC Corporation jointly launched the verification of the effectiveness and practicality of quantum cryptography technology in financial practice for the first time in Japan. The main focus is the applicability of quantum cryptography in the financial sector. Nomura Securities plans to use pseudo-data (fictitious data) such as customer information and stock trading information to verify the impacts of quantum cryptography on stock trading operations. It requires transactions to be processed within a millisecond and requires high-capacity, high-speed communications.

10.4 Singapore Uses Big Data and Blockchain Technology to Promote PE Investment

Singapore is a model for the growth of the PE industry. Singapore's PE industry attaches great importance to the application of technology, establishing special departments or institutions to promote the use of technology and innovation and using blockchain technology to enable individuals and organizations to control their data. Meanwhile, Singapore actively implements favorable policies to guide the development of the fintech industry (Monetary Authority of Singapore 2020). In 2015, against the backdrop of building a "smart country", the Singapore government actively promoted the development of fintech industry ecology in combination with its financial industry foundation. In 2016, Singapore established a Fintech Office to promote the development of Fintech, designated a National Research Foundation to fund fintech companies and researchers, and introduced the "regulatory sandbox" to provide a good institutional environment for the development and innovation of the fintech industry. In 2023, with the US increasing scrutiny of crypto platforms,[15] other jurisdictions have gained more prominence in the eyes of investors and start-ups, including Singapore and Japan (KPMG 2023). This subsection explores Temasek and CapitaLand practices as examples.

10.4.1 Temasek Creates a Platform to Optimize Financial Services Using Blockchain Technology

Temasek, founded in 1974, is a privately incorporated holding company overseen by the Singapore Ministry of Finance and is a major player in Singapore's national economy. The Ministry of Finance has 100% ownership of the company. Temasek's primary business is asset management, focusing on capital investment and financial management. It primarily makes equity investments without setting limits on geographic regions, industries, or asset classes. The investments focus on financial services, favoring technology industries and emerging services.

1. **Establish Aicadium,[16] a global center of excellence**

In August 2021, Temasek's AI Working Group established Aicadium, its global AI technology and solutions center of excellence. It works with Temasek's portfolio companies to attain better business outcomes and explore new business opportunities. It promotes the adoption of AI technologies and related solutions to meet better the needs of its global portfolio companies and other enterprises to deploy AI technologies to improve business conditions.

With its global team of scientists and engineers, Aicadium is unique that its process of building platforms using AI algorithms, models, and tools is repeatable and scalable. It can provide customers with novel, high-quality, low-risk solutions to address challenges such as predictive maintenance, quality assurance, and employee safety, or high accuracy natural language processing across languages and scenarios. For example, suppose a regional bank's asset management department wants to increase the asset under management by improving the accuracy of demand prediction. In that case, Aicadium's predictive engine can analyze relevant market indicators and other quantitative data to derive critical determinants, accurately predict the retail demand for funds over the next three months, and inform the regional bank which funds to promote next.

2. **Make full use of blockchain technology to optimize financial services**

[15] In 2023, the SEC took significant steps to strengthen its enforcement of crypto platforms and exchanges, initiating legal proceedings against Coinbase, Binance, and Bittrex.

[16] https://aicadium.ai/.

According to Temasek's 2021 Annual Report,[17] after a year of incubation, the Temasek blockchain pod has founded LemmaTree, a group of blockchain companies that uses decentralized technologies to empower individuals and organizations to control their data. For example, Affinidi,[18] a LemmaTree company, has developed a digital identity platform that companies such as Singapore Airlines use. The platform verifies health credentials from other countries, including Covid-19 testing and vaccination status, via a mobile app.

On November 9, 2021, Affinidi launched a new business unit, Finnovate, aiming to serve underbanked individuals and under-served small-medium enterprises (SMEs) by adopting Web 3.0 technology. Deploying Web 3.0 innovations such as decentralized protocols and Verifiable Credentials (VCs), Finnovate partnered with stakeholders across the financial services sector, including banks, insurers, asset managers, fintech companies, and regulators, to achieve this goal.

10.4.2 CapitaLand Set up a Laboratory and Used Big Data to Promote the Digitalization Process

CapitaLand is a well-known large diversified real estate group in Asia, headquartered in Singapore and listed on the Singapore Stock Exchange. With Singapore and China as its core markets, CapitaLand continues to expand into India, Vietnam, Australia, Europe, and the United States. Its portfolio spans a wide range of real estate categories, and the scale of its real estate investment management business is one of the largest in the world. It manages six listed real estate investment trusts (REITs), business trusts, and over 20 PE funds.

1. **Set up smart urban co-creation lab**

In October 2020, CapitaLand launched the Smart Urban Co-Innovation Lab, supported by the Infocomm Media Development Authority (IMDA) and Enterprise Singapore, to create and test smart cities with local built environment and technology companies in a 55-hectare Singapore Technology Park. Singapore), aiming to develop and test innovations of smart cities with a localized environment in the 55-hectare, 5G-equipped Singapore Science Park.[19]

The lab is the first industry-led smart city solution development lab in Southeast Asia, supported by cutting-edge technologies such as artificial intelligence, 5G technology, and cloud computing. It focuses on six core industry verticals: advanced manufacturing, digital health, intelligent estates, smart mobility, sustainability, and urban agriculture. The Smart City Co-Innovation Lab has hosted more than 500

---

[17] https://www.temasek.com.sg/en/news-and-resources/news-room/news/2021/temasek-review-2021-bounce-forward.

[18] https://www.affinidi.com/enterprises.

[19] https://www.capitaland.com/international/en/about-capitaland/newsroom/inside/2021/dec/2021-year-in-review-for-capitaland-2.html.

companies and has over 70 members in its network to drive the development of smart city solutions.

2. **Use big data and other technologies to promote the digitalization process**

CapitaLand actively uses big data and other technologies to promote its business, increasing productivity and cost efficiency through digitization and developing digital strategies to expand revenue sources. CapitaLand has established core competencies in data center design, development, and operation. Meanwhile, 5G, artificial intelligence, and big data drive growth in the digital economy and create strong demand for data centers. The data center, a growing asset class, represents a global investment opportunity and is also one of CapitaLand's strategic focuses.

CapitaLand has supported its retail tenants in adopting an omni-channel strategy by launching the IMM virtual mall in partnership with Shopee, thereby opening up a new sales channel for retailers in addition to Capita3eats and eCapitaMall.

10.5 Implications

Digitization and leveraging big data are now widely recognized as strategic differentiators for the PE industry. Many PE firms are actively introducing technologies such as cloud platforms, blockchain, machine learning, and artificial intelligence to improve business operations, service quality, and market competitiveness. The following insights can be drawn from relevant practices in the United States, the United Kingdom, Japan, and Singapore.

First, a specialized agency or department should be set up to actively bring in talent to build a professional technology team and provide technical support for technology development for enterprises. Specialized agencies or departments can serve the companies, the regional and global PE industry, and the economy. For example, Ant Capital has established an AI/DX support office that can provide the best strategic planning and advice according to the invested company's environment and help companies make better-informed decisions with timely data and analysis. Another example is CapitaLand's initiative to set up a "Smart Urban Co-creation Lab" to bring innovative products and services to its customers.

Second, the digital transformation of enterprises can be promoted through blockchain and big data. The digitalization wave is an inevitable trend. How to grasp the development direction of enterprises in the era of intelligent technology is an issue that every PE institution should consider. Introducing blockchain, big data, and other technologies have opened up new horizons for developing the PE industry. And seizing the opportunity for digital transformation is conducive to improving the core competitiveness of enterprises. The financial services industry, faced with evolving customer needs, dynamic markets, complex regulatory environments, and increasing cyber threats, requires secure and scalable solutions to enable enterprises and customers to manage complex data tasks, address growing risks and meet the growing demand for real-time insights. For example, Morgan Stanley and cutting-edge technology companies have reached a strategic cloud partnership to accelerate digital transformation and shape the future of innovation in the financial services industry. The two companies collaborate to explore the opportunities brought by cloud platforms and enable Morgan Stanley to accelerate the modernization of its Internet technology environment to enhance customer, employee, and developer experience. Nomura Group jointly verified quantum cryptography for financial applications in Japan. Exploring the potential of emerging technologies such as blockchain, quantum computing, and augmented/virtual reality is undoubtedly necessary for companies to innovate digitally. Driving the adoption of advanced technologies and methodologies and accelerating digital transformation is the only way to continuously improve the service quality and the ability of companies to address risks and challenges.

Third, the cooperation between PE institutions and high-tech companies should be strengthened to complement the industry's shortcomings and achieve win–win results. Cooperation is an essential bridge between technology and financial networks. Technology can be more effectively introduced into the PE industry, customized technology solutions and technology services for enterprises through strategic cooperation. Citigroup, Actis Capital, and Man Group are actively seeking cooperation with high-tech enterprises, and are committed to building data platforms and research centers. Through cooperation, on the one hand, PE institutions can effectively use technologies to improve the industry's competitiveness. On the other hand, technology companies can obtain investment support to promote technology innovation and development further, forming a virtuous circle. For example, Actis Capital partnered with Accenture to accelerate Actis's growth and also promote Accenture's cloud-based digital claims, billing, and policy management software, expanding its reach in key markets.

Fourth, establishing a characteristic technology platform should fit the conditions and development targets of the company. It needs to be designed based on the PE fund company's customer situation and strategic objectives to solve current problems and promote development in the PE industry. For example, Actis Capital conducts a scientific analysis of its business environment, identifies market needs and gaps, and builds a data center or cloud platform that meets the company's development needs. Establishing data centers in Asia and Africa aligns with the company's strategic requirements and enables the company's data centers to operate faster and flourish. Driven by capacity flexibility, reduced upfront costs, and increased security, the company continuously adjusts the construction of its cloud platform to accommodate objective environmental changes.

Fifth, the public sector should provide appropriate support to stimulate industry innovation by holding competitions. Led by Citigroup in partnership with its allies in the public and private sector, the global open innovation competition seeks innovation in some areas, including government transactions and procurement, culture, ethics, citizen engagement, and information security and identity. Through Tech for Integrity Challenge (T4I), Citi and its allies have helped identify many promising solutions to financial development problems worldwide. China can also learn from that experience and inspire more PE and technology companies to innovate through the competition.

References

Bank of England. Embracing the promise of fintech. Quart Bull. 2019; Q1. https://www.bankofengland.co.uk/quarterly-bulletin/2019/2019-q1/embracing-the-promise-of-fintech.

Carstens A, Claessens S, Restoy F, Shin HS. Regulating big techs in finance. BIS Bull. 2021; 45. https://www.bis.org/publ/bisbull45.htm.

Chen YZ, Zhang WG. Research on the construction and countermeasures of the science and technology financial ecosystem in the Guangdong-Hong Kong-Macao Greater Bay Area. Urban Observ. 2019;3:20–35 (in Chinese).

China Academy of Information and Communications Technology. White paper on big data (2022); 2023. http://www.caict.ac.cn/english/research/whitepapers/202303/t20230316_416841.html

Choo TL. Application of blockchain technology in private equity. World scientific book chapters. In: Lee DKC, Ding D, Guan C, editors. Financial management in the digital economy, chapter 5. World Scientific Publishing Co. Pte. Ltd.; 2021. pp. 85–104.

Ernst and Young. UK FinTech: on the cutting edge; 2016. https://fintechauscensus.ey.com/2018/Documents/EY-UK-FinTech-On-the-cutting-edge.pdf.

Financial Conduct Authority. Business plan 2017/18; 2017. https://www.fca.org.uk/publication/business-plans/business-plan-2017-18.pdf

Financial Stability Board. FinTech and market structure in financial services: market developments and potential financial stability implication; 2019. https://www.fsb.org/wp-content/uploads/P140219.pdf.

Financial Stability Board. FinTech and market structure in the COVID-19 pandemic: implications for financial stability; 2022. https://www.fsb.org/wp-content/uploads/P210322.pdf.

Gensler, G. Testimony before the subcommittee on financial services and general government, U.S. house appropriations committee; 2021. https://www.sec.gov/news/testimony/gensler-2021-05-26#:~:text=While%20the%20SEC%E2%80%99s%20formal%20budget%20request%20will%20be,Purpose%20Acquisition%20Companies%20Private%20Funds%20Crypto%20Assets%20Fintech.

Gispert TA, Chatain PL. Embracing the promise of Fintech responsibly through regulation and supervision; 2023. https://blogs.worldbank.org/psd/embracing-promise-fintech-responsibly-through-regulation-and-supervision.

Guan XL. The road of financial technology development in private equity industry under the new situation. Tsinghua Financ Rev. 2017; 12:90–1. https://doi.org/10.19409/j.cnki.thf-review.2017.12.027. (in Chinese).

Hu M. Application and enlightenment of fintech in the private equity investment industry in the United Kingdom and the United States. Finance. 2022;3:89–94 (in Chinese).

Thomson Reuters Regulatory Intelligence. 2023 cost of compliance regulatory burden poses operational challenges for compliance; 2023. https://legal.thomsonreuters.com/content/dam/ewp-m/documents/legal/en/pdf/reports/cost-of-compliance-report-final-web.pdf.

JD Finance. Global fintech report 2017: industry development and legal frontier; 2017. http://www.199it.com/archives/621150

KPMG. The pulse of fintech H1; 2023. https://assets.kpmg.com/content/dam/kpmg/xx/pdf/2023/07/global-pulse-of-fintech-h123-report-web.pdf.

Li YL. When finance meets technology-global financial technology development trend report. Technol Finance. 2019;6:42–9 (in Chinese).

Mahoney J. The rise of Chinese fintech: lessons for the United States. New York: Columbia University Press; 2019. https://www8.gsb.columbia.edu/leadership/newsn/6881/the-rise-of-chinese-fintech-lessons-for-the-united-states.

Monetary Authority of Singapore. MAS Commits S$250 million to accelerate innovation and technology adoption in financial sector; 2020. https://www.mas.gov.sg/news/media-releases/2020/mas-commits-s$250-million-to-accelerate-innovation-and-technology-adoption-in-financial-secto.

Pan FH, Liu YF. Research progress on the distribution and influencing factors of global financial technology industry. World Geogr Res. 2021;4:696–707 (in Chinese).

Wang HD, Wu JW. Changes in innovative corporate financing from the shrinking IPO market in the United States. China Secur Futures. 2018;5:86–96. https://doi.org/10.19766/j.cnki.zgzqqh.2018.05.014. (in Chinese).

World Economic Forum. Deloitte. Beyond fintech: apragmatic assessment of disruptive potentialin financial services; 2017. https://www.weforum.org/reports/beyond-fintech-a-pragmatic-assessment-of-disruptive-potential-in-financial-services.

Xu Z, Xu RH. "Chapter 7: Regulating FinTech for sustainable development in China. In: Amstad M, Huang B, Morgan PJ, Shirai S, editors. FinTech in Asia: policies and practices. Tokyo, Japan: Asian Development Bank Institute Press; 2020.